The

of Thai M·   Singapore

The "Bare Life"
of Thai Migrant Workmen in Singapore

Pattana Kitiarsa

Silkworm Books

ISBN: 978-616-215-075-3

Earlier versions of chapters 2 to 6 have appeared in the following publications. Each is reprinted here by permission of the publisher.

Chapter 2: "The Lyrics of Laborious Life: Popular Music and the Reassertion of Migrant Manhood in Northeastern Thailand," *Inter-Asia Cultural Studies* 10, no. 3 (2009): 381–98.

Chapter 3: "Village Transnationalism: Transborder Identities among Thai-Isan Migrant Workers in Singapore," Asia Research Institute Working Paper No. 71 (2006), accessible at SSRN: http://ssrn.com/abstract=1317160 or http://dx.doi.org/10.2139/ssrn.1317160.

Chapter 4: "Thai Migrants in Singapore: State, Intimacy, and Desire," *Gender, Place & Culture: A Journal of Feminist Geography* 2, no. 6 (2008): 595–610.

Chapter 5: "Masculine Intent and Migrant Manhood: Thai Workmen Talking Sex" in *Men and Masculinities in Southeast Asia*, edited by Michele Ford and Lenore Lyons, 38–55 (ch. 2) (New York and London: Routledge, 2012).

Chapter 6: "The Ghosts of Transnational Labour Migration: Death and Other Tragedies of Thai Migrant Workers in Singapore" in *Asian Migrations*, edited by Lorente, Piper, Shen Hsiu-Hua, and Yeoh, 194–222 (ch. 11) (Singapore: National University of Singapore, 2005).

First published in 2014 by Silkworm Books
6 Sukkasem Road, T. Suthep
Chiang Mai 50200 Thailand
info@silkwormbooks.com
www.silkwormbooks.com

Typeset in Chaparral Pro 10 pt. by Silk Type

Printed in Thailand by O.S. Printing House, Bangkok

5 4 3 2 1

In Memoriam

Pattana Kitiarsa was born in Nong Khai in northeastern Thailand. He studied anthropology at Khon Kaen University and completed his doctorate in sociocultural anthropology at the University of Washington in the United States, after which he returned to Isan and taught at Suranaree University in Nakhon Ratchasima Province. He later became an assistant professor in the Department of Southeast Asian Studies at the National University of Singapore. As a Thai-Isan ethnographer in diaspora, he worked on a wide range of research topics, including popular Buddhism, religious commodifications, masculinity, popular culture, and transnational labor migration. His engaged ethnography focused on marginal subjects whose voices and stories are often unheard. He is author of several English-language publications, including the edited volume *Religious Commodifications in Asia: Marketing Gods* (Routledge 2008) and a single-authored monograph, entitled *Mediums, Monks, and Amulets* (Silkworm Books and University of Washington Press 2012). Dr. Pattana Kitiarsa died of cancer at the age of forty-five on January 10, 2013. This book has been published posthumously in honor of the significant contributions he made towards an understanding of contemporary Isan culture and the ongoing evolution of Thai society.

Contents

In Memoriam   v
Preface   ix
Acknowledgments   xi

Chapter 1 Introduction   1

Chapter 2 The Lyrics of a Laborious Life   19

Chapter 3 Village Transnationalism   49

Chapter 4 State, Intimacy, and Desire   75

Chapter 5 Male Workers Talking Sex   91

Chapter 6 Death, Tragedy, and Ghosts   113

Chapter 7 Conclusion   131

Notes   139
References   157
Index   179

Preface

Labor transnationalism, as an emerging theoretical concept and global cultural phenomena, is wrought with contentious meanings, given the diversity of actors and their experiences as overseas migrant workers. Such meanings are deeply embedded in and contingent on certain historical and cultural circumstances and contexts. This book tells "many stories" of Thai contract workers in Singapore's transnational labor market. It reveals some of the complex phenomena and processes that have stripped bare migrant workers' social life as it is lived away from home. In their efforts to stay the course of extended employment, these workers have had to re-craft their masculine selfhood. I argue that, like most migrant workers of other national origins, Thai migrant workers in Singapore live and endure their migrant social suffering as a "bare life." This book builds its argument based on migrants' assumption that they must travel abroad to make a living. The human venture to cross territories in order to earn an income over an extended duration of time is not a new social phenomenon. However, the initial process, intensification, and interpretation of transnational gendered experiences among various groups of border-crossers demand critical exploration and explanation.

This book covers multiple aspects of Thai migrants' bare life in Singapore, such as tragic death, hardship, sexual desire and intimacy, religious beliefs, and popular music. The book analyzes personal tales of transnational migrant workers in the Southeast Asian context. It shows how narratives of the human experience of the labor diaspora can contribute to both the scholarship on labor transnationalism and public understanding of diverse groups of people who make their living in transient places and whose lives span social ties and imaginations between host and home destinations. This book can also be read as a contribution by Thailand and

Southeast Asia to an understanding of transnational mobility based on in-depth analyses of border-crossing, migrant social life, and male migrant gendered identity-negotiating processes. I believe that some fascinating stories of Thailand's working-class men (and women, to some extent in this study) deserve their place in the transnational folklore.

Observing Thai migrants in Singapore for more than seven years, I have always felt that their lives are extremely tough, stressful, and sorrowful. As members of the transnational working-class, these individuals are barely able to keep their noses above the rippling waves of rough waters. They have shouldered heavy financial and social burdens as heads of households and breadwinners for their families back home. At the same time, they have had to come to terms with some of the challenges in their diminishing gendered roles as male overseas migrant workers. As migrant laborers from a cultural background where the male is sexually and culturally privileged, such as in Thailand, these men have had to re-craft their shattered confidence and pride as a result of being poorly paid construction workers in a global city like Singapore, and have had to struggle to negotiate their masculine self-identity. It is safe to say that Singaporean society has cast some ambivalent prejudice and stereotypes against foreign talent, both high-skilled professionals as well as low-skilled workers. While the government and labor market in Singapore rely on migrants' contributions to sustain the country's economic growth, in everyday life foreign workers are not whole-heartedly received by the majority of the public in Singapore.

Acknowledgments

Throughout the course of my research on Thai migrant communities in Singapore, I have been indebted to many individuals and organizations. I will always be grateful to my "folks" from Isan (northeastern Thailand) who, between 2004 and 2010, were "selling their labor" in Singapore, particularly active members of the Friends of Thai Workers Association (FTWA). Likewise, I will always treasure some of the finest moments in my life as a *luk Isan* (a child of the Northeast), engaging in various volunteering activities with groups of displaced Thai workers, men and women, and monks in the city-state of Singapore. Among the many volunteers and friends at FTWA, my heartfelt thanks go to Wichai Sumanatkhajonkul, Supaluk Balcer, and Sing Rachahong for their generous assistance and unfailing friendship over the years. These people played multiple roles in this book project, serving as informants, discussants, participants, facilitators, and critical observers. With them and through them, I have learned what it means to be a Thai diasporic scholar and person.

The embryonic stage of my research was funded in 2005 by the Center for Research on Plurality in the Mekong Region, Khon Kaen University. My gratitude goes to Achan Yaowalak Aphichatvullop and Achan Dararat Mettarikanond for their encouragement and enthusiasm. I wish to express my heartfelt thanks to the Royal Thai Embassy in Singapore and the Office of Thai Labor Affairs for their kind assistance. Support from Ambassadors Thakur Phanit, Chalermphol Thanjit, Nopadol Kunavibul and their staff, especially Panpimon Suwannapongse and Saranyu Ampatrakan, were invaluable to my research. I will always be indebted to the minister councilors in charge of labor affairs, Somthawee Kopatthanasin, Nutcha Trithanyaphong, and Kanjana Wongsuwan, and their staff, especially Patana Phandhufalck, Latthaphan Walsh, and Dr.

Sakdina Sonthisakyothin, who shared with me their views and information pertinent to the making of the community of Thai construction workers in Singapore.

I am grateful to the Asia Research Institute (ARI), National University of Singapore (NUS) for its excellent research facilities and stimulating academic environment throughout my three-year appointment there (2004–2006). My interest in the subject of transnational labor migration was ignited by the encouragement and support from my ARI colleagues, especially Chen Kuan-hsing, Chua Beng Huat, Arianne Getano, Gavin Jones, Beatriz Lorente, Nicola Piper, Mizanur Rahman, Anthony Reid, Shen Hsiu-Hua, Mika Toyota, Bryan Turner, Brenda Yeoh, and Teo You Yenn. I wish to thank them all. I am also grateful to Eric Thompson and Vineeta Sinha for their thoughtful advice and genuine interest in my work. The Department of Southeast Asian Studies at NUS allowed me to take a short research leave in Bangkok to prepare the book manuscript in the first semester of the 2008/2009 academic year. The final revision of the manuscript was made possible through a FASS Writing Semester Grant, awarded August–December 2011.

Achan Biff (Charles) Keyes has always been a source of moral support and a professional model. The chapter "Village Transnationalism" was partly inspired by his pioneering work *Isan: Regionalism in Northeastern Thailand* (Keyes 1967). Another chapter, "The Lyrics of Laborious Life," was originally presented at a panel honoring Prof. Keyes's career contributions to Asian Studies at the 2006 AAS Annual Meeting in San Francisco. This book owes its existence to the encouragement and enthusiasm of Trasvin Jittidecharak and her staff at Silkworm Books, Chiang Mai. They share my dream to tell some of the transnational tales of overseas Isan and other Thai workers to our English-speaking readers. I truly appreciate their patience and understanding. I will always be thankful to Achan Chris Baker who provided sharp, constructive comments on how to improve the manuscript.

My family is the watershed of my moral strength. My father inspired me to search for my own dignified path of becoming a *luk phuchai*. My late mother fondly imbued in me an ethics of "showering oneself with sweat" (*ap nguea tang nam*) in work and in life. Achan Phoyai Suriya has always been there with me and my family over the years. I truly appreciate his invaluable contribution to the fieldwork stage of this book. Nan, Tan, and

Tukta are the love of my soul. They have virtually co-authored this book and my other works. We have grown up together as a transnational Thai family in Singapore. This book indeed forms a crucial milestone in our diasporic endeavors to make sense of our Thai-Isan ethnocultural roots in the wide, wild transnational world.

PK
Singapura
April 2012

Note on Romanization

The romanized spellings of Central Thai and Thai-Isan terms and names in this book follow the general guidelines for transcription issued by the Royal Institute of Thailand on January 11, 1999. Originally, the guidelines were described in detail in the Journal of the Siam Society, vol. 33. The guidelines are also available online at www.royin.go.th. Translations are the author's unless otherwise noted.

Chapter 1

Introduction

The community of Thai migrants employed as construction workers in Singapore is known to the world primarily through general public information and various impressions. Most Thai migrants are working-age males from the Thai countryside—especially the northern and northeastern regions of Thailand. They have temporarily moved away from a traditional land-based economy to a modern wage-based economy through the rather dangerous and risky venture of transnational labor migration.

Media reports on the problems faced by Thai migrant workers in Singapore focus on the harsh treatment they receive from job placement agencies, employers, and to some extent, governmental authorities due to Singapore's strict law enforcement. Violations of the law committed by Thai workers in Singapore range from careless littering, smoking in prohibited areas, and drunken behavior (for which fines are administered) to drug trafficking and murder. Corporal punishment, such as canning and execution, is not uncommon.

Thai foreign workers in Singapore are an unusual group with high rates of death due to a mysterious sudden death syndrome. Doctors and medical researchers call this cause of death "sudden unexplained death syndrome" (SUDS) or "sudden unexplained nocturnal death syndrome" (SUNDS). This deadly killer is widely known back home in Thailand and among members of Thai overseas communities as *lai tai* (lit., floating into death while sleeping, or dying in deep sleep). There have been cases of death among seemingly healthy Thai workers in Singapore since the early 1980s (see chapter 6). The real-life situation of Thai migrant workers in Singapore has subversively defied the Thai government-promoted and popular image of Thai overseas workers as "economic warriors" (*nakrop setthakit*) who have sacrificed themselves to earn hard currency so as to help their impoverished families and the nation's ailing economy. The life of Thai migrants working and living in foreign environments away from the comforts of home is extremely difficult. This life experience is overwhelmingly dominated by discomfort, stress, suffering, and death. In northeastern Thai society, a prominent cultural perception describing someone who has had to endure such a migrant life is usually rooted in the Buddhist notion of human suffering (Thai, *thuk*; Pali, *dukkha*). Living a migrant life is one of the major forms of human suffering, because one has to leave the comfort and intimacy of home, family, and the community of relatives and friends. Migrant workers, with their limited knowledge and capital, often feel the whole world is forever against them. Once away from their home base, their lives become displaced and uncertain. They become strangers working on contracted jobs with foreign employers and colleagues, and must adjust to new daily routines. For many of them, simple daily activities become a struggle, such as living in a crowded dormitory room with international colleagues or attending to basic needs such as cooking, washing laundry, and managing their own salaries without the help of wives or girlfriends. In short, displacement as a consequence of labor migration is a major cause of human suffering in the Thai Buddhist cultural perception.

In this book, I focus on three topics: the re-crafting of masculine selfhood, suffering, and death within the context of transnational labor migration. The subjects under investigation comprise a sampling of Thai migrants working and living in Singapore during the period of this study (2004–2010). The book addresses such questions as: How do Thai workers participate in a social life away from home? What does it mean to be a member of the transnational working class from Thailand working and living in a neighboring country like Singapore? How is labor transnationalism practiced in a host country known for tight legal and market regulations? How does a marginal male migrant population (e.g., contracted foreign workers from Thailand) live its transnational life, especially with the impossibility of citizenship and a certain degree of social exclusion? As migrant laborers, what are their responses to legal, cultural, and economic barriers to legal and social membership in the society where they live and work? How have they negotiated their migrant manhood away from home? Why do Thai workers die, especially as a result of sudden death syndrome? What are the root causes of death and suffering in the context of transnational labor migration?

In response to these questions, I argue that death and suffering within the context of transnational labor migration, as illustrated by the case of Thai workers in Singapore, is best understood as an immense human struggle to make the Agambenian "bare life" bearable (further discussion on Giorgio Agamben's works follows shortly). Surviving a bare life is the major characteristic of being an overseas migrant worker. Death, injuries, and other forms of physical and emotional suffering is the price migrant workers must pay for their transnational migration venture. Their overseas employment and work conditions are known as "3D jobs," which generally stands for dirty, dangerous, and degrading. By definition, the bare life in the context of transnational labor migration entails economic, cultural, emotional, and legal constraints as well as everyday hardships, as a result of the worker's individual decisions and action and the acts of sovereign powers operating within the modern state and the global market economy.

I further argue that Thai men as contracted foreign workers are a group of transnational migrant workers who are stripped bare of the powerful sociocultural, economic, and legal processes that govern their existence at home and govern the citizens of their host countries. These processes are generally structured to function beyond the control and agency of migrant workers. No one is fully immune from such complex modern processes. The moment a person makes a decision to enter the transnational labor market is a decisive time—it is when a worker enters into the bare life of labor migration. Consciously or not, the worker will lose some control over his own destiny and become an extremely vulnerable person on the move, even though he may be well equipped with supporting networks of experienced friends, family members, and relatives. With limited knowledge and skills in the vast global labor market, migrant workers are often powerless when it comes to negotiating the terms and conditions pertinent to work, wages, and living conditions in the host country.

In addition, I also argue that by living a "bare life" in the context of transnational labor migration, one inevitably encounters social suffering and sometimes even tragic death, as well as the intensive process of re-crafting gendered selfhood and identity. These experiences are interactive and integral parts of the migrant life. After being stripped bare, migrant workers are economically and socially naked. Their bare life in the host country is thus interpreted as a deliberate effort to re-craft themselves in order to regain self-confidence and identity as men and foreign workers. I do not mean to say that living a bare life is totally destructive and tragic. What I intend to show is the multifaceted sides of the bare life as experienced during transnational migration. Enduring a bare life as a transnational migrant laborer can, nevertheless, be a matter of life and death. One can return home as a new, reformed man with redefined masculine selfhood and identity, or as a dead body, as will be illustrated in the coming chapters.

"Bare Life" as an Analytical Concept

My arguments about migrant life are basically drawn from two theoretical sources. The first one describes the migrant experience as an unusual bare life full of physical and social suffering, including the risk of injury, illness, and death. The concept of a "bare life" is based on key works by political philosopher Giorgio Agamben (1993, 1998, 2005), while the idea of social suffering is borrowed from the work of medical anthropologists Arthur Kleinman, Veena Das, and Margaret Lock (1997). The second theoretical source uses the notion of hegemonic and subordinate masculinities to understand the transnational labor migration experience, as discussed by a number of scholars such as Robert Connell (1995) and Mike Donaldson, Raymond Hibbins, Richard Howson, and Bob Pease (2009). Migrant workers do own and exercise their gendered agency. In the pursuit of economic opportunities abroad, male migrant laborers have developed certain masculine sensitivities and pride as foreign workers.

Agamben's studies do not directly discuss workers in the context of transnational labor migration. His works *Homo Sacer* (1998) and *State of Exception* (2005) are attempts to establish interconnections between a bare life, sovereignty, and the modern state. In general, the state has sovereign power to establish certain forms and institutions of political relations with its subjects through law. By imposing legal systems, the state creates the "state of exception," which Agamben defines as a "zone of indistinguishability between law and life" (Agamben 1998, 56) or an ambiguous zone "between the political and the juridical, and between law and the living being" (Agamben 2005, 2). The state of exception is more apparent in critical situations, such as civil war, insurrection, and resistance, in which a human being is turned into *homo sacer*—an "accursed man" according to ancient Roman law, who has been "excluded from the human world and who . . . could be killed without committing homicide" (Agamben 1993, 86). Agamben, with some influence of the Foucauldian notion of biopolitics, outlines how the modern state works out sovereign power over its subjects. He shows how legal bans, the state of exception, the bare life, and the "camp" are highly interrelated because they are imposed by the modern state's institutions and technologies of power. He explicitly demonstrates such interrelations as follows:

1. The original political relation is the ban (the state of exception as zone of indistinction between outside and inside, exclusion and inclusion).

2. The fundamental activity of sovereign power is the production of bare life as originary political element and as threshold of articulation between nature and culture, between *zoē* and *bios*.

3. Today it is not the city but rather the camp that is the fundamental biopolitical paradigm of the West. (Agamben 1998, 181 cited in Laclau 2007, 11–12)

Why are Agamben's thoughts useful in understanding the migrant life of Thai workers in Singapore and elsewhere? First, Agamben provides a systematic analytical model to gauge the harsh realities migrants face away from home. He reminds us that there are certain institutionalized patterns behind the bare life. Second, migrant suffering and death, as Agamben would remind us, result from the activity of sovereign power. They do not randomly stem from individuals' poorly informed decision-making or misshaped behavior alone. Like other population groups, migrant workers live and work under the close control of state authorities and market institutions. Finally, Agamben's thought points to the way that the modern state and its sovereign power work hand-in-hand with capitalist market institutions in extracting economic value out of the bodies of migrant workers.

The modern state imposes laws and regulations on foreign workers—in this book's example, inside and outside of construction sites in Singapore. It arranges for them to stay in designated dormitories and living quarters located away from city centers designed for foreign workers. The state issues these workers—mainly men—various types of work permits, tightly regulates their working and off hours, and controls their sexuality by not allowing their wives or girlfriends from home to accompany them to Singapore. Foreign workers are then reduced to laborers, subject to stringent jurisdiction, which is a common but effective way to put these men into a state of exception and a bare life. Confined into a regulated space between the Thai home and the Singaporean host country, workers, in some respects, represent *homo sacer* who live and work in a transnational migrant zone indistinguishable not only between life and law, but also between life and death.

"Bare Life" as Social Suffering

The bare life in the context of transnational labor migration is a form of social suffering, which I describe in this book as "migrant social suffering." Social suffering is not confined to an isolated individual fate and it is not a form of an isolated, private life which is endured or suffered separately by individuals. Rather, the socially collective aspect of the bare life is deemed important here. In this respect, I benefit from the conceptual discussion of "social suffering," set forth by Kleinman, Das, and Lock (1997, ix), who rightly argue that suffering is a social experience because there is always a close linkage between personal problems and societal problems. The authors remind us that human sufferings have "their origins and consequences in the devastating injuries that social force can inflict on human experience" (ibid.). Injury, illness, and other forms of suffering are multifaceted, interpersonal human experiences. Individual bodies serve as the physical canvas or site of suffering, but they are not mere living organisms or biological phenomena. Human bodies are the products of complex and intensive power relations. Human suffering is thus rooted in the complex linkages between bodies, social actions, and institutions. According to Kleinman, Das, and Lock (ibid.), "social suffering results from what political, economic, and institutional power does to people, and, reciprocally, from how these forms of power influence responses to social problems. Included under the category of social suffering are conditions that are usually divided among separate fields, conditions that simultaneously involve health, welfare, legal, moral, and religious issues." The conceptual strength of the notion of social suffering is twofold. First, it highlights the importance of power relations underlying such human social experience. Unbalanced social relations manifest in social exclusion and marginalization, which limit equal opportunity for gaining access to education, healthcare services, and other resources necessary to improve one's quality of life and social mobility. Second, the inclusion of social suffering into my conceptual framework draws attention to the migrant reality of being a working-class, disadvantaged population, because social suffering is likely a key symptom that is synonymous with the powerless, the poor, and the migrant both in host and home countries. As Kleinman, Das, and Lock (ibid., ix–x) point out, "social suffering is shared across high-income and low-income societies, primarily affecting, in such different settings, those who are desperately poor and powerless. This is not merely a statistical correlation, but a causal web in the global political economy. Many of the same sources of breakdown, violence, emerging infectious diseases and mental and social health problems are at work among poor populations worldwide."

This study demonstrates that the socioeconomic and cultural aspects of social suffering are imminent in the context of transnational labor migration. Workers are desperately powerless, poor, and struggling to survive their bare life away from home. The mysterious death of Thai workers in Singapore is evidence of migrants' most severe social suffering.

Gendered Agency and Emotional Sensitivity

I am aware that describing the lives of Thai migrant workers in Singapore as marked by the bare life and social suffering may seem overly simplified and one-sided. Foreign workers have ups and downs in their transnational migrant lives. They are not passive social actors who are incapable of handling their personal affairs. As I show in this book, male migrant workers have gendered agency (Constable 2005) and emotional sensitivity that reflects their autonomy, responsibility, and self-definition. This includes their conscious ability to reinterpret and re-craft their masculine ways of action based on culturally conditioned norms and expectations. The concept of gendered agency deals with the question of how and why to behave properly as men in the transnational migration context. Male migrant workers are first and foremost men with masculine dignity and pride. They are experienced men with the sensitivities and capabilities to handle their own migrant life situations.

It is also my argument that male migrant workers' gendered agency is made possible through the practices of transnational migrant self-situatedness. Scholars like Bourdieu (1977), Geertz (1973), and Giddens (1979) showed us a few decades earlier that subjects are involved in producing and reproducing social meanings and imaginations through practices. Acts and habits in everyday life always open up the possibility of interpretive reading and comprehension. Giddens' theory on "structuration" is useful in my understanding of transnational gendered agency. He suggests that "every social actor knows a great deal about the conditions of reproduction of the society of which he or she is a member" (Giddens 1979, 5). The fact that actors know so much about their social world is crucial. In his ethnographic records of pre-World War II British workers, Zweig (1952, 19) suggests that "the world seen through his [a worker's] eyes is different from the world seen by another man. In the account a working man gives of his life can be seen the whole outlook of his class, and its entire background of conditions and situations." Knowledge, awareness, and purposeful conduct provide workers some capability as well as potentiality to make sense of, transform, and/or reproduce their structural conditions. I take Thai migrant workers as situated transnational actors with a specific form of agency who arm themselves with cultural capital and male gendered modes of social action.

In my discussion of the notion of gendered agency, I wish to add gender aspects into the juncture of the structure-agency framework. Transnational male actors as gender-conscious beings produce and reproduce specific forms of masculine transnationalism. Inspired by works such as Giddens (1992) and Herzfeld (1985, 1997), I suggest that transnational migrant actors are capable gendered actors who have actively defined and redefined their transnational migrant social fields both at the sending and receiving destinations. Gendered agency contains both rational and emotional sides. Labor transnationalism consists not only of rational ties and networks (Faist 2004) as well as flows of capital and travels across borders (Appadurai 1993, 1999; Clifford 1997), but it also consists of various forms of gendered emotional intimacy. In this respect, Giddens (1992, 130) argues that "intimacy is above all a matter of emotional communication, with others and with the self, in a context of interpersonal equality."

In their attempts to exercise gendered agency, male Thai workers in Singapore must manage their emotional desires and expression. They, too, must come to terms with the various forms of emotional management, which Hochschild (1983) calls "emotional labor." Emotional management through facial and other bodily expressions is a form of gendered laboring. Parrenas (2001a, 2001b) and Constable (1999) remind us, from their studies of Filipino migrant mothers and contract domestic workers who have spent extended periods overseas away from their children and families, that emotion plays a major role in migrants' lives, both in their relationships with their employers and in handling their long-distance, transnational families. Transnational migrant life is indeed composed of sets and scenes of emotionally soaked and gender-contested actions that contain a great potentiality to transform institutional orders and structures.

Emotional labor is usually associated with the construction of gendered self-identity inspired by modern sensibility. Mills (1997, 1999b) argues that female factory workers from the northeastern countryside migrate to work in Bangkok suburbs not only for economic reasons, but also as an aspiration to be modern (*than samai*). It is part of their desire to immerse themselves in or acquire some of the latest versions of Western-style modernity in the Thai capital's cosmological world. The Western-style modernity, which the Thais call *khwam than samai*, indeed makes up a good portion of "social remittance," which Levitt (2001) explores among Dominican migrant workers in areas of Boston and their extensive social networks at both ends. Some of the modern American ideas and patterns of behaviors that are transported back to Dominican home areas are American-style Christianity, participatory democracy, hygienic practices, and gender-based consciousness. In this respect, transnational migrant self-fashioning and its impact on both ends resembles the concept of "gendered migrant social capital" (Curran 2002; Curran et al. 2005), which has sustained the social life and imagination of both domestic migrant workers such as Isan female factory workers in Bangkok and their male counterparts as "transnational villagers" (Levitt 2001) in Singapore.

The practices of migrant gendered agency imply some varied degrees of interpersonal closeness, comfort, and hierarchy. In Singapore's transnational migrant world, male Thai workers are conscious of their working-class, socioeconomic, and marginal immigration statuses as low-skilled foreign laborers. When it comes to the domain of sexual intimacy, they are aware of existing as well as perceived distances between themselves and women of many different nationalities that they meet in Singapore (see chapters 4 and 5). In places like the Thai-style shopping mall of the Golden Mile Complex, roadside brothels and hostels for foreign workers, as well as the night marketplace in the Geylang area, Thai workers enjoy the possibility of intimacy. Despite being away from their families and home communities, being deprived of their supportive social networks and resources, and being subject to strict regulations, surveillance, and harsh treatment imposed on them by the state and their employers, Thai workers and other groups of transnational migrant actors, such as sex workers and transborder tradeswomen, have created certain channels to express emotional and rational forms of communication. They are subtle and calculated negotiators of the constraints and obstacles they face as migrant workers and find ways to express their desire for emotional intimacy.

This book discusses the intimate aspects of how male Thai workers in Singapore have embraced their migrant employment and social life in Singapore. Indeed, these individuals represent an important example of how men have re-crafted themselves emotionally and socially within the context of transnational labor migration in order to come to terms with the deprivation of their masculine pride.

Singapore as a Transnational Labor Market

Sowell (1996, 2) reminds us that "the story of migration is not only about people who migrate but also about the lands to which they go and their impacts on those lands." Singapore stands out as one of the most prolific lands in the world filling up with migrant stories and folklore. As a country built by immigrants, Singapore has relied on immigrants' contributions to its economy and culture since its founding in 1829. In fact, one could argue that the history of Singapore is the history of migration (Warren 2003a, 2003b; Yao 2007). With its strategic geographical and cultural location, Singapore has for centuries been a receiving destination of immigrants from diverse ethnic, religious, and other cultural backgrounds. Unlike most immigrant societies, Singapore's most consistent role in the world map of international migration lies perhaps in the fact that it has consistently retained its status as a receiving destination. Singapore exists as a key regional labor market and has been prosperous over the centuries due to its success in managing its labor market. It remains the destination for flows of foreign workers from traditional labor supply sources (e.g., Malaysia, China, South Korea, and Hong Kong) as well as non-traditional ones (e.g., Bangladesh, India, Myanmar, and Thailand).

Labor migration is a social force and cultural practice. As the history of modern labor migration in Thailand and Southeast Asia suggests, transnational labor migration is no longer a seasonal or temporary occurrence (Ananta and Arifin 2004; Rafael and Abraham 1997). Since the 1990s, Thailand has imported, exported, and provided a transient space for transnational workers (Stern 1998; Supang 1999). Transnational labor migration for Thais has become a normalized everyday event and cultural practice. Curran et al (2005, 225–55) views the rural-to-urban migrant cultural practice in northeast Thailand through the concept of "gendered migrant social capital or networks," while Mills (1997, 1999b) observes how the transient culture of female migrant workers from the same region is embedded in their "explicit desire to be 'up-to-date' (*than samai*) and to participate in Thai modernity" (1997, 42). Mills (1999a, 4) develops some further arguments regarding young women's labor migration as a "powerful vehicle for—and an expression of—profound social and personal transformation." Elsewhere, in Mexico, a culture of migration is characterized by long-standing and high rates of international migration (Kandel and Massey 2002, 981). In the busy traffic lanes across "transnational social spaces" (Faist 2000), transnational labor migration appears as a dynamic site shaping and reshaping the changing faces of the global-local continuum of particular cultural settings.

Labor migration provides not only an escape from poverty and unemployment, but also a chance for "capital accumulation" (Osella and Osella 2000a, 75). Labor migration from the Thai countryside to

Singapore has expanded rapidly since its beginning in the early 1970s. Thai migrant men "who built Singapore" (Wong 2000) have constituted one of the largest portions of Singapore's multinational foreign workforce, especially in the construction industry. According to Low (1995), Singapore has always been an open door for skilled and professional workers. No unskilled workers were permitted before 1968. In the 1970s, Singapore's policy to import foreign unskilled workers was relaxed for the construction and manufacturing sectors. A wholly Singaporean workforce became unrealistic and foreign labor grew, reflected in 72,590 noncitizen and nonresident (foreign) workers in 1970 and 119,483 in 1980, or 11.5 percent and 11.09 percent, respectively. Huang and Yeoh (2003, 80, table 1) show a very steady growth in the percentage of foreign workers out of Singapore's total workforce in the last four decades, beginning from 3.2 and 7.4 percent in 1970 and 1980 respectively to 16.1 and 29.2 percent in 1990 and 2000. In 2000, Singapore had a record 612,200 foreign workers out of its 2,094,800 total workforce. It is estimated that foreign workers will make up more than 60 percent of Singapore's workforce in 2020 (see Rahman 2003, 81).

Wong (2000, 58) shows that Thai workers have reportedly been coming to Singapore since the early 1970s, but statistics made available by Thailand's Ministry of Labor and Social Work date only from 1978 onwards. Boonruang Chunsuvimol (1980) reports that approximately five hundred Thai workers came to Singapore in October 1978 to work in the electronic and textile companies of the Jurong area. This was the beginning of the rapid expansion of the importation of unskilled and semiskilled workers from Thailand in the 1980s and 1990s, which sustained the construction industry boom in Singapore that was sparked by the gigantic public housing program undertaken by the Housing and Development Board (HDB). During these times, due to the critical shortage of domestic labor, the government allowed workers from "non-traditional sources" (e.g., Bangladesh, India, Indonesia, Myanmar, Philippines, Sri Lanka, Thailand) to take up employment in the construction sector (Porntipa (2001, 128). By 1981, it was estimated that there was a critical shortage of some three thousand construction workers needed to work on HDB building sites (Wong 2000, 66).

The high demand for noncitizen workers in Singapore's construction industry in the mid-1980s brought not only documented workers, but also undocumented or illegal workers from Thailand and other non-traditional sources to this island republic. The peak of illegal workers seeking employment was during the second half of the 1980s. When an amnesty was declared for illegal workers in the country in 1989, almost ten thousand Thais working illegally in the country registered themselves for repatriation, as against twenty-five thousand Thais who were employed with work permits (Wong 2000, 58). It was around this time that Singapore's authorities began to systematize and implement a stricter and more effective policy toward the management of its foreign labor affairs. While Singapore has recognized and valued foreign workers' contribution to the impressive growth of its economy (Wong 2000, 63), the country needs to find ways to manage its foreign workforce effectively, as international labor migration is a delicate, highly dynamic, and complicated issue. Singapore also has to make sure that it does not overly depend on an imported workforce lest it make the whole economy and society risky and vulnerable. Huang and Yeoh (2003, 80–81) show that Singapore's authorities have adopted three key measures, namely, the work permit system, the dependency ceiling (regulating the proportion of foreign to local workers), and the foreign levy to manage unskilled and low-skilled workers as a "temporary and controlled phenomenon" (see Rahman 2003, 62–76).

Attaining accurate numbers of Thai migrant workers in Singapore has long been problematic. Major studies on the subject by Porntipa Atipas (2001) and Wong (2000) admit that numbers of both illegal and legal Thai migrant workers in this country are only estimated figures "due to the lack of official data" (Porntipa 2001, 130), and "no exact figures on the size and composition of the foreign labor workforce in Singapore have been released by the Ministry of Labour" (Wong 2000, 58). One of my interviews with a labor councilor at the Office of Thai Labor Affairs, Royal Thai Embassy in Singapore, also confirms that no one knows the exact number of Thai migrant workers in the country, since Singapore has never disclosed this data, and only a small portion of Thai workers report themselves to the office upon their arrival. The statistics reported by Thailand's Ministry of Labor Affairs are also too broad to establish the actual number of Thai workers present at their workplaces in Singapore.[1]

As indicated by Porntipa Atipas (2001) and Wong (2000), the number of Thai migrant workers in Singapore has increased steadily from the late 1980s until the present. Indeed, Singapore is the only country receiving Thai labor that has maintained "the highest degree of continuity in employing Thai laborers during the last decade . . . where legal employment figures rose from 25,000 in 1988 to 50,000 in 1994 and 60,000 by the end of 1997. Thai workers represented one sixth of the total foreign workforce in 1995" (Supang, Germershausen, and Beesey 2000, 2). A more recent report by the Office of Labor Affairs in Singapore (2006) indicated that the total number of Thai workers in the first half of the 2000s seemed to be stable at around forty-five to fifty thousand, as the arrival of newly recruited workers has very significantly slowed down. Singapore's Ministry of Manpower (MOM) has maintained tight regulations since the mid-1990s regarding a standardized skill test that foreign workers must pass. Foreign workers also have to pay high job placement fees to private agencies (80,000–100,000 baht). In addition, Singaporean employers tend to look for workers from cheaper sources such as Bangladesh, India, and Myanmar to replace Thais who have received higher wages as trained and semiskilled workers. This has prevented more Thai workers from coming to Singapore in recent years.

Ethnographic Common Sense and the Study of Thai Migrant Workers in Singapore

My fieldwork experience in Singapore can be characterized as a committed process to ethnographic common sense. I have attempted to dig deep into the textures of everyday life for those on cross-border, contracted-employment missions. Cultural sensitivity and courtesy are among the key ingredients for successful fieldwork, which permitted me to "adjust [my own] role-repertoires to research objectives" (Gold 2005, 100). I stepped into the world of Thai migrant workers in Singapore with a sense of curiosity. Doing fieldwork requires common sense as much as scientific enquiry in order to enter the social field and establish rapport with the people one wants to study. I found myself talking to male workers (*khon ngan/raeng ngan*) sitting on the floor on top of used newspapers drinking beer or rice whisky and nibbling on snacks inside the Golden Mile shopping mall, or sitting with them under their residential flats or in the park. Cross-border tradeswomen (*mae kha*) from Hat Yai came to sell these workers snacks and occasional sexual services on weekends via the air-con buses that travel between Hat Yai, Malaysia and Singapore. Sex workers (*phuying ha kin*) also plied their trade in these areas.

Most of my informants were men and women speaking a distinctive Thai-Lao dialect. I usually began asking them such questions as how long they had been working in Singapore, which part of northeastern Thailand they came from, and what job they were on at the moment. Besides our common linguistic dialect, we develop rapport by sharing our places of origin. I come from a rural village in Nong Khai province. My informants came from various districts in the same province or neighboring provinces, such as Sakon Nakhon, Nakhon Phanom, Udon Thani, and Khon Kaen. They were more comfortable once they learned as a professor working in an established university in Singapore, I was interested in studying the livelihood of Thai workers in Singapore. They identified me as a Thai *achan* (teacher/instructor) who came from their home region of Isan and spoke their dialect. We were *khon ban diao kan* (people coming from the same village of origin). From my side, I was conscious of their status and identity based on Thai cultural conventions of seniority and fictive kinship. I therefore addressed my older tradeswomen informants as pa or na (aunt) and male workers as *phi* or *ai* (older brother) or *nong* (younger brother).

A few months after I arrived in Singapore, I discovered the Friends of Thai Workers Association (FTWA), located on the third level of the Golden Mile Complex. The FTWA is sponsored by the Office of Thai Labor Affairs and the Royal Thai Embassy and runs educational and cultural activities for the benefit of Thai migrant workers. It was looking for a volunteer teacher for their English classes and I decided immediately to take on that role. Most Thai workers have attained only four- or six-year compulsory education, and as a result overcoming language barriers in their workplaces was a daunting task. They speak neither English nor Hokkien nor Mandarin, the three main languages spoken in Singapore. It was difficult for them to communicate with their employers and co-workers from countries like Bangladesh, China, India, and Malaysia. My basic English course for Thai construction workers held on Sunday evenings eventually was opened to more than one hundred workers and students over the course of three years. Later, a number of Thai women married to Singaporean men as well as domestic workers, clerks, and sex workers joined my ever-expanding language classes. Through the act of volunteer teaching, I learned not only my proper field role, but also my true identity that makes up my selfhood. I always felt at home teaching and conducting research as an ethnographer from Isan with a strong Thai-Lao cultural sensitivity. My ethnographic fieldwork provides an opportunity for me to serve the community of Thai migrants in Singapore, especially those sharing my ethnocultural background. I identify myself with my own displaced people and our temporary sojourn away from home.

Headnotes, Heartnotes, and Thai Workers

Ottenberg (1990) argues that "headnotes" are fundamental for an ethnographer both during and after fieldwork investigation. By headnotes, he simply refers to the notes that are in the researcher's head. He maintains that "I remember many things, and some I include when I write even though I cannot find them in my fieldnotes, for I am certain that they are correct and not fantasy" (ibid., 144). Headnotes refers to mental note-taking and can include audio, visual, and graphic traces in one's memories of the field experience. Headnotes are the product of memo-faculties and can be recalled, retrieved, or reproduced in service of complementing the fieldworker's first-hand accounts of "being-there-in-the-field." Headnotes are specifically useful in certain sensitive field situations, where fieldworkers cannot make use of pens, pad-notes, or cameras.

My head and my heart usually go hand-in-hand. I learned how to take "heartnotes" over time and through cultivating close social relationships with groups of Thai workers as well as officials in charge of Thai labor affairs in Singapore. My "heartnotes" usually led to some further intriguing and exciting headnotes, as well as constant fieldnotes. This is illustrated by the ethnographic convention that "the ethnographer is engaged in 'writing down' what goes on" (Atkinson 1990, 61). With an extended period of contact with Thai workers in the classroom and by joining other Thai migrant activities, such as May Day celebrations, Thai football tournaments, and events commemorating Thailand's National Day, His Majesty the King's birthday on December 5, I gradually built rapport with a group of male informants who allowed me to visit their dormitories and observe their off-duty nightlife activities. These men invited me to join them on numerous occasions in the Kallang Riverside

Park, at the beer bars and pubs in the Geylang area, the Golden Mile Complex, and the Orchard Tower, as well as at their living quarters. They willingly cooperated with me throughout my semi-structured interviews and participant observations, even to the extent of allowing me access to their private lives.

Wolcott (2005) examines fieldwork in terms of its "basic arts," yet the art of studying the social life of a people must be firmly embedded in human relations. The social life of Thai migrants in Singapore is largely governed by forms of transient culture in which men and women struggle to survive on their menial labor wages in a given limited space and time. I developed good relations and trust with many of my informants. My straightforward approach was well-accepted by most of the male workers, whom I could comfortably engage in conversation. They knew me as a teacher/researcher and gave me full cooperation. Occasionally, I was met with suspicion and skepticism over my role as an ethnographer. Ket, for example, a veteran cross-border tradeswoman, initially believed I was a secret anti-narcotics police officer from Bangkok (see chapter 4). She had been searched and interrogated rather roughly by both Singapore's immigration officials and Thai police over a period of several years. The officials treated her as if she were a criminal suspect, instead of a small trader who was trying to earn a living to support her family. Her suspicion of me was valid given that no Thais or foreigners spend Sunday afternoons with tradeswomen in the Kallang Riverside Park. When I asked Ket if I could join her overnight bus trip to Hat Yai in southern Thailand, she sarcastically told me to prepare rolls of film and a good camera, so that I could take plenty of photos of her and her friends. I shrugged off her remarks, recognizing an ethnographic fieldwork truth: observers are constantly observed by their informants in the field (Stocking 1983). Natives and informants are keen observers, too.

Both headnotes and heartnotes guided me in the conscious process of "constructing the field" (Amit 2000). My fieldwork in Singapore among Thai migrant workers forced me to define and redefine Singapore as a fieldwork site. I had initially failed to see Singapore as an ethnographic field beyond its cosmopolitan, global images.[2] But my close relations with Thai migrant workers soon led me into social spaces which are usually hidden away or suppressed in Singapore's official and academic discourses. My perception of Singapore forever changed with these trips to marginalized places that were reconstructed and redefined by the migrant worker population.

Organization of the Book

This book consists of seven chapters. Following this introductory chapter, chapter two explores the multiple representations of migrant reality and masculine identities of Thai overseas workers in Singapore through popular music. It provides some background of popular culture in northeastern Thailand, and examines the musical representations of changing selfhood and sensibility among migrant men and their women. Chapter three looks at an example of village transnationalism set against the backdrop of Thai workers crafting their male gendered agency while living under Singapore's strict regulations and law enforcement governing foreign workers. Chapter four unfolds with a look at Thai men and Thai women's sexual desires and intimacy. I expand (and complicate) the model of transnational intimacy by introducing sex workers and tradeswomen from Thailand and juxtaposing men's voices to women's narratives. Chapter five examines male Thai workers' private sexual lives and the intimate patterns of desire that dictate their migrant pastimes in Singapore. It reveals channels of transnational intimacy between the Thai men and migrant women of different nationalities and cultural backgrounds. Chapter six uncovers the tragic side of transnational labor migration. Various causes of death, injury, and other calamitous incidents are examined as sets of common occurrences for Thai migrant workers. Chapter seven provides brief concluding remarks on the findings and implications of this study.

Chapter 2

The Lyrics of a Laborious Life

In Thailand, popular music represents a cultural site where labor migration and its consequences are narrated and performed. It is from this unusual place and mediation that I begin my discussion of the bare life of Thai workers in Singapore. The focal subject under investigation here is the gendered identities of male migrant workers as presented in contemporary song lyrics from northeastern Thailand. A selection of lyrics from popular Thai music genres, such as *phleng lukthung,*[1] *molam,*[2] and *phleng phuea chiwit*[3] forms the soundscape of transnational life realities, involving endless flows of migrant workers between home and host destinations. Produced and consumed by the masses, popular music creates as much as reflects the dynamic culture of migration.

By transcribing and reading a collection of hit song lyrics pertinent to the human experiences and sensibilities of Thai-Isan overseas migrant workers since the late 1970s, I intend to uncover some of the complex, cultural junctures of transnational labor migration. These cultural junctures are where men, mobility, and music meet and form a social force that reshapes the cultural imagination of migrant manhood. I argue that the popular music of Thailand, implicitly and explicitly, celebrates the male heroism of overseas migrant workers. Instead of challenging existing structures of hegemonic masculinity, popular Thai song texts poetically reaffirm and reassert traditional gender ideology and cultural practice. Overseas workers are usually depicted as hard-working, self-sacrificial heroes in their attempts to rescue their families from economic hardship, as well as romantic, caring lovers and morally responsible fathers. I define masculine heroism as a constructed dominant form of migrant male subjectivity and sensibility. However, heroic migrant manhood, as indicated in the lyrics of popular Thai-Isan songs, does not stand alone. Its existence as a dominant gender ideology depends very much on how it is related to and conditioned by the female presence. More often than not, overseas migrant workers' women at home—usually a wife, lover, or mother—are portrayed as either supportive or dishonest homemakers or partners. Hayes (2004) suggests that Thai popular music does not openly produce the discourse of resistance to existing structures of power relations and, in this case, of dominant gender ideology. Rather, it sustains or supports them.

Men, Migration, and Popular Music[4]

I, who worked myself to death like a *khwai Thai nai Singkhapo* (lit., Thai water buffalo working in Singapore), was dumped. After three years away abroad to earn money for our family, I returned home only to find that my wife had gone away with her lover, leaving my children with their grandmother. My entire savings was also gone. I can't believe it! My wife "put a pair of buffalo horns on my head." Is this what I deserve after years of sacrifice and hardship abroad? (Lukphrae and Maithai 2002[?])

The lyrics of this top hit song by the *lukthung-molam* duo Lukphrae and Maithai Uraiphon feature some of the familiar repercussions associated with overseas labor migration—broken families, lovelorn episodes, shattered dreams, and a sense of betrayal. The song depicts the painful consequences of transnational migration after returning home. A despairing husband/father narrates a tearful lamentation over his bitter shame and shattered masculine pride after learning his hard-earned savings have vanished and his wife has run off with her lover. The song exposes a deep emotional soul-searching moment of how the traditional ideal of Thai-Isan masculine heroism has come under threat in the "age of migration" (Castles and Miller 1998).

I use the lyrics from the song "Thai buffalos working in Singapore" (*Khwai Thai nai Singkhapo*) as a starting point to explore issues concerning human experiences and sensitivities in the complex processes of transnational labor migration from northeastern Thailand. Baily and Collyer (2006, 18) remind us that "lyrics are the element of music most similar to creative literature and they can be analyzed in similar ways to shed light on processes of transnational cultural production."

Labor migration is a productive form of social force and cultural practice. Castles and Miller (1998, 1) argue that the emergence of international migration is also a "force for social transformation." Labor migration, as a social force and set of human experiences, cannot be fully understood by statistics, survey data, or economic development indicators alone. Music and other popular cultural forms, such as film, literature, and art performance, are equally prominent data sources, which reflect the human experience and emotions that are part of transnational labor migration processes (see Bottomley 1992; Connell and Gibson 2004; Naficy 2001).

Men, migration, and music mark a critical intersection in studies of transnational labor migration. Men have remained important transnational sojourners despite an increasing number of female domestic workers and caregivers during the last decade. Men's roles as family breadwinners and their struggles in international labor markets are well-documented, but I suggest that representing male migrant workers through popular song lyrics provides an opportunity to examine male migrant selfhoods and sensibilities. Some key questions concerning the constructions of gendered migration culture include: What is the male dominant ideology performed in transnational settings, which is often part of the cultural practices of many labor exporting countries such as Bangladesh (Rahman and Lian 2005), India (Osella and Osella 2000b), and the Philippines (Marigold 1995; Parrenas 2001b)? And how is such male dominant gender ideology narrated and expressed in and through popular music genres?

The gender culture among Thai overseas workers is culturally constructed as "hegemonic masculinity" (Connell and Messerschmidt 2005). Broadly referred to as a cultural norm and ideal of male behavior, such a form of masculinity is meant to encourage the dominant position of some men over others, and the subordination of women. Thai foreign workers' identities and sensibilities are deeply embedded in the Buddhist culture of gender (Keyes 1984, 1986). They are culturally created throughout the life passage from boyhood to manhood. Males grow up with a strong motivation to assume a leadership role as well as to be providers for their families. When they become overseas migrant workers, they carry the masculine burden of "being *good at* being a man" (Herzfeld 1985, 16) with them from their home; they also must adjust their masculine sensitivity within the transnational context.

Individuals engaged in transnational labor migration are first and foremost men. The gender culture of Thai overseas workers contributes to the way one behaves as a man and creates symbolic masculine pride, which constitutes a gender-based ideology and practice. The culture of overseas migrant manhood produces a range of outcomes. On one side of the spectrum, these workers' masculine culture can be described as a *"nakleng-like"* model of social action that can be seen in the workers' passion for drinking, gambling, smoking, and womanizing. *Nakleng*—literally, rogue, tough, fearless, and influential—is an ideal type of Thai masculinity (Thak 2007). Yet these workers' masculinity also acts as a source of inspiration and moral commitment to their families and communities of origin. Masculine culture reinforces working-class migrants' responsibility to excel at being breadwinners and leaders in both the household and society at large. It encourages men to work hard, earn money, and redistribute some of that money to their family and others at home. Strong moral commitments to family members through regular remittances and the funding of Buddhist merit-making projects help support the welfare of their community back home (see chapter 3).

Popular music has emerged as a cultural medium, conveying and reflecting gender and other cultural aspects of transnational migration. The landscape of transnational labor migration is demarcated and redefined in and by certain musical traditions. In other words, transnational labor migration is registered in the domain of public culture as well as individuals' consciousness through the subtle works of popular music. Travel away from home and overseas employment are major factors contributing to altering or transforming the migrant's cultural "habitus" (Bourdieu 1977), with popular music emerging as one of the dynamic cultural sites recording and commenting on the impacts of transnational labor migration. As Deborah Wong (1998, 97) suggests, travel and music "map out decades-old processes of labor migration and speak on the emotional language of displacement and nostalgia."

Music migrates as its audiences move socioculturally and geographically.[5] Both internal and transnational labor migrations are exciting economic and cultural venues from which to observe the subtle power of popular music beyond "its naked commodity" (ibid., 26). "Music is performative and it 'speaks' with considerable power and subtlety as a discourse of difference," argues Wong (2004, 3). It is music's performative power and subtlety that makes transnational labor migration a cultural practice and "constructs new critical realities" (ibid.) out of the transient transnational social fields. In recording social dramatic events, popular music appeals and speaks to its audiences, turning them into "the person[s] for whom the song ideally speaks" (Adorno 1962, 27). In this respect, transnational labor migration has been registered in the public awareness and consciousness through song lyrics and musical performances that are centered on the lives of migrant workers and those people and communities left behind.

Pai Krungthep: Isan Migrant Workers' Lives Prior to Transnational Labor Migration

Labor migration is not new in Thailand (Supang 1999). An early pattern of rural-to-urban migration emerged in Thailand and became rather prominent in the seasonal labor movements of peoples from the high plateau of Khorat to the central plains of Thailand and further south to Bangkok. Working-age individuals from Isan migrated because of the region's poverty, drought, and limited natural resources. Prior to the beginning of each rice-planting season, lengthy droughts often required the movement of people in search of alternative livelihoods, at least for a few months (Curran et al. 2005, 230). This seasonal labor migratory flow began as early as the late nineteenth century when the central plain of Rangsit was developed as irrigated rice plantations to meet the high demand for rice on the world market. Isan supplied menial labor to this early agricultural development program, as the region's labor forces were abundant and already familiar with geographically constrained movements.

Labor migration from the marginal periphery of Isan to the modern center and further on to the world beyond is a fundamental part of life for the population of Isan. Kampoon Boontawee (1976) tells stories set prior to the Second World War in the early decades of the twentieth century[6] that reflect his own biographical account of how young men in his village escaped drought and hardship in search of cash income, valuable knowledge, and beyond-village world experience. These men journeyed to distant places like Bangkok, Luang Prabang, and Vientiane. Both Luang Prabang and Vientiane are located on the Lao side of the Mekong River and were then considered the center of the world for the Lao-speaking Isan people (Dararat 2003). However, beginning with the era of "development" in the 1950s and 1960s, Bangkok became the center of their universe. This was despite the rise of "Isan regionalism" (Keyes 1967), which involved Isan people's political loyalties to their ethnocultural and linguistic brethren in Laos during the height of the US-led Indochinese War.

Internal rural-to-urban labor migration is made possible through, and facilitated by, cultural channels of social and geographical mobilities. Isan villagers' perception of labor migration is viewed through three everyday colloquial terms: *pai thiao* (to go around), *pai Thai* (to go to a Thai-speaking area/region) and *pai Krungthep* (to go to Bangkok). These channels represent major *pai*-patterns of labor mobility in the region. Kirsch (1966) suggests that the term "*pai thiao*" (to go around) represents a social mobility channel for traveling in search of seasonal wage employment and adventures to Laos, Bangkok, southern Thailand, and other areas. These young men, it is assumed, will return home with some savings, considerable skills, and an experience of the "world," which will enable them to get married, settle down, and start their own families. The term "*pai Thai*" shows Isan migrant workers' perception of ethnocultural differences between themselves and Central Thai speaking employers/people, whereas *pai Khrungthep* once again reveals Bangkok as the most desired migrant destination and the encompassing influential center of Thai modernity (Mills 1999b). The musician Su Su (1997a) sings about an Isan reed piper (*mo khaen*) who goes to Bangkok to play his music in exchange for money. In the song, Su Su uses the vernacular expression "when I do not have money, I go to *Krungthep*" (*mai mi ngoen ko pai Krungthep*).[7] These three terms marking Isan's active routes of mobility—*pai thiao, pai Thai*, and *pai Khrungthep*—reflect the popular discourse of internal labor migration in the region. The gradual vanishing of *pai thiao* and *pai Thai* from people's everyday vocabulary suggests the ever-increasing prominent role of Bangkok and its vicinities as top employment destinations (Ayal 1992; Curran et al. 2005; Fuller, Lightfoot, and Peerasit 1985; Mills 1999a; Penporn 1978; Wilson 2004; Yang 1994). It further reveals, more than ever, the physical and cultural closeness and familiarity with the Thai capital that Isan villagers have accumulated over years of their labor migratory experiences.

Bangkok has long been a prime destination for young migrants from Isan. The popular lyrics of *molam* and *lukthung* during the decades after the Second World War introduced Bangkok as the country's Mecca of economic prosperity, political power, and Western-style modernity. The classic *lam klon* and *lam long* lyrics of great national artists like Bunpheng Faiphiewchai, Chawiwan Damnoen, Khen Dalao, and Thongmak Chanthalue regularly featured accounts of Bangkok's Western-style modernity (Charuwan Thammawat 1997; Phaibun Phaeng-ngoen 1991). In the song "The ex-novice Bua takes a train ride to Bangkok" (*Siang Bua long krung*) by Saksayam Petchomphu (1975[?]), young men from Isan villages who are traveling by rail from Ubon Ratchathani to Bangkok share their mixed feelings of the sorrow they feel for leaving home and the excitement of their first-time experience of "arriving" in Bangkok.[8] They bid farewell to parents and beg their lovers to wait for them until their return. In the song, these young men tell their beloveds: "I am going to work as a wage laborer in Bangkok. My dear love, please wait for me for a year. We shall have a grand wedding when I return" (ibid.). This song was released in the mid-1970s, which was the period when train transport had established itself as a prime mode for migrant workers to travel to and from Bangkok. The song records events and places along the main railway stations from Ubon Ratchathani through Khorat and on to Bangkok. For young village boys-turned-migrant workers, it was a memorable expedition filled with excitement before being pulled down into the harsh realities of Bangkok's third-world factory environments.

Music often narrates the difficult and emotional realities of transient life. Hardship and suffering, homesickness, loneliness, poor living and working environments, and the transformation from rural rice farmers to urban migrant workers are some of the most common themes in the *phleng phuea chiwit* movements. This music genre billed itself as the champion of the underprivileged and the poor by the time it made its musical breakthrough in the early 1980s (Wong 1998). Both Caravan and Carabao, arguably the founders of the *phleng phuea chiwit* genre, produced songs and marketed their works by advocating for the rights and welfare of migrant workers and other underprivileged people.

In 1985, Caravan's song "Homeless fish" (*Pla rai wang*) portrayed construction workers as roving men who sell their labor for cash, and constantly move from one construction site to another. It depicts migrant workers' life as hopeless, with a sense of no tomorrow. Carabao (1983), adopting a pair of buffalo horns as its logo to represent the Thai working class, refers to migrant workers from the northeastern region as *khon niranam* (nameless people). Millions of workers from the countryside were hardly treated as fellow human beings in the eyes of the urban public. Their employers tended to see them as a labor commodity rather than persons with unique identities and lifestyles. They were known as workers (*khon ngan/kammakon*) who roamed Bangkok streets, factories, and construction sites in search of daily wage employment. Isan workers were known to be diligent and industrious. They escaped drought and poverty from their home villages and were able to work every type of construction job, from steel, concrete, and carpentry to road construction projects. Their labor was cheap and in abundant supply, flowing down from every corner of the vast, high plateau region. But the question remained: Who will employ these "nameless people" (*khrai cha chang phuak khao khon niranam*)? Through a sampling of lyrics, one fact stands out: Isan men preceded their female counterparts in the musical representations of early-day rural-to-urban labor migration.

The emotional sense of displacement and nostalgia of home along with strong cultural roots appears as a prominent theme of musical narratives pertaining to migratory life. Isan as "birthplace" (*ban koet*) and "home" (*ban*) is often imagined as the prime object of nostalgic narrations despite the region's poverty and natural impoverishment. The nostalgia of home is emotionally felt deep in the hearts and souls of displaced migrant workers, particularly "when they are comfortably removed from it" (Chang 1999, 37).[9] The term "comfortably" requires some further clarification. It only makes sense for Isan migrant workers when the term refers to being situated far from home in geographical and imagined realities. Homesickness and loneliness in harsh urban environments provide the time and distance to internalize their memories of "home" and village life into mental material for nostalgia. The famous *molam* epic "The life of Isan rice farmers" (*Chiwit chao na*) by Chawiwan Damnoen (1974[?]) is perhaps the most powerful narrative of rain-fed rice farmers' memories of Isan's old days. It tells of life at home and the hardship of its people, whose survival heavily depends on the mercy of mother nature. "Rice-cultivating villages as heaven on earth" (*Sawan ban na*) by Phonsak Songsaeng (1986b[?]), "I love my rice-farming village" (*Chan rak ban na*) by Siriphon Amphaiphong (1987), and "Come home to Isan, my dear brothers!" (*Klap Isan thoet ai*) by Phikun Khwanmuang (1997b[?]) are three examples of *molam* hits with lyrics pertinent to Isan workers' deep longing for a reunion with their rice-farming village life at home.

The manner in which the farmer's life is lexically put into lyrics and melodies is filled with a sense of nostalgic pride in Isan's self-sufficient village traditions. As in the timeless hit song "Isan, our homeland" (*Isan ban hao*) by Thepphon Phet-Ubon (1975[?]), Isan village life is firmly attached to the fond scent of water buffaloes lying in the muddy ponds, the memory of *molam* performances during festivals, the haunting soundscape of *khaen* (reed pipe) from young men displaying their musical skills to attract lovers, and the delicious taste of local food. The village as a living place in time is even more special in one's memory. Siriphon Amphaiphong (2005) fondly recaptures memories of her family and home village when thinking about the rice harvesting season and kite-flying against the cold wind. The attachment of Tai Orathai (2003b) to her home surfaces when in bed at night she listens "to the sound of rainfall on the roof" (*non fang siang fon*). As she lies there, she recalls, "I played with my brother and sister in the rice field when it was raining last year. This year I sleep alone in a rented factory dorm when the rain comes." The comfort of home is a formidably powerful force that brings out the perennial homesickness of each migrant worker. The memories of Isan village life are sustained and reproduced during migratory flights away from home.

The nostalgic sentiments of the "imagined home" often overshadow Isan village real-life, bone-breaking hardships. In the migrant worker's mind, Isan as "home" is always imagined as the most heavenly place on earth. Unlike the "paradise" of the old days in Chawiwan Damnoen's (1974[?]) song "The life of Isan rice farmers" (*Chitwit chao na*), poverty-stricken Isan villages in the 1980s had to rely on mother nature (rainfall) and remittances from young men and women working in Bangkok and other urban areas or overseas to sustain themselves. Poverty and drought forced many to leave their homes. They flooded the streets of Bangkok in search of wage labor in factories, gas stations, restaurants, service industries, and the entertainment industry. Some drove taxis; many sold food. They made up Bangkok's underclass population, yet nostalgic memories of home and their folks left behind in Isan were always with them. Rainfall is like a "divine calling" for them—a return to refresh or renew their bonds with their village paradise. However, "when there is no rainfall, rice farming is suspended. Young people have to head back to Bangkok, leaving behind their 'village heaven' and old folks" (Carabao 1984).

The emotionally painful nostalgia of "home" is made bearable through a psychological negation that comes with hopeful upcoming holiday visits. The nostalgic attachments to home villages, together with regular communications through letter-writing, telephone calls, and remittances, encourage migrant workers to make trips home. Their constant transient life is endured by the conditioned promises of homecomings and family reunions during the major annual holiday seasons such as Songkran (traditional Thai New Year), *trut Chin* (lunar/Chinese New Year), and the Western New Year (January 1). Their rooted homes loom large in their transient emotions of joy as well as loneliness and sorrow. Traffic jams during the long holidays and festive celebrations in villages across the vast region are among major themes in popular songs, which include the hits "Returning to celebrate Songkran in our home villages" (*Klap pai Songkran ban na*) by Su Su (1997b) and "A call for Isan migrants to return home" (*Isan khuen thin*) by David Inthi (2003[?]). Both songs celebrate the Songkran festival as memorable moments of annual homecoming and family reunion for young Isan workers. "The promise made in front of the *lukthung-molam* concert stage" (*Sanya na han*) by Tai Orathai (2003c) unfolds at the festive celebration of a *pha pa* (merit-making) ceremony, organized by returning migrant workers. Amid their happiest moments of celebration, young migrant men and women vow to keep their promise to return for annual homecomings as part of their "routine job" (*ngan pracham*). These festive occasions present migrant workers with opportunities to leave behind the harsh realities of work and life in the city and to re-embrace their Isan's sweet home once again. Deep in their hearts, they know that their pleasant breaks from the city and holiday homecomings do not last long. Nonetheless, they are a way to throw themselves into temporary suspension and escape.

Pai Nok: Isan's Embracing of Transnational Labor Migration

By the early 1980s, Thailand's Isan community had intensely embraced transnational labor migration, as can be seen in the terms used in the vernacular language of rural villagers. Throughout the region, transnational labor migration is perceived through everyday colloquial terms such as *pai nok*, literally "to go abroad."[10] Despite the existence of the Thai official expression *kan doen thang pai tham ngan tang prathet* (a trip to go and work abroad), the term "*pai nok*" has gained overwhelming acceptance among ordinary people in this historically labor-exporting region. Sometimes, seeking employment abroad is understood through the terms used by well-known musicians; example lyrics include *"pai ha kin mueang nok"* (to go make a living abroad) by Carabao (1985) and *"pai ha ngoen ha thong/kham"* (to go seek money and valuables) by Phonsak Songsaeng (1982a[?]). These terms effectively imply that working at home in Isan or elsewhere in Thailand is insufficient to make a living for rural villagers. As Bunchu Buaphang (2002[?]) points out in his VCD, "I have to flee Thailand—the land of so little money (*ni Thailand daen ngoen noi*) to become a wage laborer in Taiwan. I am poor and heavily indebted, so I have to go."[11] Rural villagers are forced to leave home and enter the international labor market. Phonsak Songsaeng (1986c[?]) confesses in one of his songs that "because of poverty (*khwam chon*), I have to leave home, leave my birthplace, family and parents, to become a temporarily diasporic person (*khon klai ban*)." The same reasoning lingers in certain later *lukthung-molam* lyrics: "I am sad. I miss home so badly. I am very poor, thus I had to leave home. I have to endure hardship and sell my labor to feed my own mouth [and my family left behind at home]" (Lukphrae and Maithai 1998[?]). Through these self-reflexive expressions emphasizing the active movement away from home (e.g., *pai* = to go; *ni* = to flee or escape; *chak* = to leave or depart), Isan's route to transnationalization from below has gained increasing momentum involving a large-scale movement of a rural workforce.

The mirage of overseas labor migration as a "gold mine" was created and produced by the pioneering generations of Thai workers heading for construction jobs in the oil-rich Middle East, which has been a region-wide phenomenon since the early 1980s. At the time, Saudi Arabia employed the majority of these Thai workers. Labor migration to the Middle East created waves of region-wide awareness of *pai khut thong mueang nok* (going to dig gold abroad) and *pai Sa-u* (to go work in Saudi Arabia).[12] This early *pai nok* labor migration was largely exaggerated as a quick, profitable investment for rural villagers. Its lure of money-making is reflected in the expressions, *pai khut thong mueang nok* (to go digging for gold in a foreign country) or simply *pai khut thong* (to dig for gold). Since the wages in the Middle East were "often five times higher than Thailand's" ("Letter from Bangkok" 1984, 26), migrating there was simply irresistible for rural villagers.

Overseas remittances became a new-found source of unimaginable wealth by poverty-stricken, rain-fed rice farming families in rural Thailand. *Pai nok* labor migration quickly became a social phenomenon as millions of rural families pinned their hope on overseas employment for their male members, usually the father or an unmarried older son. "Saudi Arabia" (*Sa-u*) by Phonsak Songsaeng (1982b[?]) describes the large numbers of Thai workers in Saudi Arabia: "The cement specialist, the carpenter, the menial laborer are all Thais. Some are diligent, others are always lazy, but everybody is happy by the end of the week (payday). During their pastime, they sing songs or engage in Thai boxing. They expect to be rich (*ruai*) with some bundle of cash by the end of their contract, unless they lose it in gambling with their fellow workers."

The Birth of Migrant Working-Class Romanticism

Pai nok migrant workers are primarily rural villagers, but they are not necessarily the poorest in their villages. The majority of them have considerable experience with internal labor migration to Bangkok and other industrial centers in Thailand prior to their overseas trips.[13] This trend conforms to a general thesis that internal migration is "often the first step in a process that leads to international movement" (Castles and Miller 1993, 141). In the Thai official and academic languages, *pai nok* migrant workers are known respectively as *nakrop setthakit* (economic warriors), *nakrop raeng ngan* (labor warriors) and *raeng ngan kham chat* (transnational laborers). The first two terms are used to acknowledge these workers' contributions to the national economy through their remittances, while the last term provides an overarching description of the movement of workers across international borders. However, the identity associated with *pai nok* migrant workers is rather broad. This was especially the case when the term was used in the late 1970s and 1980s. There is virtually no Thai term that differentiates between internal and overseas migrant workers. The terms for internal labor migration such as "*kammakon*," "*chap kang*," "*phu chai raeng ngan*," and "*raeng ngan rap chang*" are commonly also assigned to menial *pai nok* overseas workers. *Khon ngan* (worker) is another widely used colloquial Thai term that functions as a general reference for both internal and overseas migrant workers. These terminological nametags suggest blue-collar occupations, and they further stamp a particular identity on the public's perception of these men and women as working-class with underprivileged social distinctions. As a result of the country's large-scale transformation from industrialization to urbanization since the 1960s (Pasuk and Baker 2002), these workers' rural background is constantly looked down upon by the general public at large.

Early musical accounts of Thailand's overseas labor migration appeared soon after the conclusion of the Indochinese War in the mid-1970s.[14] With a sudden void of employment opportunities created by the expulsion of US military personnel and services from the country, skilled and semiskilled Thai technicians and menial workers headed to the Middle East, where demands for foreign workers were at an all-time high. As a result, a large number of Thai prostitutes, GIs' lovers, and "rented wives" (*mia chao*) were unemployed. It was these women who first became the objects of sarcastic remarks in popular *lukthung* lyrics. One famous *lukthung* song posed these questions to Thai sex workers at the time: "Why don't you go to America as a GI's wife and enjoy the [US] dollar-filled life? Why do you have to come back to Thailand? Why don't you go to the US, *maem pla ra* (lit., Ma'am Fermented Fish)?" (Sayan 1975[?]). This song criticizes GIs' wives from a specific Thai male perspective prominent in the mid-1970s, when the presence of US military and Western cultural influences in Thailand were considered sources of both political dependence and social vice. Another hit song, adopting the sarcastic tone of Thai men, carries this lament: "I hate to say it but I am sick of you, you the GI's woman. You always look down on me (a local Thai man). You pretend as though I do not exist at all. You adore your *farang* man as if he was a deity (*thewada*)" (Sayan

1975[?]). These popular sentiments from the 1970s reveal that not only was the whole decade one of political turbulence, but it was also a historical moment of cultural transition due to the onset of high mobility into global junctures among the local population.

Overseas migrant workers are often given an identity marker based on their specialized skills, particularly within the construction industry. Phonsak Songsaeng (1982b[?]) noted in one of his songs that in the early 1980s there were a large number of Thai electricians, welders, bricklayers, carpenters, and general laborers in Saudi Arabia. In the 1980s and 1990s, Phonsak Songsaeng (1982a[?]) and Phongthep Kradonchamnan (1992)[15] both produced lyrics about "young construction workers" (*num ko sang*) who urged their lovers to wait for them until they could save enough money to return home. Later, Phongsit Khamphi (2000a) employed the general term "*kammakon*" to refer to menial workers and sang a song with the lyrics: "My father is a *kammakon* who has to go and work abroad because wages in Thailand are too low and the voices of workers usually fall on deaf ears." Carabao (1985) referred to overseas migrant workers as the poor (*khon chon*) who "were born poor and vulnerable" and who "never have the upper hand in dealing with people," further noting that they are cheated and victimized when applying for employment abroad.

One particular noted identity of Thai-Isan workers is that they possess limited social assets and privilege and thus must rely heavily on their manual labor to earn a living, as noted in the songs "Wading into Kuwait" (*Lui Khuwet*) by Su Su (1991) and "Wandering hard-working Isan people" (*Khon sing Isan*), also by Su Su (1997a). The first song describes Thai-Isan workers as "*phuak kha mai kaen lon Isan*" (lit., Isan wooden log traders). Here, the wooden log (lit., *mai kaen lon*) is used metaphorically to refer to the workers' hard-shelled, muscular bodies. These workers are seen as unsophisticated, as revealed by physical attributes. The second song refers to Thai-Isan workers as "lions who feed on daily wages" (*sing rai wan*) and portrays these workers as men who work with their hands and feed on their daily minimum wages.

By the late 1990s and 2000s, migrant workers' social identities shifted. No longer were they seen as individuals with low social status. Now, the ideal of migrant romanticism took over. I employ the term "migrant romanticism" to refer to an emerging view of the migrant lifestyle that focuses heavily on the ways of life away from parents' gazes and home village comforts and male-female courtship. From the 1980s onwards, internal labor migration was no longer seasonal or marked by male-dominated flows of working-age rural populations to urban settings. The feminization of the migrant workforce became highly visible as young women began to make up more than 60 percent of the migrant workers from the countryside (Curran et al. 2005; Mills 1999a).

The shift of social identities and the response to the rise of migrant romanticism owes a great deal to the arrival of Thai-Isan-style *luk-thung* superstars like Chintara Phunlap, Mike Phiromphon, Siriphon Amphaiphong and Tai Orathai. Ethnoculturally labeled by some music critics in Bangkok and central Thailand as Lao-speaking *lukthung* (*lukthung Lao*), these singers come from Thai-Isan rural villages and were themselves migrant workers in Bangkok. Sponsored by the country's giant Grammy Records and the gifted Isan composer Sala Khunawut, they were heavily marketed as the romantic voices of migrant workers.[16] Top hits by these famous musicians portrayed young migrant workers, both male and female, as devoted heroes and heroines who worked hard for their families and lovers. Two hits by Siriphon Amphaiphong (2003a, 2003b), "For my mother, I can't give up" (*Phuea mae phae bo dai*) and "Moral support for daily-wage workers" (*Raeng chai rai wan*), show the double burden on young female workers who toil hard to send remittances back home to their mothers, while also trying their best to cheer up the men they have left behind. These songs seem to replicate the traditional roles of village women in the complex rural-urban ties that bind them. The song "Selling my labor to marry my love" (*Khai raeng taeng nang*) by Mike Phiromphon (2002c) is about a young man, rather than a woman, who, speaking from the bottom of his heart, is determined to leave home to work and save enough money to fulfill the promise he gives to his lover. "Each drop of my sweat is dedicated to you. I can always endure physical fatigue for my dear love at home." In two megahits by Tai Orathai (2003e, 2003a), "Honey, have you eaten yet?" (*Kin khao rue yang*) and "Young girls' moral support to their dear workers" (*Kaem daeng raeng chai*), young village girls are shown as supportive and cheerful toward their men who have left the village to find work. They encourage their men to work hard and save money in order to realize their dreams. "I will always be loyal to you and will wait patiently until you can save enough money for our marriage. I am looking forward to our promised date with faith and love" (ibid.).

In short, the lyrics of these songs glorify men and reproduce images of migrant men fitting well with Thailand's dominant gender ideology, in which a young single man is expected to prove his manhood by earning enough money to build his own family. A young single woman is traditionally taught to be supportive and committed both to her family and to the man she loves. Heterosexual romanticism tends to be heavily idealistic in recent *lukthung* musical representations. Male and female migrants appear intensely in love and as responsibly faithful to each other. This type of romantic love is exemplified in Mike Phiromphon's (2003b) song, "The white towel on my left shoulder" (*Pha khao bon ba sai*), which tells the story of why a young man always keeps a white towel, a gift from his girlfriend, on his left shoulder. Having the beloved towel on his left shoulder is not only convenient as it allows him to use it to wipe away his sweat while he is working, but it is also physically and symbolically close to his heart. The towel helps remind him of the promise that he and his lover made to each other before he left on his "sweat-for-money" (*nguea laek ngoen*) undertaking. Crucial to the masculine pride of young male workers is having girlfriends who inspire and motivate them to leave home and work hard to earn enough money. "I am a man. I have to leave home to work. I can endure the hard work, but I can hardly stand to endure the longing love I have for you when we are apart" (Mike Phiromphon 2001c).

Some co-habiting internal migrant couples make their living at the lower end of the city's economic sphere, selling noodles or chicken rice, or working in factories. They are represented as cheerful and supportive lovers who are always there for each other. These characters show up in megahits like "Are you tired, my dear?" (*Nueai mai khon di*) by Mike Phiromphon (2001f) and Siriphon Amphaiphong's (2001b) "Certificate of the Heart" (*Parinya chai*). Moral support and inspiration (*kamlang chai/raeng chai*) to delight each other's spirit in the form of a sweet smile, a simple small gift, a telephone call, or a kind word means much to struggling migrant workers who must sustain their romantic lives while in transit.

Pai Nok Workers as Poor Water Buffaloes at the Hands of Wicked Middlemen

The romanticism associated with internal migration is also attached to transnational migration. Hardworking, yet romanticized portrayals of Thai-Isan overseas migrant workers usually exist hand-in-hand with images of them as innocent and victimized. These workers are represented as unsophisticated countrymen that stand in stark contrast to the urban-based recruitment agents (widely known as *nai na*) and their international networks. Two prominent messages of *pai Sa-u* (lit., going to Saudi Arabia) labor migration, as it is widely known to the public, are its high wages and rumors or news via popular media outlets about job placement agencies cheating and overcharging these migrant workers. Family tensions also surface as a topic of public discussion due to the extended periods of absence of the *pai nok* workers from their wives and children. Thai society as a whole has learned about corrupt placement and recruitment agencies through such popular sayings as *pai sia na, ma sia mia* (lit., you lose your rice land [mostly to the bank mortgage] when you leave and you lose your wife [either to adultery or divorce] when you come back). The songs, "Saudi Arabia/Udon Thani" (*Sa-udon*) by Carabao (1985), "Three days to fly" (*Sam wan bin*) by Phonsak Songsaeng (1979b[?]), and "Saudi Arabia" (*Sa-u*) by Phonsak Songsaeng 1982b[?]) are musical hits from the late 1970s and early 1980s, all of which tell heartbreaking stories of poor workers that were deceived by wicked middlemen and job placement agencies. As innocent and unknowing, these men completely trusted the middlemen. They unquestioningly followed their instructions and paid air fares, recruitment fees, and other charges in advance. Nonetheless, they ended up facing a series of broken promises and deceptions, such as "you will be flown abroad within three days." In one of the worst cases of labor scams, false recruitment agencies flew migrant workers-to-be on a Thai Airways' domestic flight back to the heartland of Isan in Udon Thani, instead of taking them to Saudi Arabia where well-paid jobs were promised.[17]

The "gold mines" of Saudi Arabia and other Middle Eastern countries proved to be an illusion. What emerged at home were rumors and news items in the press involving one-sided battles between "poor water buffaloes" and "wicked middlemen/wolves." As reflected in the popular saying *pai sia na, ma sia mia,* if overseas labor migration fails, it can be a disastrous, loss-incurring venture for village men, who are seen as *khwai* (lit., water buffaloes) on each leg of their trip—going and coming. Overseas labor migration can effectively turn proud, industrious men into hopeless, near-bankrupted persons whose life-risking venture often ends in shame and dismay.

The middlemen and recruitment agencies play a crucial part in determining the workers' success or failure. In most cases, *nai na* are urban-based business persons with distinctive ethnic markers like Sino- or Vietnamese-Thai, whereas local villagers are predominantly Thai-Lao. The villagers are typically known for their keen profit-making attitude and skills. In the song "Do not risk your future by taking a side route" (*Thang biang ya siang doen*) by Mike Phiromphon (2001a), the middleman is described as *nai na chai dam* (lit., black hearted or cold-blooded), who mercilessly scams money and assets from rural villagers and their families. Isan villagers who make the decision to *pai nok* gamble with the family's future by mortgaging or selling their families' most valuable assets and last resources, namely farm lands and houses. When their trip abroad fails, it means they are virtually bankrupt. Their own life is also at stake. The worst scenarios are cases where they are killed in workplace accidents, or imprisoned or sentenced to death by foreign authorities due to their involvement in criminal or illegal activities (Pattana 2005b). Transnational labor migration thus takes on the stunning metaphor of a gambling bet (Aguilar 1999). It is a high-risk and dangerous venture for rural villagers, who necessarily are in a very disadvantageous position. As in the culture of gambling, success or failure, life or death in the context of labor migration is a matter of fate and luck (Pattana 2005a). You win some; you lose some.

One veteran transnational migrant worker from Nong Khai used a boxing metaphor to explain his overseas labor migration venture. "One has to endure hardship and patiently wait for the golden moment to throw a knock-out punch. Every migrant worker has lived his life for this golden moment to strike his goal. Persistence pays off as every dog always has its day."[18]

Transnational Romances

Popular music in Thailand has long recounted both romantic and tragic long-distance love stories. Once again, the song lyrics show that transnational labor migration is bound up with a variety of human emotions. Longing for love and care when young lovers or a husband and wife must be separated from one another is rather common. Phonsak Songsaeng (1979a[?]), the perennial king of the *lukthung-molam* genre, released one of the first songs on Thai migrant workers in Singapore in the late 1970s entitled "My heart is off to my lover working in Singapore" (*Fak chai pai Singkhapo*). The song is sung from the perspective of a young man whose "factory girl" (*sao rong ngan*) was among the first batch of Thai workers employed in Singapore's electronic and garment industries (Wong 1996). The song registers the intimate feelings of love and longing across seas of distance in a foreign land in the closing years of the 1970s. "Singapore is too far away. My lover has left me behind a long time ago, and I can't wait until the day she comes home" (Phonsak 1979a[?]).

A more familiar romantic tone adopted in Thai popular music is the voice of young girls and wives who *song chai* or *fak chai* (lit., send their hearts wrapped up with long-lasting love and care) to their lovers working in faraway lands. Siriphon Amphaiphong (2002b) sings powerfully on behalf of Isan girls whose lovers work in Taiwan. "Sea, mountain, and sky separate us, but our love always sails through barriers. We stay apart, but our hearts remain as close as ever. Taiwan and Thailand are so near and so real, at least in my heart." In "I wait for my lover working in a foreign country" (*Khoi rak chak tang daen*), Chintara Phunlap (1987[?]) sings about how an Isan girl is committed to her man in the Middle East from the day he boards the plane until the day he returns. When Iraq invaded Kuwait and ignited the Gulf War in 1990, Chintara Phunlap (1999) sang the hit song "I am worried to death for the safety of my lover working in Kuwait" (*Huang phi thi Khuwet*) to express her deep concerns about the well-being of her lover during that critical time. She urged her lover to "write a letter home if you are still alive because I am sick of worrying. I can't even eat since I do not know what your situation is out there." In the song "I love the foreman" (*Rak num fomaen*), Siriphon Amphaiphong (2002c) sings about the moment when an Isan girl sees her lover off at Don Muang International Airport, as he leaves to go work as a foreman in Bahrain.

"Tears have blurred my eyes and my heart beat so loud as the plane took off." She reminds her lover to concentrate on his work and save money. She even cautions him not to eye the girls while he is away.

Musical representations of long-distance romantic love tend to be excessively idealistic. These representations sometimes speak to the lonely young overseas female workers in many Asian countries as well as European ones,[19] such as Germany and Switzerland, who, from a distance, express their love towards their men back home in Isan. In the song "I am lonely in a foreign country" (*Ngao chai nai tang daen*), Chintara Phunlap (2005) tells a story of a young Isan girl who cries on her international flight from Bangkok to Germany, and how she must adjust herself to factory work in a cold, foreign environment. Her only goal is to make money, hoping to save some "hundred thousand or a million baht" to bring home. She will not cast an eye on *farang* men. Her heart is loyal to her lover in Isan who is always present in her dreams." In reality, the girl may or may not work in a factory at all, but she nonetheless insists that "I will not forget my dear lover, even though I am far away from him. When I have some good food, it reminds me of my love at home. I wish we could be together. I wish to remove the sky [and sea so that we can be closer to one another]."

The lyrics of *lukthung* songs about transnational romances can also function as social and ideological restrictions toward female migrant sexuality, mobility, and the desire to be modern and independent from traditional institutions such as the family and home village (Mills 1999a, 4–5). These restrictions often appear in the form of an authoritative male voice speaking out against the decision of their girlfriends or wives to move abroad.[20] This can be seen in two songs by Maithai Uraiphon that express the bitterness felt by two Isan men when their wives leave them and their children to marry foreigners and go to live with their new husbands in Switzerland and Germany, respectively (Maithai, n.d.). In the first song, a young woman, who marries a Swiss man, is dumped and has to return to Isan heart-broken and face her former husband's and relatives' harsh condemnations. She learns the lesson that "Thailand is always better than Switzerland." In the second song, a young woman lives happily with her German husband, but is criticized for having forgotten her own roots (*luem kamphuet tua eng*). "She has a *farang* husband, so she ignores her mother's land and her rice-farm ex-husband who once took her and their children on an ox cart ride. She has had enough of *mueang Thai* and has managed to change her nationality to German."[21]

Heartbreaking Tales and Resentment

Intimacies concerning long-distance love portrayed in popular music do not always highlight the romantic side of love. Often they reveal a dark, tragic dimension. In the 1990s, a large number of Thai women were forced or lured into the Japanese sex trade (Suriya and Pattana 1996). In "Letter from Japan" (*Chot mai chak Chepaen*), Siriphon Amphaiphong (2001a) sings about a group of Thai-Isan girls who had been forced into the sex trade by the yakuza and then wrote a letter to their parents and sent it via the Thai embassy in Japan. Living away from home, they suffered dearly in order to earn *ngoen yen* (Japanese yen). Phongsit Khamphi's (2000b, 2000c) songs "Girls to export" (*Sao song ok*) and "*Yokohama*" provide a much more tragic picture of the same story. Phongsit criticizes Thailand's large-scale flesh trade involving young girls from the countryside who are usually forced into heavy debt and have to work for years in brothels and karaoke bars in Japan to pay it back. He warns "made in Thailand" girls not to fall prey to the myth of getting rich quick and easy. In "*Yokohama*," he dramatically recaptures a tragic tale of a "good daughter" in the port city of Yokohama, Japan, who built a big modern house for her parents with her remittance, but never returned home alive. "She sells her *na phuen noi* (lit., a small rice field, but colloquially refers to female genitalia) to feed many lives at home" (Phongsit 2000c). No one knows how difficult her life is as a sex worker in Japan. She becomes addicted to drugs and gambling, is forced to serve sexually abusive Japanese male customers, and is cheated by her Thai pimp lover. Finally, she commits suicide by hanging herself and only her ashes are quietly mailed back to "live" in her newly built house.

Homecomings can be stunning and shocking moments for overseas worker-returnees. Adultery, broken homes, and the mishandling of overseas remittances have been among some of the most publicized subjects of families left behind in villages across the region since 1980s. The megahits, "Tears of the wives whose husbands are working in Saudi Arabia" (*Nam ta mia Sa-u*) by Phimpha Phonsiri (1982[?]) and "My wife left me because I went to Saudi Arabia" (*Mia pa phro Sa-u*) by Somphot Duangsomphong

(1984[?]) created region-wide debates concerning the moral and familial tensions that ensued from the large-scale labor migration to the Middle East. The lyrics of the two hits are written as husband-wife dialogues and involve accusations of who was really responsible and should be held accountable for their broken home. Each side takes a turn to tell his or her story. In Phimpha's song, the *Sa-u* wife argues that she is forced to commit adultery because her husband has left her and the children for too long without sending her any money. Her husband's remittances go straight to his parents and relatives. She is deeply disappointed since the money the family paid to the recruitment company came from her own family land given to her by her parents. She is judged badly by her husband and the people around her. No one understands what she has actually endured as the wife of a *pai nok* worker. The tone of the woman's voice in this song is self-defensive and unconvincingly apologetic, as if she is under heavy pressure. Through his song, Phimpha warns the public that it should not stereotype every *Sa-u* wife as "bad."

In Somphot Duangsomphong's song, the husband tells his side of a story, and speaks in a very authoritative voice. His wife, who goes everywhere with her lover, is strongly condemned. She wastes her husband's remittance as if the money earned through his sweat is a "worthless thing" (*khong bo mi kha*). The husband counters his wife's argument about why she committed adultery by saying, "before my trip to Saudi Arabia, I reminded you to be faithful. My heart breaks to find out that you are having an affair. My wife now belongs to another man. She gives him my money, too" (Somphot 1984[?]). The husband's heart-shattering bitterness is expressed at the end of the song when he curses his wife saying that "if you are such a bitchy girl, why don't you just drop dead! Shame on you, woman" (*sang bo tai sam sa, ha kin phu ying ai*). Losing both his savings and his wife is seen as coming very close to the end of the world for a *pai nok* man. Wages from years of his sweat and fatigue abroad are taken away. While it is a total loss in the economic sense, it is an inestimable personal loss in terms of his shattered masculine pride. The shame inflicted on him by his wife runs deep in his self-image as a man (*saksi luk phuchai*). Resentful and shameful feelings among men are evidenced through the metaphor "my wife put a pair of buffalo horns on my head" (Lukphrae and Maithai 2002[?]), which was quoted earlier in this chapter.[22]

The proper handling of remittances and their wives' sexual lives are often what overseas workers think about most. They know that their extended time abroad means familial and parental voids for their wives and children. These men have a common dream that they "will be richer with a big new house equipped with luxuries like a TV, stereo, and more when they return home" (Carabao 1985). Some even dream of being "rich . . . rich for sure this time. I will return a respected millionaire. I should have enough money to marry my love, buy a new house, and more rice fields after repaying my debts" (Mike Phiromphon 2001d).[23] Overseas migrant workers are also deeply concerned with their wives' sexuality during their absence. They beg their wives to be faithful. "Do not have an affair with another man" (Carabao 1985). An Isan man working in Taiwan tells his wife to "wait for me. Do not take another man. I miss you night and day. I am faithful to you while I am in Taiwan. All of my wages will be remitted to your bank account. Please keep it well and spend it wisely" (Bunchu 2002[?]).[24] A voice representing Isan men working in Kuwait whispers to his wife that "when you go to bed at night, make sure that your room is well-locked. Hug our children for me. I promise to build you a new, big house within three years. Please wait for me. Don't have affairs behind my back" (Su Su 1991).

Tragic Deaths in Singapore

Singapore as a destination country for Thai-Isan workers has occupied special status in local folklore. In particular, Singapore is marked by tragic and controversial events, despite the fact that the island state is the most reliable and steady market for Thai labor forces. Throughout Thai labor's three decades in Singapore, workers from Thailand have experienced mysterious death (*rok lai tai*), deportation, the death penalty, and countless cases of fines or imprisonment for violating Singapore's laws. These events were circulated among Thai audiences in a series of popular songs in the 1980s and 1990s. When the mysterious death controversy broke out, a pop band called Sam Thon had a *lam toei*[25] hit entitled "A lament on a mysterious death in Singapore" (*Toei lai tai*). The song speaks on behalf of thousands of young "sticky rice-powered workers" (*raeng ngan luk khao niao*) in Singapore. Amid panic and fear of the mysterious death, the lyrics cite how Thai workers "died in their sleep like falling leaves," while the living ones wish to go home to be with their lovers.[26] The mysterious death phenomenon created waves of political tension between the Thai and Singapore governments when groups of Thai officials revealed the substandard working and living conditions of Thai migrant workers in Singapore.

Some popular songs expressed some of the negative perceptions the Thai populace had toward Singapore following two controversial cases involving Thai migrant workers. "Singapore," by Carabao (1989), squarely accused the Singapore authorities of insensitivity and a lack of humanitarian judgment and mercy when they deported Thai workers who had overstayed their work permits following an amnesty deadline. The Thai Navy sent a carrier to take the workers home. Carabao described Singapore as a country "oriented only to profit-making" (*khit phiang kamrai kan kha*). Phikun Khwanmuang (1997a[?], 1997c[?]) released two modern *Phuthai*-style *lam* songs in the late 1990s, entitled "My lover was hanged to death in Singapore" (*Faen tai yu Singkhapo*) and "My dear, you must be honest when you work abroad" (*Pai mueang nok hai sue sat*). The first song draws on an incident in which three Thai workers were sentenced to death by a Singapore court in August 1996. In the song, a female voice laments over her tragic love—her lover, who promised to save money and come back to marry her, was one of the three dead inmates. She cries in despair when his ashes arrive home. The only thing she can do is wish for a happier life when her lover is reborn in the next life, according to popular Thai Buddhist beliefs. The song expresses soul-searching narratives about the death penalty and international labor migration. In Phikun Khwanmuang's second song, using a feminine voice of maternal care, Isan men are reminded of the dangers of working in foreign countries. In the song, a woman urges her lover and other Isan men abroad to behave honestly and abstain entirely from legal and moral wrongdoings. "The foreign lands are different from ours on all accounts: religion, law, custom, and even the weather. Please think twice before doing anything as you have parents, wives, and children left behind at home. You must have strong morale and be honest; otherwise everything will come to a disastrous end."

Thepphon Phet-Ubon (1998a[?], 1998b[?]) also reminded his fellow Isan men, who were heading to Singapore and Taiwan for employment, to abide by the laws and customs in their host countries and behave well. He adopted the chanting melodic mode of *bai si sukhwan*, which is a soul-tying ceremony that parents, family members, friends, and relatives organize to bid farewell to *pai nok* workers. The ceremony is intended to ensure that the workers are in good spirits and mentally ready for their overseas venture; it also reveals the high expectations of the families left behind.

Reaffirming and Reasserting Male Migrant Heroism

Transnational labor communities not only listen to various musical genres that correspond to their transient life realities, but they also embrace, support, reproduce, and, in effect, own them. Overseas migrant workers from Thailand's northeastern region have their musical trademarks in *lukthung, molam,* and *phleng phuea chiwit.* In and through these "murky and self-evident" (Adorno 1962, 21)[27] popular musical genres, homesick migrants can "assert a kind of regional identity and pride" (Miller 1998, 332), despite being looked down upon by their employers and urban folks. I have demonstrated that popular music is capable of more than appealing to lonely and homesick crowds of migrant workers both in transit and at home. It mirrors how a culture has been transformed by transnational labor migration and allows actors caught in the midst of such transformation to speak their mind. I term a specific emerging cultural trend in Thailand's Isan region since the 1980s the "culture of *pai nok* labor migration," which is largely characterized by changing personal, familial, and societal relations and intimacies as a result of labor migratory flows and displacement between home and host destinations.

The ideological foundation and material outlook of Isan culture has been radically transformed by "*pai nok* labor migration." Such transformation assumes many forms and content, as evident in the musical landscape. Cultural ideas of love, family, home, and gendered self-identities of working-class individuals have been under a considerable degree of transformation and readjustment since the impact of transnational labor migration began to take shape in the region in the 1980s.

The traditional romantic love of young peasant men and women from the same local or neighboring areas is replaced by long-distance love affairs between migrant workers and those left behind at home. Young men and working-age fathers play their part as "breadwinners" in this long-distance affair, which sees its communication channels shifting from slow-paced letter writing or verbal networks of villagers to personal mobile phones, modern banking transference of remittances, and travel via low-cost airlines. Two megahits by Tai Orathai (2003d, 2003e), "Please give me a call, my dear" (*Tho ha nae doe*) and "Honey, have you eaten yet?" (*Kin khao rue yang*), vividly capture the working-class romantic intimacies of daily tele-chats via cell phones. "Talking to you daily is like taking an energy vitamin to prevent my loneliness. If a day has passed without hearing your voice, I feel something is really missing, as though I hadn't eaten all day" (Tai 2003d). A pre-paid phone card is used metaphorically as a card filled with love and care. When it operates in a cell phone, it converts a regular phone call into a magic cloth of caring love given to the migrant worker to "wipe away [his] sweat and freshen up [his] day" (Tai 2003e).

The family left behind as a social institution appears under severe threat due to the impact of overseas labor migration. Working-age fathers are absent for extended periods. This can create familial tensions over sexual relations between husband and wife and the management of remittances. A large number of workers I observed in Singapore have to work abroad at least three years in order to repay the loans and save enough money for their families. I found many Isan workers have been working in Singapore for over ten years, with one serving twenty-one years. Their absence has put strains on the familial relationships with their wives and children. It has created a pattern of a displaced family, in which the father lives and works apart from the mother and their children. Paternal figures and authority have minimal roles in this type of family. One worker shared his personal experiences on this subject with me: "I left home when my wife was pregnant. I returned home again when my son was three years old. It was painful when he did not call me *pho* (father)."[28] However, these workers are proud of their idealized roles as the breadwinners for their families. On top of their wish list is supporting their children's education. None of them want their children to become overseas construction workers like their fathers.

"Home" is imagined differently when one becomes an overseas migrant worker stationed abroad for years. It remains the subject of nostalgic sentiment as much as ever, but the actual location of home and the placement of overseas workers mean an impossible distance is "separated by foreign land, sea, and sky." Overseas migrant workers need to rely on both psychological channels such as dreams and "being there with someone in spirit" (*fak chai*), and affordable technologies like cameras to produce pictures and mobile phones to talk and listen to someone's voice from home. The lyrics of the Mike Phiromphon's (2002a) song "I miss someone who lives far away" (*Khoet hot khon klai*) speaks of a time in the evening when his father and his brothers would return home from their daily work in the rice fields and his mother would prepare dinner for them. This was the most intimate moment in his memories of home. A more transformational idea of home is the building of a new house using hard-earned remittances. It transforms a lifetime dream into a reality. Fully furnished, modern houses are "monumental" social-status markers distinguishing overseas workers from non-migrant families in their villages. This is a common desire reflected in the song "A letter to my father [who works abroad]" (*Chot mai thueng pho*) by It Futbat (1999[?]). It depicts a mother responding to her children's question about why their father had to leave to work overseas. "Your father has to go earn money for the future of everyone in our family. We will have a big house and a beautiful car. We will be respected like other people in our village."

The gendered self-identities of working-class individuals that appear in Thailand's popular music are bold and markedly pronounced. The lyrics fully acknowledge the arrival of migrant workers as socially, economically, and culturally distinctive persons and as specific members of Thailand's working class. They have emerged as diasporic migrant workers who travel between their home and host destinations to "sell their labor" (*khai raeng*) in order to earn a living. This kind of work requires them to journey across international borders and to remain abroad for extended periods of time. Migrant men from Isan sometimes become attached to the symbolism of the region, including the more masculine symbols of *khaen* (bamboo reed pipe) and *molam* as well as the staple food of the region, *khao niao* (glutinous rice) and *pla ra* (fermented fish). Emerging as *khon khai raeng* (people selling their labor) in recent musical hit songs, these men are effectively categorized as members of local as well as transnational labor forces. This new identity marker underlines a rather self-proclaimed personhood. It includes intimate human experiences and sensibilities, and it exposes a more humanized dimension of young men and working-age fathers as individuals that take great pride in their hard work and dedicate their earnings to their families and loved ones. In this respect, the popular lyrics carefully capture, coin, and publicize this identity marker in order to counter previous identity markers of being rustic, poorly educated, and underprivileged working-class individuals associated with terms such as *kammakon* (laborer), *khon ngan* (workers), *num ko sang* (construction worker), and so on. Mike Phiromphon's (2003a) song entitled "People behind the scenes" (*Phu yu bueang lang*) aptly demonstrates this point. It tells his audiences that the hands of migrant workers, both male and female, are the hands that nurture the world. From garbage collectors and factory workers to construction workers, "we dedicate ourselves to serving the people."

My reading of the lyrics of popular songs pertinent to the lives of overseas migrant workers shows that male workers are rather similar to their female counterparts in their economic and cultural attachments to their families and home villages, unlike studies such as Curran et al. (2005) and Mills (1997, 1999a), which suggest that daughters—not sons—are more economically responsible to their families left behind. In the case of remittances, greater pressure is placed on daughters than sons to send money home on a regular basis. Moreover, the village and overall Thai cultural values tend to nurture this expectation and gender role (Kirsch 1982; Nidhi 1995). However, my studies of male Thai-Isan workers in Singapore and the reading of popular song lyrics suggests that gender makes little difference in the commitment to families and home villages. Perhaps, overseas labor migration as an economic venture has imposed duty and responsibility on male migrant workers—not simply moral obligations as is the case of internal migration. This duty and responsibility is imposed on male migrants because the decision to seek employment abroad is often made by the entire family and requires the mobilization of large sums of family savings and resources. This then becomes a rather high-risk investment. It is, therefore, rather common that male migrant workers feel obliged to remit their wages back home to their parents and immediate families.

Conclusion

Through the reading of song lyrics as texts of "new critical migrant realities," we can see how intimate selfhoods of migrant actors—male and female workers, family members and relatives left behind, as well as middlemen—have been constructed and construed in popular perceptions of the overseas labor migration experience. In this sense, popular music has established itself as a cultural trope that produces multidimensional and dialectical gazes upon the transnational effects imposed on local settings and vice versa. It helps migrant workers and those left behind to make sense of transient experiences ranging from sorrow, shame, guilt, and loneliness to humor and joyfulness. Popular music returns to them their agency and autonomy by telling stories in their own narrative modes and from their perspectives. In the soundscape of popular music, transnational and local junctures are imagined and translated into a complex performance of the "narratives of the self" among Thai-Isan overseas migrant workers. I suggest that the transformation of cultural intimacies involving transnational migrant actors reflects how Thailand has been deeply drawn into the problematic of local-global trajectories due to the intensive movement and displacement of its labor force.

Scholars in migration studies have shown only minimal attention to the representation of overseas migrant workers in and through popular media. In my readings of popular song lyrics, music is the key portion of the soundscape of labor migration at home and in transit. It configures the voice culture of human realities, especially the emotional experience of nostalgia and the displacement felt by both overseas migrant workers and their families back home. Looking at labor migration through the lens of popular culture is an intellectually stimulating and creative way to understand human flows across international borders. At the least, it uncovers what the home society really knows and feels about the effects of labor migration, and it helps us to critically capture human agencies and the voices of the people involved in the complex processes of overseas labor migration. The popular music lyrics presented here poetically illustrate how these Thai-Isan workers remain true to their ethnocultural roots and move in and out of their villages, transforming themselves from "*pai* Thai/Bangkok" to *pai nok* workers.

Chapter 3

Village Transnationalism

What does it actually mean to be a Thai-Isan construction worker in Singapore? How does one define oneself? What are Thai-Isan construction workers' life and work experiences like away from home? How do they react to their socially marginalized status and the stereotypes ascribed to them by their Singaporean hosts? Viewing Thai (and other foreign) migrant workers as part of Singapore's society and economy provides only a partial perspective on these men's lives since they have never been fully integrated or assigned a proper place in the rigidly defined and competitive structure of Singaporean society. We cannot understand migrant workers' lives and their temporal communities in Singapore without taking into account the "rural-based moral community" (Keyes n.d., 36) or the "common moral economy" (Keyes 2002, 1). The sense of moral economy and community is persistently redefined and employed as cultural and symbolic capital to form the foundation of Thai-Isan identities. It further renders itself as a key resource, as well as a cultural mode that helps displaced migrant workers construct their transborder identities. Although they live and work here, they have always belonged elsewhere, as they maintain strong emotional, moral, cultural, and economic attachments to their places of origin. Thai-Isan construction workers in Singapore need to be resituated and reconceptualized within the framework of village-based transnationalism.

The term "village transnationalism"[1] is treated as an explanatory model as well as an analytical construct in order to come to terms with the lived experience of Thai migrant workers in Singapore. Hired as semiskilled contract workers in Singapore's construction industry (see Porntipa 2001; Wong 2000), they have remained rural villagers at heart despite their increasing cross-border mobilities (Hugo 2004, 29). Their temporary lives in transit, social relations, and communities away from home have very little to do with their Singaporean hosts. Their everyday life has also transcended traditional identities and cultural worlds back home in the Thai countryside.

The social lives and transborder identities of migrant workers from Thailand or elsewhere should not be viewed as an extended part of Singapore society and culture. Rather, they are part of the migratory flow of temporarily displaced persons in the late-capitalist, borderless world, which Ong (1999, 10–12) describes as "cultural globalization." These workers come to "sell their labor" (*khai raeng*) in this island republic, but their home—imagined or real—has never been here. For them, Singapore is simply a marketplace where they come to sell their labor and "earn money" (*ha ngoen*).

Sorachai, a thirty-year-old male construction worker from Udon Thani in northeastern Thailand, spoke on behalf of his fellow workers when he said: "You know what? Thai workers in Singapore bear a very heavy pressure on their shoulders."[2] With their average daily wage of 23 Singapore dollars (14 US dollars; 552 baht),[3] Thai workers in Singapore have the burden of debt bondage as a result of borrowing money from relatives or private money-lenders, which is used to pay recruitment and job placement agents to secure jobs in Singapore's construction industry,[4] plus they remit money back home to support their families.[5] They also must live with Singapore's harsh realities, where they are often looked down upon as "3D workers," with "3D" referring to difficult, dirty, and dangerous jobs, a term used in international migration studies. These Thai workers speak neither English nor Mandarin, and thus they are not capable of communicating with their employers and supervisors. They must unconditionally obey their bosses and supervisors since their lives totally depends on them. They have no rights and no voice in the workplace, even though their work can be very dangerous.

Thai workers' lifestyles and community networks while living and working in Singapore are modeled on village transnationalism, which is largely consistent with Parnwell's (2005, 21) explanation that "a continuing cultural-socio-psychological or nostalgic attachment to 'home' leads to the persistence of living and acting translocally, and holding on to the 'myth of temporariness'/denying the 'myth of return,' in spite of the growing apparent permanence of residence 'there.'" The difference in the case of Thai contract workers in Singapore is that the return home is not a myth. It is a reality due to Singapore's strict immigration policies and employment laws regarding foreign workers (see Ewing-Chow 2001; Huang and Yeoh 2003, 75–97; Wong 1997, 135–67).[6] Every migrant worker must return "home" once his work permit expires.

Transnationalism and globalization not only overlap, as Kearney (1995, 548) suggests, but also need a localized ground on which to operate and involve actors with certain characteristics and identities. Smith (2001) characterizes this specifically localized ground and subject as a "transnational optic." In the case of Thai contract migrant workers in Singapore, it is true that they "move into and indeed create transnational spaces that may have the potential to liberate the nationals within them" (ibid., 553). They also possess multiple identities and are involved in "multi-stranded social relationships." This "illustrate[s] how they are sustained through multiple overlapping of familial, economic, social, organizational, religious, and political practices that transcend borders" (Schiller, Basch, and Blanc 1995, 684). However, the multiplicities of these transborder identities among transnational migrants are not necessarily "new." Transborder identities are made possible by appropriating and articulating one's "home" cultural and symbolic capital into new cultural experiences while abroad with the aid of borderless telecommunication and transportation technologies.

As an entry point to discuss issues concerning transborder identities and transnationalism in the Southeast Asian context (Ananta and Arifin 2004; Parnwell 2005), I use ethnographic accounts of Thai-Isan migrant workers in Singapore. My discussion is conceptually framed and guided by two principal assumptions: (1) "what is transnational is embedded in the local" (Schiller, Basch, and Blanc 1995, 684; see also Kearney 1995; Yeoh, Charney, and Kiong 2003) and (2) "people's lived realities and ideological constructions . . . transgress, though they do not always subvert, the territorial boundaries of the nation-state" (Duara 1997, 1030). Personal accounts of lived experiences endured by a group of male contract workers from Isan in Singapore represent one of many localized realities in a specific transnational setting, allowing us to rethink ongoing international labor migration in this part of the world at the turn of the twenty-first century. The migrant workers presented in this chapter tell stories of what Willis, Yeoh, and Fakhri (2004, 11) call "the materiality of how individuals experience [state/nation/transnation]."

The "Golden Mile" Story: Displaced Migrant Villagers and Their Shopping Mall

The most popular place outside of work for Thai workers in Singapore is the well-known Golden Mile Complex or simply "Golden" or "Golden Mile," as Thais refer to it among themselves.[7] The building houses a shopping mall, eateries, clubs, offices, supermarkets, and apartments and is also known among Thais as "Golden *Mao*," literally the golden place [and time] where workers can meet up with fellow Thais. It is quite common to find small groups of Thai-Isan workers gathering to talk, drink, and have fun both inside and outside this commercial complex. Often they will be approached by female vendors selling snacks. The peak time when crowds of Thai workers congregate here is during the weekend, especially the first and third weekends of the month, which are paydays for most Singaporean companies and construction contractors.

Typical scenes at the busy Golden Mile are captured by these journalistic accounts (see also Chia 2002/2003):

> On Sundays, as many as 5,000 Thais may visit the complex as it has money services open seven days a week, enabling them to send cheques home. The complex is also the terminal for buses linking Hat Yai and Singapore. Many locals and foreigners consider the complex dangerous—full of thieves, brawlers, and killers, and keep away. They see it as dirty, with Thai workers sitting on the floors and footpaths while they drink. (Wuth 1996)

> The Thai crowd was right in front of one of the biggest supermarkets in the complex. Some hummed Thai tunes, others were drinking Thai beer. Some had plastic bags of bamboo shoots or raw papaya. Many of them read Thai newspapers. Just around the street corner, some Thai men were drinking Thai beer. A Singaporean policemen kept an eye on them. (Supara 2002)

In the eyes of the media, Thai and Singaporean officials, and the general public, this three-story shopping complex on Beach Road is a "3D place for 3D workers." Media representations of the place can be unambiguously negative.[8] The mall's identity as a social space has been linked to male workers' drinking sprees and other illegal activities. Singaporeans will remind their relatives and friends that this is a place to avoid. While Thai workers are widely regarded as diligent, hard-working, and obedient people in their normal selves, they can become a problem when they get drunk.[9] Most Singaporean employers share this stereotypical perception of Thai-Isan workers, such as Darren, who is quoted as saying that "when they are sober, they are the best workers, but when they get drunk, they can be real troublemakers" (cited in Supara 2002).

The Golden Mile Complex, as a public space, is one of Singapore's urban development projects from the early 1970s. The complex as it stands today represents part of the failed urban renewal program known as the Golden Mile district. According to Chia (2002/2003, 21–23), the Golden Mile district program grew out of the government's intention to transform the area from a slum into a first-class commercial, residential, and hotel district, but it failed miserably due to poor accessibility and competition from other development sites in the vicinity. Built in 1972, the Golden Mile was originally known as the Wah Hup Complex. It was designed as a mixed-use commercial and residential building. In the 1970s, the business performance of the shops in the Golden Mile Complex was poor and it resembled a ghost town. However, it was gradually revived as Thai workers began to arrive in Singapore and businesses associated with the Thais flourished in the early 1980s, which is why Chia referred to it as "the birth of Little Thailand in Singapore."

The physical setting of the Golden Mile is not fixed or limited only to the three-story building space. Its boundaries are rather complex, expansive, and flexible, particularly during peak business hours on the weekend. As Thai workers, female vendors, cross-border tourists, travelers, and visitors arrive in the area, they gradually occupy and make use of most of the available space within the complex and its surrounding areas. Footpaths and some small vacant spaces in front of the Golden Mile are used as meeting points. Most of the corridors on the ground floor and the parking lot are occupied by workers engaging in leisure activities. A large number of workers also use the spaces provided by the stalls and other available ground space under the Housing and Development Board (HBD)[10] apartment flats opposite the Golden Mile for entertainment activities. Many of them go to Kallang Riverside Park at the intersection of Beach Road and the highway and use that area as an alternative leisure space. They sit or squat on the floor to enjoy drinks, snacks, and food with friends after their long week working on construction sites and in factories across the island. It is not unusual to witness workers lying passed out on the footpaths or under the HDB apartment flats after long hours of heavy drinking or fighting with other fellow workers.

Most Thai workers seem to have balanced views regarding the presence of Golden Mile on their "labor migration map." They recognize both positive and negative aspects of the place. For instance, Anuchit, age thirty-one, a veteran worker from Udon Thani, wrote in his diary that "the Golden Mile is the meeting point for the Thais. Friends, relatives, and people coming from the same village meet here. They also come to have fun in their free time. The Golden Mile offers all kinds of entertainment, such as karaoke bars, discotheques, and a snooker club. People usually visit the place at the end of the month or on payday. Some people come to remit money home; others just come to spend money on things they want."[11] Another Thai worker said it is the only public space in Singapore where they can truly feel at "home." Lili said, "this is really 'Little Thailand.' The shops do not sell Singaporean products. Everything is made in Thailand, even the vegetables. Every morning, fresh vegetables from Thailand come here on buses. Every day, flowers, *padi* (rice plants), chili, and spices coming out from Hat Yai are sent here. You name it, they have it" (cited in Chia 2002/2003, 24).

Yet Thai workers are aware of the danger of the noisy drinking scenes in and around the Golden Mile Complex on the weekends. Anuchit wrote in the same diary that

> both good and bad people come to the Golden Mile. There are illegal migrants, male and female, looking for jobs. They go underground, hiding with friends. Some occasionally visit the Golden Mile; some illegally hang out and camp in the forests. This is the reason why the police come to inspect the place frequently. The Golden Mile is also a place of sin. Many workers get lost amid tempting seductions like girls, drugs, and drink. Some people get killed in fighting after heavy

drinking. Many forget that they have their families back home under their responsibility. It is heartbreaking for their parents, wives, and children.[12]

Janta, age twenty-nine, agrees that the negative image of the Golden Mile has to do with the fact that Thai workers come to drink, and when they drink too much, fights break out.[13] Some people drink until they pass out and many have their personal items pick-pocketed. Nonetheless, a Thai worker insists: "The place has more pros than cons. I will always go the Golden Mile, no matter what."[14] Another worker emphatically noted: "Even if its location is remote or far away from my construction site, I will always try to be there."[15]

The Golden Mile on the weekend resembles the festive atmosphere in Isan's rural villages. Mostly middle-age and older men gather together to have a meal and a drink over lively conversation in corners of the buildings or in the parking lots and footpaths, reminiscent of scenes common to household ceremonies or village festivals (*ngan bun*), especially those during the post-harvest period when villagers might find themselves with the luxury of time to celebrate and enjoy themselves after heavy work in the field. Noise, drinking sprees, enjoying abundant meals together, urinating or spitting in public, and even putting up a fight are all considered normal behavior during village festivals. They are a way of life in village festivals, although they are also considered "out of place" and socially unacceptable at times, and can be regarded as antisocial behavior. Many of these activities border on being illegal in Singapore, given the country's legal codes and public social norms. Thais who are educated, professionals, and middle-class or elite working in Singapore, often see the Golden Mile as degrading, dirty, and exclusively for working-class people. Some of the more blatant anti-social behavior during festive weekends at the Golden Mile could perhaps be interpreted as a symbolic "slap-in-your-face," registering a kind of protest against the strictly regulated nature of everyday life in Singapore as well as a way to reflexively apprehend one's own marginalized life and hardships.

As transnational contract workers, Thai-Isan men find themselves caught up in an extraordinarily complex situation. They live their lives "selling their labor" (*chiwit khon khai raeng*) as temporarily displaced and culturally uprooted persons. These workers have rather suddenly and cruelly become men without families or village communities over a sustained period of time. They are men away from parental and customary influences, husbands separated from wives, fathers far away from their children, and good community members leaving behind relatives and neighbors. Many of them are frustrated with the unfriendly and discriminatory gestures they receive from their Singaporean employers and people they meet on their worksites and within everyday life.[16] They have become mentally, culturally, and socioeconomically handicapped strangers in an unfamiliar workplace and society. What the Singaporean public witnesses during weekends at the Golden Mile is, in part, Thai workers' imagined attempts to keep in touch and reinforce their nostalgic sense of Isan village-style "home." They unconsciously wish to make the Golden Mile their "community" in their own impossible way, given Singapore's strict law enforcement and the public's attitude toward foreign workers.

The Golden Mile offers Thai workers not only a "mirrored sense" of home and community, but also a "real, touchable" physical communality in transit. Golden Mile is, indeed, a "contact zone" for Thai migrant workers in this ethnoculturally pluralized island republic, where groups of foreign workers need their marked "home" away from Isan's social and physical space. It is perhaps the only place in Singapore where Thai workers can come together and make a "village" out of their social networks, which, during weekdays, are kept to a minimum through face-to-face contact and via popular mobile phones. A large number of Thai workers possess mobile phones. Wireless technology has made it possible for them to keep alive their social networks and community through instant live chats and SMS messages.[17] It is, therefore, understandable why Thai-Isan workers are easily stimulated and fling themselves deep into a rare joyful mood at the Golden Mile while they are away from the menial jobs and hardships they endure on the construction sites throughout the island of Singapore. This shopping mall's spatial identity, as marked by a Thai-style fresh market, a village festival atmosphere, and a miniature replica of the famous Bangkok Erawan shrine that represents a major spiritual demarcation, is indeed a "home away from home."

Pha Pa Raeng Ngan: Transborder Buddhist Merit-Making Endeavors

Isan workers in Singapore, in addition to sending remittances to family members, also send a certain amount of money back home to help their communities build Buddhist temple halls, school buildings, asphalted roads, and other public utility projects. This is known as *pha pa raeng ngan*—one of the most important Buddhist merit-making activities organized by Thai workers in Singapore. For some reason, this activity has been overlooked in existing studies on Thai workers in Singapore, even the most comprehensive ones like Porntipa Atipas (2001) and Wong (2000). At the outset, *pha pa raeng ngan* may be viewed as a simple and familiar fund-raising project initiated by groups of male Isan workers. However, after a series of interviews and participant observations, I realized that the collective effort of organizing a *pha pa* could be seen as a form of culturally/religiously organized social remittances, through which Thai migrant workers have maintained their connections with "home" while living and working abroad. It is illustrative of the moral obligation these men feel to "give back" to their homes, where they have always belonged.

A *pha pa* project is organized through personal leadership and social networks, not only between a group of migrant workers and their original home villages, but also through strong social reciprocal relationships and network organizations among workers on different worksites throughout the island. Each year there are a large number of *pha pa* fundraising projects among Thai workers. The gathering to collect and remit donations takes place every week around the Golden Mile and its nearby meeting spots. The peak of this seasonal activity is seen around January and April. January and February are highlighted by the Western and Chinese New Year holidays. These are the times when most workers are on their long holidays with some of them receiving *hong pao* ("red envelope") money from their employers. March and April are particularly auspicious times for Buddhist merit-making and public festivities in Isan, where most temple fairs and village festivals are organized around the Songkran festival in April to celebrate the Tai/Thai traditional New Year.[18]

The *pha pa* is a joint effort between leaders in the host village in Isan and their fellow villagers/workers abroad. In most Thai Buddhist villages, it is an annual event and is considered one of the grand Buddhist

57

merit-making projects to mobilize money and resources for specific civic development projects. During this event, labor, money, and other material resources are sought after from virtually every reliable source inside and outside of the village. Members of the village by birth, residence, or other means of social membership are requested to make a donation in the name of making merit for "our village" (*tham bun huam kan/het bun nam kan*). In the past few decades, young migrant workers and their social networks at their workplaces in Bangkok and overseas (e.g., Brunei, Israel, Japan, Middle East, Singapore, Taiwan) have been viewed as very significant contributors to the village *pha pa* fundraising activity.[19]

Not every migrant Thai worker is capable of putting together a *pha pa* project. As a cultural and economic capital mobilization endeavor at the community level, it requires leadership and organization. Chai, age thirty-eight, a veteran worker in Singapore and *pha pa* organizer from Udon Thani, explained that the committee leader and committee members are very important. They need to have strong and reliable networks of fellow workers, whose construction sites are located in different places throughout the island. They also need to have accumulated a sufficient degree of trust and charisma (*barami*), which is demonstrated through one's past record of contributing to or assisting with previous *pha pa* projects organized by their fellow workers. A successful leader of a *pha pa* project, widely called the president (*prathan*), usually has a personal reputation as being fair, sportsman-like, and a giver and taker. He must also have strong reciprocal relationships with a large number of friends (*pen phu kwang khwang*). He needs to have excellent skills of social reciprocity. He also needs to have enough support and cooperation from his fellow committee members in order to carry out different tasks such as distributing and collecting the *pha pa* envelopes (*song pha pa*), preparing and organizing food and drink for the gathering to "open *pha pa* envelopes" (*poet song pha pa*), and remitting the donated money home.[20]

Every *pha pa* project needs a village host, and the proposal begins from there. In most cases, the leaders of the hosting village in Thailand, such as a village headman, schoolteacher, local policeman, or member of the Subdistrict Administration Organization (*ongkan borihan suan tambon—o bo to*) initiates a plan for organizing this annual fundraising activity among fellow villagers. Potential outside donors, including overseas migrant workers, are invited or requested to contribute as part of an extended social network to raise further donations. Most *pha pa* activities in Singapore belong to this category. Charoen and his fellow workers from Udon Thani were requested by the local police in Udon Thani to contribute money to a local road construction project. Nak and his friends were invited to make a donation for a *pha pa* activity in Nakhon Phanom to build a library within the village school. Vira and his friends organized their *pha pa* to help their village erect a temple preaching hall in Nong Khai.[21] However, there are also cases in which *pha pa* activities have been proposed by the migrant workers themselves who wish to contribute to their home village. They volunteer to gather donations from their contacts in Singapore to contribute to the merit-making activity at home. Most overseas *pha pa* projects, as I observed in Singapore, fit into the category of invited or requested contribution to the ongoing merit-making activity in a particular host village.

The *pha pa* proposal reaches its overseas donors in the form of a bunch of *pha pa* envelopes that are widely known among Thai-Isan workers as *song* or *song pha pa*. Printed on the front of the envelope is the merit-making event's details, indicating what, where, why, and when the *pha pa* is to be held. It also provides blank spaces for donors to fill in their name, address, and the amount of their donation. Inside the envelope is a letter that again outlines the event's details as well as provides a list of organizing committee members from both the hosting village and the overseas workers. Man, age forty-five, a veteran migrant worker and frequent *pha pa* donor from Buri Ram, explained that since most of the listed names are real and respected persons, the letter is proof that the *pha pa* is creditable intention and represents an auspicious undertaking. The title of a *pha pa* project is written in a way to honor the contribution from workers in Singapore in their joint merit-making efforts. Examples include: "You are cordially invited to host the Yasothon-Singapore Pha Pa Project to help with funding the construction of the temple's fence at Ban Na-ngam, Tambon Sompho, Amphoe Thai Charoen, Changwat Yasothon, dated Thursday, March 1, 2005," and "You are cordially invited to host the Singapore-Nakhon Phanom Pha Pa for an Education Project at Ban Dong Khwang Village School, Tambon Saen Phan, Amphoe That Phanom, Changwat Nakhon Phanom, dated on Saturday January 8, 2005."[22] These messages are commonly printed on every *pha pa* envelope, pamphlet, and advertisement. The intention is to provide necessary information and proof of authenticity and originality, as cases of fraud are frequently reported in the Thai media.

Although it varies from case to case, most *pha pa* projects among Thai workers in Singapore involve sending out between eight hundred and two thousand envelopes. The *pha pa* organizer roughly calculates a return of around 70 to 80 percent of the distributed envelopes. While most non-committee and general workers tend to donate between one and two Singapore dollars (0.60–1.20 US dollars; 24–48 baht) per envelope, committee members, especially the president and vice president, who are members of the hosting village, are expected to contribute up to several hundred Singapore dollars. Panya, a recent president of the *pha pa* from Udon Thani, spent 500 dollars[23] with almost half of this amount allocated to organizing expenses such as food, drink, and other allowances. He donated 300 dollars to the *pha pa* fund for his village temple.[24]

It was my observation that most *pha pa* envelopes rarely contained more than ten dollars (6 US dollars; 240 baht), except those belonging to organizing committee members. The largest proportion was envelopes containing a two-dollar Singapore banknote. Many contained coins. A number of Thai workers revealed that they often felt there were too many *pha pa* envelopes coming to them throughout the year. Although they are willing to help out friends and organizers by making merit with them, they cannot afford to spend a large portion of their precious earnings, since their salary is limited and they need to remit a portion of their earnings to support their families or pay off their debt bondage. This is the major reason why the majority of them usually donate only one or two dollars in each *pha pa* envelope. Pornchai, age forty-two, a veteran worker from Kalasin, told me that each year he receives between fifteen and twenty *pha pa* envelopes and spends up to fifty dollars (30 US dollars; 1,200 baht) on this activity. Although making merit is a voluntary activity, most Buddhist Thais feel a strong moral obligation to contribute what they can, especially when they are requested.[25]

The exact amount of remittances sent via *pha pa* fundraising projects is still unknown, as no one has ever kept any records. Yet, as a number of workers and experienced organizers of this annual merit-making activity told me, it could be as much as millions of Thai baht per year. One of my informants estimated that there are at least two hundred and fifty *pha pa* projects (*kong*) per annum. An average project is usually reported to raise around 2,000 dollars. It means each year *pha pa* remittances could pump as much as 500,000 dollars (304,068 US dollars; 12,006,345 baht) of foreign currency directly into the Thai rural economy.[26]

The most important stage of *pha pa* organization is the quasi-ceremonial gathering called *poet song* (lit. to open the envelope). It is a time when organizers and friends from different worksites agree to bring together the *pha pa* envelopes, which they had distributed earlier though their connections with fellow villagers and friends known as *sai* (a key person with a chained social connection). They normally choose to get together to open the *pha pa* envelopes at their favorite place at the Golden Mile Complex, the HDB flats near Golden Mile, or Kallang Riverside Park on Sunday afternoons or holidays. Key members in the organizing committee play the role of the *pha pa*'s host (*chao phap*), adopting the same function as in a genuine *pha pa* and other ceremonies back home in Isan. The hosts have to prepare food, drink, and snacks as if it were a real feast. Reed mattresses are spread on the ground under trees in the park or on the cement floor inside the building of the meeting spot, where around twenty to thirty *pha pa* donors and their friends come to witness the sorting and collecting of the final donations.

In most circumstances, *poet song* starts with donors, guests, and hosts having a meal together. Eating, drinking, having fun, and enjoying social greetings are the most fundamental aspects of village festivals in Isan and elsewhere. The hosts prepare a variety of food, but the main dishes are traditional Isan cuisine, including glutinous rice, papaya salad (*som tam*), grilled chicken (*kai yang*), and cooked or raw beef/pork with Isan-style ingredients (*lap* or *koi*). Drinks, especially rice whisky and beer, are bought from a store inside the Golden Mile or on the spot from female vendors mostly from Isan. In some cases, the host does not have time to cook as most construction workers rarely have time off from their tight schedules and demanding employers (*thao kae*). They buy cooked food and vegetables from the Golden Mile stores. When everybody is well fed, the president of the *pha pa* activity calls for the attention of those gathered, so they can begin to open the envelopes and count the donations. It is time for all of the *pha pa* participants to join and witness the counting of monies towards a particular *pha pa* project and find out how much their overall collection efforts produced. In most of the events I attended, the envelopes contained both Thai and Singaporean currency with larger contributions being in Singapore dollars. While committee members were busy counting and sorting the money that came in various coins and banknotes, the rest of the participants stayed on to give moral support and witness that the donations were handled in a proper and transparent manner.[27]

An additional step to raise more money is through what is known as *to yot* (to extend, or top up, the donations already collected from the envelopes). When the amount of the collected donations is finalized, the president, who also acts as the master of ceremonies, announces to the gathering the total amount of the donations and asks whether it is an appropriate amount to be remitted to their folks back home or if anybody wants to make an additional top-up donation. This is another way to call for donations on the spot, where the name of the donor and the amount of his donation are publicly acknowledged, usually accompanied with compliments and cheers from fellow workers. Some say that they need the final amount of the donation to end with the number nine (i.e., 799, 899, 999, or 1999 Singapore dollars), which is considered an auspicious number in Thai popular belief because it is pronounced with the sound "*kao*," which indicates growth and progress. In some cases, the topping-up session encourages more donations from both committee members and fellow workers, as it usually ends up raising a couple of hundred additional dollars.[28]

Many workers agree that the call for *to yot* is the most interesting and entertaining part of the *pha pa* gathering. It allows people in their social circle to step up and display their generosity by making an extra donation in front of their fellow workers. In other words, the *to yot* demonstrates the individual's "face" and "honor" beyond an ordinary contribution, thereby allowing those gathered to recognize and remember this person's act of special merit making. When the *to yot* finally comes to an end with no further donations, a group of organizing committee members brings the donated money to the remittance service located inside the Golden Mile Complex. The donation is usually remitted to the bank account of the village headman, the abbot, a schoolteacher, or a reliable villager, who in turn will bring the donation to the local *pha pa* organizing committee. To ensure that donations are handled properly and used for totally legitimate purposes, a group of key persons in the committee are present during the transaction of the remittance.

The *pha pa* project among Thai men working in Singapore represents an exercise of male networks that aim to renew and reinforce a masculine reciprocal prestige and to strengthen their social and religious commitment to their "home." It is representative of their prime role as "breadwinners" for their immediate families. The men's contributions to *pha pa* projects confirm and reinforce their moral and social obligation to fulfill some of the needed financial funds for public development projects at the village level. The *pha pa* project also helps overseas migrant workers who have been absent from their villages over a sustained period to renew their Buddhist faith through merit making, as they rarely go to a Buddhist temple while working in Singapore (Wong 2000, 105). This activity allows them to maintain their social relationships among male friends working on different worksites in Singapore in addition to their normal contact via mobile phone or social meetings at the Golden Mile Complex.

The Thai Labor Football Tournament

Football (soccer) is one of the ultimate outdoor activities for young Thai construction workers played on weekends and in the late afternoon during their off hours. It is not only the most popular sport in Thailand and the Southeast Asian region,[29] but it also displays characteristics that well suit the excessively masculine community of male Thai workers in Singapore. For them, football is their passion and pride. It represents an identity marker of their working-class lifestyle and offers a cultural mode of how men from different villages and provinces throughout Isan and Thailand deal with one another. Football is a game that male workers play to define and redefine their masculine selves outside their extremely physically demanding jobs and the socially suppressed and marginalized social milieu.

Thai-Isan workers in Singapore bring with them not only their manual labor skills, but also their multi-sports talents, which they acquire in their village school and daily village sporting events. The workers' sports talents include football, volleyball, *sepak takraw* (kick volleyball), and of course Thai kickboxing (*muai Thai*). They regularly play these sports for exercise and to pass the time. On the weekends, some of them manage to practice their football skills with fellow foreign workers from Indonesia, Malaysia,

Myanmar or with their Thai counterparts from different companies or worksites. Once a year, they eagerly participate in a football tournament organized by the Office of Thai Labor Affairs of the Royal Thai Embassy in Singapore, known as the "Thai Labor Cup." It is the only major sporting event among the community of Thai workers and had been organized for four years running at the time of my field research.[30]

The Fourth Thai Labor Cup, like any public event, required considerable effort and input from both the organizing committee under the guidance of the head of the Office of Labor Affairs (Mr. Somthawee Kopatthanasin) and the staff from Friends of Thai Workers Association (FTWA) as well as from the participating teams. On the side of the organizing committee, key members sat in a meeting at the FTWA office at the Golden Mile in late October 2004, just one month prior to the event. They did not require much in the way of public relations, since most of the team managers from different construction sites and companies were familiar with one another and most were already looking forward to the football tournament. The organizing committee agreed to have a fourteen-team event due to time and budget limitations, including rental of the football pitches and referees' wages. They needed to hire a team of professional referees registered with the Football Association of Singapore to supervise the game after a series of complaints from participating teams in previous competitions.

Each team was required to pay 200 Singapore dollars for the application fee and 100 dollars as a refundable deposit to guarantee the team's participation throughout the tournament. The winners would walk away with 800 dollars in prize money plus a trophy, whereas the runners up and the third-place finalists would win 500 and 300 dollars, respectively. The tournament gained overwhelming attention from the community of Thai-workers, as the entries had jumped to twenty-one teams. The organizing committee had to adjust their plan to accommodate the worker-players' enthusiasm. They ended up handling a total of fifty-three matches and spent more than 12,000 dollars (7,300 US dollars; 288,123 baht) on referees' wages and the pitch rentals. The tournament ran from early November 2004 to late February 2005, with games held every Sunday between 8:00 a.m. and 5:00 p.m. It drew hundreds of football fans and supporters from various construction companies throughout Singapore, who participated with loud noise and passionate cheers over an endless series of popular

Thai folk music (*lukthung*), Isan/Lao folk music (*molam*), and "songs for life" (*phleng phuea chiwit*) music for their teams.[31]

Football demonstrates the workers' social organizational and networking skills as much as their sports talent. As football is a team sport, it is impossible to excel without proper management and leadership on and off the pitch. Yutthana, age thirty-eight, a veteran football player and trainer from his home village in Nakhon Phanom, told me that a successful football team needs a skillful manager who can act as a mediator on both team-sponsoring and team-building tasks.[32] Teams participating in the Thai Labor Cup were either self-financed through funds raised among players with the largest contribution coming from the team leader, or financed by "sponsors," such as private retail stores and companies doing business with Thai workers at the Golden Mile. These sponsors included some transnational companies (Siemens and Singha Beer), construction companies (Hiap Seng Engineering, Thai Jurong Engineering, Shimizu Corporation, and Bangkok Forex PTE), a VCD/DVD/cassette store (Lam Nam Phong), and a remittance service (Phuean Thae GPL). The Thai True Way team was sponsored by a Khon Kaen-based Presbyterian church.[33] These sponsors were responsible for paying for application fees, team jerseys, food and drinks, sporting palms, and first-aid kits, while the team leader took care of pre-tournament training and practice expenses. Only a few lucky teams gained full sponsorship worth more than 1,000 dollars; the rest received only partial sponsorship deals. Thus the team leader had to use personal money to run his team.[34]

Football brought the workers together and put them on the masculine playground. Som, age twenty-four, a young worker from Sakon Nakhon, insisted that it takes years to build up a good football team. The finalist teams, such as Lam Nam Phong, Shimizu, Nong Han, Nong Prachak, and A&D Siemens, had been formed for quite a while and the core members of each team (*tua lak*) had played together on a regular basis for at least two to three years. Even before the Labor Cup was organized in 2001, they played together as a team on weekends and holidays on vacant grounds on their construction sites or in public sports facilities.[35] Yutthana, the leader of Phuean Thae GPL, explained that to build up a respected football team, he had to scout for talented players, maintain good relationships with and among team members, keep up regular training, arrange friendly matches with other teams, and of course, hunt for considerable financial support. Once a month, on his trip to the Golden Mile to remit money to his family back in Nakhon Phanom, he would look around for potential team members among the armies of fellow workers at the mall. His ideal specifications were men aged between twenty and twenty-five years old with good muscular bodies, the kinds needed to play football, as well as men known to be experienced and talented players in their home villages. Sometimes he joined them in a drink and discussion to see whether they were the right "guys" for his team before extending an oral invitation to join his club.

Football has established itself as a masculine form of communication among the Thai workers in Singapore. Yutthana believes that it is easy for men who play football to connect with one another, as they speak the same language and share the same passion. The more important part is how to get team members to practice together on a regular basis. The team leader has to look for a proper practice field, communicate with players via mobile phones, and arrange agreeable times for the practice without affecting their work at various construction sites. Yutthana and his team had practiced for over a year on the vacant ground near Singapore's National Stadium in Kallang, where they played a game with five people per side known in Thai as *ko nu* (lit., "mouse goals"). He said playing this type of game is the best way to mold fast-paced teamwork strategies and to simulate the zone defense of the whole standard pitch. When they wanted to play in the "big" standard football field (*sanam yai*), his team members had to each contribute approximately five dollars to pay for the rental fees of the field. Alternatively, they can play for free if they manage to win against their opponent in friendly games, since the losers take care of the pitch fee.[36]

The way in which football brings out the working-class masculine culture among Thai construction workers is perhaps most visible when the team's spirit is materialized through the team's symbols (i.e., name, flag, and uniform) and through the passionate support of their devoted fans. No team entering the Fourth Thai Labor Cup illustrates this point better than Shimizu, which was the most well-prepared and well-funded team in the tournament. The Japan-based Shimizu is one of the largest international construction corporations in East and Southeast Asia. Its Singapore branch managed to give full sponsorship to its construction workers' team, led by Somchai, an office worker and veteran football player. Members and supporters of this team traveled in a rented coach and two six-wheel trucks along with sufficient supplies of food and drink (i.e., bottled water, energy drinks, glutinous rice, grilled chicken, and some Isan-style food). Alcohol was mostly provided by the foremen or through workers' contributions. Shimizu was the only team that played under their company's proud white flag emblazoned with the blue English letters of their company's name as well as Thailand's tri-colored national flag. Supporters and fans of the team brought with them drums, guitars, and other instruments to entertain themselves and give their team the loudest vocal support during the game. They roamed the pitch and jumped with uncontrollable joy when their team scored and won games. Some fellow workers even offered the handsome reward of ten dollars per goal to the scorer. They traveled, cheered, and supported each other throughout the tournament to the extent that Shimizu managed to enter the semifinal round. Unfortunately, they were beaten twice and ended up disappointingly as fourth-placed semifinalists. They gained neither a trophy nor a monetary award from the organizing committee. However, their Singaporean boss and foreman were generous enough to acknowledge their efforts with financial rewards, since the team helps promote the company's favorable image, displaying role-model workers with strong discipline and capable bodies.[37]

As a metaphor of contemporary Isan village masculinity, football has both physical and mental sides to it. These dual complementary aspects are essential to play this masculine contest game. Every player regardless of his amateur football skills and experience is aware of this. On its physical side, the game requires its players' to be physically fit (*mi haeng/mi khwam fit*) through regular training. Thongsuk, age thirty-seven, a veteran player for A&D Siemens, the losing finalist team, commented that his players lacked match fitness (*on som/heang bo tueng*), because they had worked so hard for their company in the past weeks, and had no time to practice football. Working out on construction sites does not help one to keep or maintain enough fitness to run and fight for the ball over ninety minutes. To make matters worse, on the day of the game, many players drank whisky or beer. Some were even mildly drunk on entering the game. A good football player must complement his physical fitness with his wit and understanding of how the game is played. Most players felt that they lost "face" and "male ego" when the ball was stolen from their possession by an opponent. They felt it was also demeaning when an opponent dribbled the ball passed them, through miscalculated steps or through a hole between their legs, a move known among players as "a through ball under one's ass" (*luk lot dak*). This Thai football slang implicitly refers to a heterosexual man forced to have anal sex against his will. It is a symbolic act in the game of football that hurts a man's masculine pride. As a masculine and contact sport, football players have to play with heart, concentration, and determination to win. Yutthana once stressed to me that "if we do not play to win, why bother to enter the competition. We want to win for the reputation of our team."[38]

The Fourth Thai Labor Cup ended with one of the most competitive and exciting finals, between Phuean Tae GPL and A&D Siemens, on February 27, 2005. In the presence of high-ranking officials and guests of honor from the Royal Thai Embassy and the Office of Thai Labor Affairs, Yutthana's team (GPL) won the championship after a wild penalty shootout. The game had finished in a 1–1 draw within regulation time, so a tenth player from GPL was needed to slam home the winning goal after a series of heartbreaking spot kicks and saves. At the end of the day, Yutthana and his captain led their team members, mostly comprised of young men from neighboring villages in Nakhon Phanom and Udon Thani, to collect their winning trophy and individual certificates from the officials. Posing before the camera, they were truly proud players and winners enjoying one of their most memorable moments long yearned for as male Thai-Isan migrant workers in Singapore.

Hunting and Gathering Away from Home

"Village transnationalism" among Thai-Isan workers in Singapore is far from complete without taking a close look at these men's fishing trips and outings to gather wild food in parts of Singapore's abandoned farming areas and forests. On the last day of the Chinese New Year in late February 2005, Prasong, age twenty-two, my informant from Sakhon Nakhon, invited me to join what he called a "picnic" outing to a forested area in Choa Chu Kang. "I will take you out 'to go have a meal in the forest' (*pai kin khao pa*). My roommates are already there. They have been out fishing and gathering wild vegetables since last night," he informed me in our telephone conversation.[39] I gratefully accepted his invitation and off we went to join the group of workers/fishermen/wild food gathers around noon. We got off the main north/south MRT line at Choa Chu Kang station, walked through rows of HDB flats, and crossed the highway deep into the forested areas near a military barracks. A number of workers I met at the Kallang Riverside Park also proudly told me their stories of how they went fishing, collected bamboo shoots, wild vegetation, roots, honey, and tropical fruits, like durian, rambutan, and jackfruit from the reserved forests or abandoned fruit orchards in areas like Woodlands, Boon Lay, and elsewhere near their construction sites away from Singapore's populated areas.[40]

Khondker (2003, 322), speaking of the communities of Bangladeshi migrant workers in Singapore, points out that the migrant worker is a "hunter and gather in a global landscape of capitalism." Thai-Isan workers demonstrate that the hunter and gather is not a mere metaphor. From media accounts, I had already learned about how Thai-Isan workers in Singapore and elsewhere were keen on hunting and gathering game and wild vegetation. The hunting and gathering culture among Thai-Isan workers is modeled upon their village life back home in Isan, where most workers were once forest-dwellers and farmers cultivating their land and natural habitations. This forms an important part of a traditional self-sufficient economy and culture, known among rural villagers and cultivators as *ha yu ha kin*. Activities such as fishing or hunting game represent culturally acquired masculine knowledge and skills among men from Isan villages. When they go abroad as migrant workers to Israel, the Middle East, or Taiwan, for example, they are frequently reported in the media as having violated the host countries' laws and customs with their hunting and gathering activities.

The cultural meaning of hunting and gathering is transported across borders from Thailand's northeastern countryside to Singapore. Migrant workers who are involved in this activity in Singapore largely consider it a combination of going out for fun in the forest (*pai thiao pa*), including going for a picnic or meal in the forest (*pai kin khao pa*) and hunting or gathering wild food in their free time. Chatri, age twenty-seven, a construction worker for six years from Nakhon Phanom, cited his trips to gather wild food in the forest as one of his favorite leisure activities.[41]

As a pastime activity for workers, "going around to have fun in the forest" provides an escape as well as a nostalgic sanctuary. On trips to the forest, as I observed, the workers feel totally at home away from the regulations of the workplace and the disciplinary gazes of Singapore society. The forest, in contrast to their construction sites and over-crowded, foreign-worker dormitories, is also a temporary outlet for self-expression. It releases them from their everyday constrictions and tensions. They can go swimming or wade in the abandoned ponds or open canals, and go fishing as well. They share jokes and stories from their various worksites. Some hum or sing their favorite songs out loud. They can cook a quick lunch under the shade of a tree, and take a precious day-time nap after the meal. Sometimes on long holidays they invite their Thai "girlfriends" (*faen* or *phu sao*), who travel to Singapore for a short social visit, to join them on their trips to the forest.

Food gathering is also a survival strategy for Thai-Isan migrant workers who have to sustain their life on the margins of Singapore's economy. While they cannot rely entirely on their wild food, it is nonetheless something they really enjoy. When they are successful in their fishing or wild food gathering efforts, they often bring the food back to their construction sites or dormitories to save on the cost of food.[42]

Conclusion

Modeled and conceptualized around their transnational realities, these men's lived experiences away from home represent "village transnational-ism." I argue that their lives provide us with the materiality to rethink and contribute to what Levitt and Nyberg-Sorensen (2004) call "the transna-tional turn in migration studies." These men illustrate what Yeoh (2003a, 3; see also Smith 2001) insists are "transnational identities" that "while fluid and flexible, are at the same time grounded in particular places at particular times." Although they are "particularly vulnerable to exploita-tion" (Allen 2003, 1), they are salient actors as they "bring a set of social and cultural tools that aid their adjustments to their new lives . . . They make sense of their experiences using the interpretive frames they bring with them" (Levitt 1998b, 930).

The practice of "transnationalism from below" as illustrated here shows that village transnationalism is a major form of transnational or transborder migration and human mobility within the Southeast Asian context (see Ananta and Arifin 2004). This form of border-crossing identity can be shared by either male or female migrants from agricultural backgrounds in the countryside with limited education, who primarily take opportunities to invest, and thus risk, their future to cross international borders to seek greater income and better life chances. This identity can be similarly extended to include transnational border-crossers such as domestic workers, farm laborers, factory workers, fishing industry workers, prostitutes, illegal unskilled workers, transborder tradeswomen on short-term social visit passes, and so on. The work and life of these men and women away from their countries of origin (i.e., Cambodia, Indonesia, Laos, Myanmar, the Philippines, Thailand, or Vietnam) in the countries of destination (i.e., Brunei, Malaysia, Singapore, or Thailand) can be relatively understood within the scope of the village transnationalism model.

Thai-Isan workers, as key actors in the village transnationalism model, are compelled to construct what Levitt (2001) calls "transnational villagers." As a model of transborder identities, village transnationalism deals primarily with how ordinary people carry out their social, political, and economic lives across borders. They are transnational subjects who are historically situated and cultural beings, as bearers of gender, ethnicity, class, race, and nationality, who at the same time are agents constantly negotiating these self-identities vis-à-vis others in transnational spaces (Yeoh 2003a, 2-3). However, due to different political and cultural contexts in Southeast Asia, transnational villagers in Asia are almost completely shut out of the political sphere in the host country. They are subject to government control and effectively manipulated by legal and political means. Citizenship, membership, or civic engagement with the intention to integrate contract migrant workers into the society and economy of the host countries has never occurred in Southeast Asia. It confirms Smith's (2001, 3) thesis that "transnationalist discourse insists on the continuing significance of borders, state policies, and national identities even as these are often transgressed by transnational communication circuits and social practices."

Village transnationalism is specifically embedded in the cultural practices of gender. It means different things to different people. It mirrors the gender identities and cultures of the dominant migrant population in question. In the case of Thai-Isan workers in Singapore, the practices of village transnationalism are predominantly male-oriented. Men from Isan who travel to work in Singapore rely on what they have "in them" and "with them" after being displaced from home over a sustained period of time. In this respect, the village transnationalism of male Thai-Isan workers in Singapore (and elsewhere in Southeast Asia) is a culture of village men at work and at play in a foreign setting. Going out, having fun, drinking, playing football, organizing pha pa merit-making projects, or going fishing and gathering wild food in the forest well demonstrate this feature.

In addition, village transnationalism represents transnational and transborder acts of transgression predicated on the use of actors' or villagers' limited cultural and symbolic capital in the context of a foreign country. Cultural and symbolic capital for migrant workers functions as "interpretive frames" used to make sense of their backbreaking realities and used to interact in varying degrees with the host society. This cultural and symbolic capital further provides transborder identity markers based on "how things were done at home" (Levitt 1998b, 930). While Thai-Isan workers may not have the requisite skills to become successful workers in a modern/postmodern society like Singapore given their limited education, capital investment, and knowledge of modern technologies and the business world, they nevertheless are able to use their physical labor as a commodity in the unskilled international labor market.[43] They also have knowledge and skills as rural villagers and land cultivators as additional cultural and symbolic capital. Social networks and activities described in this chapter demonstrate how these migrant workers have learned to survive in Singapore with such knowledge and skills.

Village transnationalism implies a complex self-reflexive sense of "displaced otherness." Transnational villagers, as shown in the case of male Thai-Isan construction workers in Singapore, have by and large become "out-classed others" and have been economically and socially confined to their worksites, foreign-worker dormitories, and certain noted "ethnoculural enclaves" in Singapore.[44] They have never been culturally or socially integrated or properly incorporated as members of the host society. Instead, they have always been given the tag of "guest" workers, constricted, confined, and segregated by Singaporean authorities and their employers.[45]

"Village transnationalism" is an important model of the social life of Thai workers in Singapore. It provides a collective model for how overseas workers can construct their migrant life and networks, including their social relationships in Singapore as well as between Singapore and their home villages in the Thai countryside.

Chapter 4

State, Intimacy, and Desire

This chapter moves beyond the social life of Thai-Isan construction workers in Singapore and takes the reader into the private, individual lives of Thai construction workers in Singapore. It examines their desire for and practice of sexual intimacy—arguably a crucial element of these men's lives. Issues surrounding heterosexuality in the context of transnational labor migration are discussed from the perspectives of the key actors at stake, namely, migrant workers, sex workers, and Singapore's state authorities. I explore what Foucault (1980, 11) calls "the way in which sex is put into discourse" in the cross-border contexts of Thailand and Singapore. Specifically, I look at how sex is practiced and defined by Thai men and women within the context of sex work. I emphasize how the "discursive practices" of heterosexuality have shaped and reshaped gendered migrant identities, focusing on male construction workers and short-term visiting female sex workers from Thailand, both of whom engage in various transient heterosexual intimacies while temporarily living and working in Singapore.

According to a number of scholars, the study of sex work has been relatively neglected in the context of transnational labor migration studies (Agustin 2006; Mahler and Pessar 2001; Pratt and Yeoh 2003; Silvey 2004a; Yeoh and Willis 1999). Yet sex work has formed an important part of the transnational labor market and cannot be left out. Indeed, "migrant women selling sex are generally neglected by migration and diaspora studies" (Agustin 2006, 29). Agustin's critical observation means that the "actual stuff of sex work" in transnational labor migration environments needs to be contextualized. The growing literature on the subject indicates that a more complex and nuanced approach is required in order to understand the situations of mobility on the ground.

In recent studies of transnational labor migration, transmigrant sexuality, specifically referring to patterns of commercial and consensual sexual intimacies engaged in by men and women in their transnational labor environments away from their homes, has emerged as theoretically problematic for three reasons. First, studies do not make strong connections between transmigrant sexuality and the complex notions of "gendered geographies of power," as argued by some feminist geographers (Gardner 1995; Mahler and Pessar 2001; Pratt and Yeoh 2003). By the term "gendered geographies of power," I follow Mahler and Pessar (2001, 447), who define it as "a framework for analyzing people's social agency—corporal and cognitive—given their own initiative as well as their positioning within multiple hierarchies of power operative within and across many terrains." Lived experiences of transnational migrants, whether they are sojourners or settlers, should be understood as those of actors whose lives are subject to tight regulation and control by state agents and employers. These people are central figures of globalization processes, which manifest unequal relationships of social, political, and economic power across geographical locations. The inscribed effects of "geographies of power" on transmigrant sexuality need to be reconsidered, particularly when both women and men are transient subjects who frequently transgress international borders to engage in their sexual activities. In short, transmigrant sexuality "cannot be understood fully without reference to power relations, both between places, and between people" (Gardner 1995, 16).

Second, the majority of studies on sex work in the context of transnational labor migration are overwhelmingly devoted to the investigation of "women selling sex," while "men buying sex" through a variety of permitted channels are apparently ignored. Transnational migrant workers' sexual lives and their roles in the global sexual economy are as important as their economic contributions (Curran et al. 2005; Osella and Osella 2000b). This scholarly trend suggests the reversal of gender issues in transnational labor migration, one that often implies "masculinist hypermobility" (Pratt and Yeoh 2003, 160).

Finally, the "victim tradition" (Cohen 1996, 513) seems to have dominated studies of transmigrant sex work that focus on women sex workers as victims of the international human trafficking networks or of an exploitative sexual economy (Bales 2002; Darwin et al. 2003; Derks

2000; Human Rights Watch 2000; Kempadoo 1998, 2005; Monzini 2005; Murray 1998, 2001). This scholarly tradition needs to be rethought and challenged. Should transmigrant female sex workers and their male counterparts be viewed as powerless and oppressed or as purposefully articulated actors in dealing with structures of power and socioeconomic processes operating in the transnational labor marketplace?

I address these problems by discussing the state's disciplinary technologies of regulation and gaze as well as their multiple effects on the practices of sexual intimacies among Thai migrant workers in Singapore. I argue that sex "sold and bought" in transient geographical locations assumes complex and diverse forms within the informal economy (Sassen 1994). Sex work or "sexual labor" (Truong 1990) in transit is not necessarily coerced or forced. In a strictly regulated geopolitical city such as Singapore, sex work within the transnational labor migration context might also be understood as mutually sought-out encounters among a displaced and highly mobile working-age population. It usually involves socially and culturally marginalized foreigners and takes place in sociocultural contact and permissive zones (Askew and Cohen 2004, 96).[1] These zones constitute the constructed space for sexual intimacies between cross-border foreign sex workers and transient overseas migrant workers in Singapore.

The Politics of Migrant Desire, Sexuality, and Masculinity in Singapore

Since the "Great Marriage Debate" in the early 1980s, the Singaporean government has obsessed over the low fertility rates of its population, especially among its "graduate mothers" (Yao 2007; Heng and Devan 1995). Homosexuality is not recognized in Singapore's state ideologies of sexual intimacies, which focus almost entirely on sexual reproduction. Heng and Devan (1995) appropriately describe such paternalistic ideological apparatuses as "state fatherhood," a concept describing the state's overall hegemonic domination over society's development and people's livelihoods, including concern over reproductive sexuality and patriarchal familial values. Unlike Singapore's habit of producing narratives of national crisis regarding its citizens' sexuality and reproduction practices, it is far less apparent how Singapore attempts to effectively manage sexual pleasure that does not involve sexual reproduction among its transient population. Policy and legislation aimed at explicitly regulating or managing the sexuality of this group is rare. Rather, the state's focus has been on the economic productivity and contributions of these migrants.[2]

Low (1995, 746) points out that "Singapore is particularly secretive about its population movement statistics. Not even the numbers and sources of foreign workers are officially released due to political sensitivities."[3] However, no state would totally turn a blind eye to its citizens' and transient population's sexualities. Sex has produced multidimensional effects that could potentially alter the country's demography, healthcare, crime, and even national security. Sex must be seen as a product of multiple social constructions and power relations. As Foucault (1980, 26) points out, "between the state and the individual, sex becomes an issue, and a public issue no less; a whole web of discourses, special knowledge, analyses, and injunctions are settled upon it."

Singapore has employed a series of calculated and specially designed disciplinary technologies to handle sexualities among both its citizens and non-citizens. Indeed, there are several legal, geopolitical, and social methods of surveillance implicitly and explicitly imposed by the state to gaze over and control the sexual practices among its transient foreign population. For instance, Singapore legally prohibits marriage between work permit-holding migrant workers, such as construction workers and domestic help, and its citizens, as well as among migrant workers themselves. Its policy for the employment of foreign workers through the complex work permit system defines them as guest workers, "who are offered employment under a contract at a monthly salary of not more than 1,500 dollars per month" (Yeh 1995, 4). They are expected to work in Singapore on a short-term basis and must leave the country at the end of their contract. "Unskilled workers can neither bring their families nor are they encouraged to marry Singaporeans" (Low 1995, 753; Wong 1997, 151). The Employment of Foreign Workers Act (chapter 91A), states:

> The foreign worker shall not go through any form of marriage or apply to marry under any law, religion, custom or usage with a Singapore Citizen or Permanent Resident in or outside Singapore. . . . If the foreign worker is a female foreign worker, the foreign worker shall not

become pregnant or deliver any child in Singapore during the validity of her Work Permit/Visit Pass. The foreign worker shall not indulge or be involved in any illegal, immoral or undesirable activities, including breaking up families in Singapore.[4]

Singapore also imposes strict medical requirements on foreign migrant workers, especially foreign domestic workers. Every foreign worker is required to pass a medical checkup in order to obtain a work permit. However, the most notable medical requirement is the bi-annual medical exam required for female domestic workers. As Iyer, Devasahayam, and Yeoh (2004, 26) point out, "the examinations were targeted at catching pregnancy or detecting an infectious disease. During the examinations, the bodies of foreign domestic workers are constructed as being sites of 'danger' in two ways: in terms of their sexuality and as potential transmitters of various infectious diseases." These medical exams aim to trace the unwanted outcomes of possible sexual encounters during the period of domestic workers' employment in Singapore and are "symptomatic of the deep-seated discomfort with, and perhaps fear of, the migrant other" (Iyer et al. 2004, 10).

Migrant sexuality in Singapore is conditioned by the politics of organized public spaces designed to segregate foreign workers from the local population. A number of "ethnocultural enclaves" (Rahman and Lian 2005; Yeoh 2004) accommodate the presence of foreign workers, namely dormitories, hostels, or living quarters in designated areas separate from local communities, new housing developments specifically tailored for foreign workers within established residential communities (Hui 1997, 109; Huang and Yeoh 2003), and red-light districts such as Geylang and Orchard Tower (Brazil 2004).[5] The Singaporean authorities carefully organize where and how the populations of foreign migrant workers are housed. The reorganization of public space permits the "processes of spatial othering" (Huang and Yeoh 2003, 90), which fosters social outings in contact zones among foreign workers during their leisure time.

Sex work and transient sexual intimacies are also made possible by certain flexible migratory regulations and flows of people across international borders. Despite the state's strict screening and monitoring, it is impossible to completely shut the door on the flows of various groups of visitors, such as tourists, students, and workers. Singapore, as a major "global ethnoscape" (Appadurai 1999),[6] has to deal with these people through authorizing social and business visit passes for tourists and other short-term visitors. These passes have opened the doors of the country to female travelers, many of whom are professional or opportunistic sex workers from countries like China, Indonesia, the Philippines, and Thailand.

Sex among the transient non-citizen population is subject to public scrutiny for healthcare reasons. A number of organizations in Singapore have attempted to curb sexual behavior of migrant workers through public health and sex education campaigns (Brazil 2004). These campaigns are conducted by the Singaporean authorities, foreign embassies, local and international non-governmental organizations (NGOs), and some charity organizations. For example, the Singapore Health Promotion Board (2003) distributes a comic book in Thai, promoting safe sex among Thai construction workers. The Humanitarian Organization for Migration Economics, a Singapore-based NGO, runs emergency shelters for foreign sex workers, domestic workers, and construction workers in Singapore and assists them with legal, financial, and moral advice (C. Sim 2005).[7]

Thai Men Who Buy Sex in Singapore

Thai workers in Singapore revealed a number of established patterns of intimacy, including paid sexual encounters and one-night stands, as well as short- and long-term relationships. It is common practice among Thai workers to use the services of a foreign sex worker when they are under the influence of alcohol. Thai migrant workers encounter sex workers in Singapore's peripheral places, such as roadside dens, vacant spaces behind the rear entrance of workers' dormitories and hostels, and forest brothels. Most of my Thai informants insist that, outside the secured areas and behind the authorities' back, night life around the construction sites' residential camps, rented public-housing rooms, living quarters, dormitories, and hostels for foreign workers is rather lively. Police raids on roving brothels, makeshift huts, and forest hideouts belonging to illegal male and female immigrants in Boon Lay Way, Jurong West, Lim Chu Kang, Tampines Avenue, and Woodlands Industrial Park have been frequently reported by the Singaporean local press (C. Sim 2005; G. Sim

2003; Yusof 2004). In these places, Thai women smuggled into Singapore by agents or pimps provide on-site sex services. Their agents and pimps, who are usually veteran Thai workers or "big brothers" among fellow workers, erect tents behind bushes or dark corners. They also prepare necessities like mattresses, mosquito coils, bottled water, and rolls of tissue paper for their nighttime underground business. Female sex workers, who often stay in a group of three to five in a cheap hotel room, come to "provide sexual services" (*rap khaek*), charging twenty dollars per service. Each sex worker has to sleep with approximately twenty men per night and share half of the earnings with the agents or pimps. Illegal gambling, such as the rolling of dice, also takes place in these dens. I witnessed foreign workers engaging in both commercial sex and gambling in the Kaki Bukit area. Some forest hideouts are large operations and can shelter up to one hundred illegal immigrants. In my several short visits to one informant's living quarters, I noticed that pornographic materials, both printed and digital forms, were common in the living quarters among Thai and other foreign men. In their dormitories, posters of movie stars or porn stars hang on the walls and pornographic magazines and X-rated VCD and DVD movies are freely circulated and shared among friends.

Several lanes in the Geylang district, together with Orchard Towers on Orchard Road, comprise Singapore's designated red-light area, where colorful nightlife businesses provide food, drink, and sex, and are always in full swing, especially on the weekends (Brazil 2004). Visitors to brothels and "love hotels" in Geylang include migrants and citizens. For those Thai men in my research study, Geylang brothels, karaoke bars, and discotheques provided them some limited social space in which to express their masculine selfhood. For example, Suwat, a construction worker from Nakhon Ratchasima, in northeastern Thailand, said: I prefer to "go up into the room" (*khuen hong*) with girls from China. . . . Sometimes, I like to try Indonesian and Filipina girls. They charge only 35–50 dollars, compared to eighty or more for younger and prettier Chinese girls.[8]

During their leisure time, Thai men working in Singapore maintain entertaining patterns that often lead to involvement in sexual intimacies. On paydays, they often start by drinking beer or whisky and singing karaoke songs in Thai-style bars and discotheques in popular places like the Golden Mile Complex and Geylang area. In these entertainment establishments, independent sex workers from Hat Yai in southern

Thailand and from Bangkok on short-term visits to Singapore often attract their attention. Tom, a Chinese-Singaporean who has spent more than twenty years running entertainment businesses catering to the Thai communities in Singapore, told me that his karaoke bar employs four or five Thai women full-time, yet more than a dozen "hostess women" who enter Singapore on short-term social visit passes can regularly be found in his bar. These women serve beer, serve as escorts to customers, and negotiate sex with the customers that takes place outside of the bar. Most Thai-owned karaoke bars in the Golden Mile Complex and the Geylang area allow these "freelance" sex workers to meet potential customers in their bars.

Another channel for sexual pleasure and romantic intimacy for Thai workers is through establishing relationships with domestic workers from Indonesia and the Philippines. Singapore employs more than one hundred fifty thousand live-in female domestic workers, mainly from these two countries (Yeoh, Huang and Gonzalez 1999). This channel is generally limited to a small number of long-term workers who have acquired some working knowledge of English (see chapter 5).

Thai Women Who Sell Sex in Transit in Singapore

Migration flows from Thailand for sex work in Singapore can be understood as "economically stimulated movements that often develop initially within a national setting, leading at a later stage to transnational job-seeking" (Hewison 2006, 2). The narratives of two Thai migrant women in Singapore, Kaew and Ket offer contrasting experiences that appear to be reflective of Thai migrant women in general. Kaew is an experienced bar girl who works at the well-known Orchard Towers on Orchard Road in the heart of Singapore's business district. Ket is a veteran tradeswoman (*mae kha*) in the Golden Mile Complex and adjacent areas on Beach Road where she has worked for more than ten years. Both are from Thailand's northeastern region and also engage in "sex work" in Singapore as a means of surviving in this global city.

Kaew, a native of Khon Kaen in her early thirties, had previously worked in various jobs in Bangkok since leaving home at the age of thirteen, including domestic work in a Sino-Thai household in the Sutthisan area, waitressing, and a factory job in Phra Pradaeng when she was eighteen years old. Her life took a series of stormy twists over the following seven years, during which her marriages failed twice. Her marriages to a fellow factory worker and Bangkok technician left her with two sons, who are cared for by her mother in Khon Kaen. On the advice of a friend, Kaew decided to try her luck in a Patphong bar in Bangkok, where she made good money, initially as a waitress and then, after a year, as a freelance sex worker. She also maintained an escort relationship that did not include sex with a wealthy banker in Bangkok, whom she regarded as a respected older friend. In mid-2001, she decided once again to follow her friend's advice and try her luck in Singapore because "I am getting too old for Patphong, but I still want to earn more."[9]

Kaew's decision to enter overseas sex work resonates with the assertion that many "women are migrating as autonomous, economic agents in their own right, trying to seize economic activities overseas" (Kempadoo 1998, 17). After the turbulent years of marital failure, Kaew's family in Khon Kaen had no influence on her decision to work abroad. Kaew, however, kept her promise to send money back home and returned home to visit her sons once or twice a year. Aside from these familial commitments, her life was very much her own. She entered Singapore on a social visit pass, but she arranged with her "agent" to work in a karaoke bar in Orchard Towers. She was frightened and frustrated during her first few months in Singapore, but she was soon able to adjust to her situation, including traveling back and forth between Bangkok and Singapore on a regular basis to renew her social visit pass.

Kaew perceived herself as a transformed woman, starting out as an innocent Isan girl and becoming an experienced sex worker in Singapore. Her view on relationships with men was more sophisticated. At her age, she knew that most men (e.g., Chinese-Singaporean men) who came to her for sex also came for long-term romantic relationships. In responding to the way these men approached her, she was ready to use sex tactically to gain something from the relationship, such as financial security, shelter, or legal status. The three most important strategies for her survival in Singapore were to do "whatever is necessary in my job to earn money, save and send remittances to my parents and sons (since they are the most important persons in my life), and give myself some rewards (hai rangwan kap tua eng). I have worked so hard all my life. I deserve whatever pleasure

I wish to have. I am not so foolish to work myself to death. I want to be happy." Kaew told me that love and sex—heart and brain—are different entities:

> I had a Singaporean police boyfriend who helped me a lot when I first arrived here. Our relationship was mutually emotional, but he was fair enough to let me go when I had another man who could give me the formal refuge I need. Yes, I have to get married to a Singapore citizen in order to live and work here. My "husband/lover" helped me apply for PR [permanent resident status], so I can continue to work while living with his family.[10]

Kaew has lived a transient life in a rather complex manner. She is married, but still works as sex worker. She is not certain whether she is truly in love with her husband/lover because he is six years younger than her. "He is not my type and not mature enough, but I need an official marriage certificate from him and a place to stay in Singapore," she said.[11]

Ket's experiences reveal that the borders between Thailand, Malaysia, and Singapore are permeable in terms of the flow of humans, goods, and services, despite heavy border regulations and controls. Ket has been commuting between Hat Yai and Singapore several times a month since the early 1990s. Although a native of the northeastern province of Nakhon Phanom, she has rented a house in Hat Yai as a base for her cross-border trade in native Isan food, snacks, fruits, and sweets, along with whisky and cigarettes. Every weekend, together with a group of her female friends and traders, she brings her goods to Singapore via an air-conditioned bus and sells them to the thousands of Thai-Isan men who gather at the Golden Mile Complex during their time off from work. In order to enter Singapore, she needs a valid passport and the sum of 1,000 Singapore dollars, which she calls *ngoen show* (show money). She also must pay 35 dollars for a one-way bus ticket. In mid-2004, fifty to seventy Thai tradeswomen commuted in and out of Singapore to do business in the Golden Mile area.[12] At its peak in the mid-1990s, the number of such tradeswomen was over one hundred. These women learned that they could earn more in the second or third week of the month, when most Thai construction workers had been paid.

Survival networks loom large in determining the existence of cross-border small-scale tradeswomen like Ket and her friends. She entered this business more than ten years ago by joining her older friends. She perceived small-scale trading as a profitable individual enterprise for a middle-age housewife from a poor Isan village, because the value of the Singapore dollar was much stronger than the Thai baht and the trade was rather reliable once a social visit pass was issued by Singapore authorities at the border checkpoint in Woodlands. Ket has built up close relations with a group of five or six women, some of whom are her close relatives from her Isan village. Together, they prepare their goods, travel, and stay in a cheap hotel room in Singapore, after which they locate good spots to do their business together in the areas around the Golden Mile Complex, as well as in some apartments nearby, and in the Kallang Riverside Park. As she is now the most senior veteran, Ket assumes leadership in the group and provides advice to her younger friends.

It is important to note that women in cross-border migration circuits have adopted a variety of migrant activities, including sex work and petty trade. Female transborder vendors in their thirties and forties, some of whom were married and have children back home, take on other kinds of small income-generating activities in Singapore as well. Besides selling their food, snacks, and drinks, they also engage in private moneylending, charging up to 20 percent interest. Sometimes, they risk smuggling in small amounts of Thai whisky and Isan-made tobacco. They also make a small profit from taking orders from Thai workers and bringing in certain requested goods from Hat Yai, where prices are cheaper, including such goods as workmen clothes, jeans, different varieties of chili paste, fishing nets, etc. Transborder tradeswomen are usually good at handling the overseas workers in Singapore. Sakhon, one of my worker-informants from Khon Kaen and an acquaintance of Ket and her friends, told me that

you have to be careful dealing with these *mae kha* (tradeswomen). They all know how to deal with men. They know exactly what they are up to. When they sell their goods, they do not mind selling their bodies too, if they are pleased and the price they quote is matched. Normally, they charge fifty dollars for one turn and a hundred dollars per night, excluding the hotel fee.[13]

My research suggests that the experiences of Thai transborder women vendors involved in sex work in Singapore resonate with Kempadoo's (1998, 4–5) observations that "sex work is not for individual wealth but for family well-being or survival," and sex workers "are able to distinguish intimacy and love from the sexual act itself." The migrant women I spoke with explained that there is a distinction between their heterosexual identities in Thailand and Singapore. For instance, Kon, one of Ket's younger friends told me that "what you hear and see from me here are definitely not what I have done at home. None of us sits, drinks, and has fun with male strangers without the company of husbands or relatives in our villages. We must be good mothers and women with our families."[14] These women must assume different identities in order to "clothe, feed, and educate their children" (Kempadoo 1998, 3), who are left behind at home.

Managing personal matters like money and sexual desire has proven to be a daunting task for many male Thai workers. Back home in Thailand, both money and sexual desire are part of their traditional domestic sphere, which is usually controlled by women. Some male Thai workers in Singapore find it difficult to handle their own financial and sexual lives without assistance from their women and families. Sakhon is a regular customer in Ket's moneylending business circle. He sometimes buys sexual services from some of the young tradeswomen in Ket's circle. His ATM card and bank account info is always kept with Ket, who demands he hand them over to her so that she can get the money she loaned him plus interest once Sakhon's employer deposits his wages into his bank account. Ket has to work hard since she is financing the construction of her new house in Thailand. Sakhon needs money to send home to his parents and to spend whenever he wants to go out drinking or to visit girls in Geyland brothels. On payday, he loves sitting on the mattresses prepared by Ket under a tree in Kallang Riverside Park having fun drinking and chatting with the *mae kha* girls. Sakhon, a young man in his early thirties who works hard and drinks heavily, told me:

> I have already slept with almost every *mae kha* you talked to in the park. You name them and I can tell you their stories. They were good housewives in their home villages, but here in Singapore, they do everything, including selling sex to make money. Of course, *mae kha*

girls are not pretty. Most of them are overweight as they are already married and have children, but I do not mind. Some of them love to have fun and some are willing to give me a credit when I run out of cash. When I have money, I use the service of young, pretty Chinese girls in Geylang brothels. Well, in my six years here, I have slept with more than one hundred women, both Thai and other nationalities.[15]

Sakhon's story seems to indicate that transient sex encounters, both male and female, are rather emotionally detachable and business-oriented.

Cross-border Thai *mae kha* women, like most women in migration circuits, are experts at migrant-style business transactions, showing their knowledge and tactics of how to deal not only with their clients but also with Singapore immigration officials and police. Ket always warns her friends that

you must be straight in dealing with the Singapore police. They have no mercy for us—foreigners. Law is law; rule is rule. Try your best to avoid quarrelling or fighting with the locals because they will always protect their people before the foreigners.[16]

Indeed, selling food, drink, and snacks without a proper license is illegal, let alone engaging in situational sex work. These women have to be extraordinarily careful and discreet. Surachai, a young worker from Udon Thani in his late twenties, had "gone to take a bath" (*pai ap nam*) with one of the *mae kha* on the day I visited the women. The term "*pai ap nam*" is a Thai expression for men that visit brothels, massage parlors, or commercial sex establishments, where a man must take a bath with his partner after they finish their sexual activity. Surachai told me, "These women are skillful at luring men to buy their goods and their 'services.'"[17] Sakhon had been in the company of *mae kha* long enough to understand these women's tactics in handling their male compatriot workers.

When Thai men gather to meet friends and fellow workers in the park or in parking lots around the Golden Mile Complex, a *mae kha* will often approach them and ask whether they want to have some beer, whisky, or snacks. Without waiting for an invitation or affirmative answer from the men, the *mae kha* will casually proceed to join the party. She treats the workers as her close acquaintances, unpacks her snacks, and offers them drinks. Men are pushed into a position where they cannot refuse her presumed business offerings and hospitality. With the men she likes, the *mae kha* does not mind touching, hugging, or even kissing in some cases. She does not hesitate to ask for a tip and is ready if a worker proposes buying sex from her. Sakhon admitted that

> men have no choice to refuse the request or offer made by those *mae kha*. How can you deny a girl begging for a two-dollar tip from you? No way. From our side we know that holding her hands, embracing her or dry-kissing or sniffing her cheeks means that you must give her some tip money. This is part of the unwritten rules of social conduct for us.[18]

Due to boredom that can set in during transnational migration sojourns, home always looms large in the Thai workers' imagination. Cross-border opportunistic or professional sex workers offer opportunities to experience a sense of home to these men who are currently without wives or girlfriends (as well as some local men). The contemporary presence of cross-border tradeswomen and female sex workers temporarily fulfills the workers' nostalgia for home comforts and their longing for the families and homes they have left behind. In these temporary moments of intimacy, these women "take over tasks previously associated with housewives" (Sassen 2002, 264) or girlfriends left behind in their home countries.

As a social field, transnational spaces (Jackson, Crang, and Dwyer 2004) tend to replicate the imbalance of power relations between men and women. Stories of both male and female Thai migrants in Singapore further demonstrate two points concerning their agency and subjectivity. One is that geographical and cultural proximity between Singapore and Thailand encourage both men and women to cross national borders in search of employment and income. Being involved in acts of selling or buying sex is part of the sexual economy of migrants. The other point is that women are more vulnerable as border-crossers than men due to their inferior position as "moving to serve" actors in masculine transnational spaces. Gendered double standards are also apparent in state-imposed regulations. Singapore's Immigration and Checkpoints Authority scrutinizes young, single Thai women more than male workers. When police raid the roving brothels or forest hideouts, more women are arrested than men. The practices of sexual intimacies among transnational labor migrants from less developed economies inserted into the complex economic and social textures of a global city are far from exemplifying cultural transformations toward gender equality and liberation.

Conclusion

In the context of Singapore, the state and employers attempt to regulate the sexuality of migrant workers but are only partially successful. There are multiple channels through which Thai migrant men attempt to satisfy their sexual desires and through which Thai women engage in sex work. In the Singaporean context, sex among the transient, non-citizen population is discouraged because it cannot lead to the legitimate conception of children, and thus will never contribute to the increase of manpower the state seeks. Sexual relations, therefore, primarily take place as commercial, illegitimate sex outside the traditional realms of marriage and families, thereby attracting state concern in the context of public health, criminal prevention, and immigration. Through sets of "technologies of power" (Foucault 1977, 30) imposed by the state, sex work in the transnational labor migration context exposes itself as the subject of strict surveillance and control.

Migrant sexual intimacy provides a case study of the representation politics of Singapore as a global city. The image and reputation of Singapore as a monolithic and severely regulated state is somewhat overemphasized (see Heng and Devan 1995; Yao 2007). Thai migrant men and women's transmigrant patterns of flexible sexuality within the Singaporean context demonstrate that it is possible for individual agents to rework, redefine, and negotiate the state's regulations and controls. Migrants' negotiations are part of broader, complex patterns of entertainment, commodified transactions, and sexual catharsis engaged in by Thai migrant men and women, as well as many Singaporeans and other foreigners. The gaze and regulatory practices of the Singaporean state are strong, but its migrant populations are capable of establishing channels of sexual intimacy within the contact spaces and highly mobile living conditions that are made available to them.

I have questioned the gender bias against women in transnational migration studies and the representation of women as victims in studies of human trafficking and sex work, by bringing into play transmigrants' agency and subjectivity in their negotiation with the state's attempts to regulate heterosexual desire among migrants. Men and women as transnational actors in global ethnoscapes are exposed to sets of economic, political, and social structures and consciousness that force them to become "moving targets" (Appadurai and Breckenridge 1989) across the transnational "sexual economy" (Warren 2003a, 59). Both male and female Thai migrants have their own complex ways of negotiating sex while temporarily residing in Singapore.

Sex as it is engaged in by transnational migrant laborers must be understood within the context of the powerful, emerging processes of the informalization of the economy in a globalizing world. Economic processes in most global cities create urban households without "primary care providers performing their traditional roles" (Sassen 2002) because both husbands and wives have become professional or skilled middle-class workers contributing to advanced sectors of the economy. At the same time, unskilled or semiskilled, low-income jobs are transferred to migrant workers, male and female, from less developed economies. My case study of Thai migrant men and women working in Singapore's informal labor market suggest that sex work emerges as a crucial arena of negotiation in these globalizing processes.

I have also demonstrated that focusing on the sexual biographies of migrant men and women allows us to better understand their agency and autonomy, which explains, in part, their transient life away from home. Sexual acts and their attached economy of pleasure allow migrant men and women to become active agents participating in both formal and informal global economies. Transmigrant men and women can indeed be thought of as "members of diasporas, as entrepreneurial women, as flexible workers, and as active agents participating in globalization" (Agustin 2006, 43). As demonstrated by Thai workers in Singapore, exploring the multiple links between individual migrants and the macro-level restructuring of gendered geographies of power through aspects of transient life identities and voices could be a focal point of further studies of sexuality and transnational migration.

Chapter 5

Male Workers Talking Sex

Desire, sexual practices, and masculine selfhood are all products of the social life of male migrant workers. These men's social lives are situated within the intertwining discourses of social marginalization, ethnocultural foreignness, and transnational labor migration. Sex as desire and practice (of this desire) is an intimate part of the male transient biography and migrant subjectivity intersecting with social conditions in which sex and sexuality are practiced. Sex and sexuality are often framed and featured in the complex narratives of the migrant experience. This chapter focuses on the construction and negotiation of masculine self-identity through migrant workers' own narratives of their sexual encounters with women. It traces male migrant intimacy through these men's own words and deeply personalized viewpoints, as displayed by their naked tales of manly pleasure and their reflexive laughter. Their stories reveal the contours of their sexually masculine lifestyle beyond the confines of familial responsibility and within the context of a new-found freedom and anonymity, despite strict control and regulation of their social lives by Singaporean authorities and their employers. While a number of these men's accounts relate to sexual encounters within the context of the sex trade, many others reflect sexual encounters outside of that trade.

I argue that these sexual-life narratives should be viewed as integral parts of male migrant workers' self-reflexivity, entailing their sudden and temporary excitement in exploring cross-cultural social life. Sexual intimacy in this respect connotes a discursive form of storytelling, generated from human experiences of migrant workers' sexual contacts and social relations in and through a life in transit. My aim in writing about migrant sexual intimacy is to portray a nuanced interpretation of the transnational migrant life. Sexual desire and acts form a core part of men's migrant subjectivity as transnational actors on the ground. Such desire brings out the humanly intimate, personal aspects of the transnational character of overseas laborers. In the narratives of migrant sexual intimacy, Foucault (1980, 6) argues that the worker talking sex "has the appearance of a deliberate transgression. A person who holds forth in such language places himself to a certain extent outside the reach of power; he upsets established law; he somehow anticipates the coming freedom."

Sex as cultural practice and lifestyle always forms a core part of men's masculine self-identity. Asian men (e.g., Bangladeshi, Indian, Myanmese, Thai) working as migrant laborers in Singapore have developed their own particular characteristics. Their sexual patterns are embedded in their transient migrant lifestyle and shaped by the wages they earn as well as the host society's legal and cultural regulations. Migrant sexuality is a form of marginally constructed social identity within foreign migrant communities.

Migrant sexuality as widely practiced among Asian men employed in Singapore's construction industry reflects the social marginalization of ethnocultural foreignness. "Migrant foreignness" refers to certain acquired ethnocultural and gendered patterns of identity and differences that migrant workers carry with them from their home countries and put into practice during their transient stay abroad. Migrant foreignness announces migrant workers' national, ethnocultural, economic, and political differences and perhaps constitutes the most visible sign of migrant subjectivity and identity. In most cases, migrant foreignness represents a constructed form of migrant otherness, which is part of the encompassing product of social marginalization. Marigold (1995), for example, shows that male Filipino workers in the Middle East were degraded and humiliated by the Gulf employers and experienced a painful crisis of emasculation as compared to their pre-migratory gender status at home.

Migrant workers have been placed at the lower end of restructured informal economies of global cities around the world (Sassen 1991, 1994). In a highly regulated and controlled labor market like Singapore, migrant workers (e.g., construction workers, shipyard workers, and domestic workers) are designated by the government's employment policies (Rahman 2006; Rahman and Lian 2005; Piper 2006) and the geographies of power (Mahler and Pessar 2001) to work and live in marginal social and economic spaces of the larger society. They are employed to work on backbreaking, manual jobs with lower income, assigned to live in isolated and congested hostels for foreign workers away from local communities, and subjected to close criminal and sexual surveillance. Off-duty, they usually spend their leisure time gathering in public spaces that feature their own home ethno-cultures. The migrant public spaces in Singapore, such as the Golden Mile Complex for Thai workers, are among public zoning spaces with multiple links to migrant sexuality. The social marginalization of migrant workers' foreignness is most visible in Singapore's politics of migrant spacing. Migrant sexuality and other leisure activities that are deemed potentially harmful forces of foreignness need to be exposed to legal and public gazes as much as possible.

In Their Own Words: Migrant Sexual Intimacy

The general characteristics of migrant male sexuality adopted by male Thai migrant workers in Singapore are described here through the accounts of Thai construction workers I met during my fieldwork for this study—in particular, a focus group discussion held on October 28, 2006.[1] Their narratives tell of their actual sexual practices as much as their biases and predicaments.[2]

Common attitudes. For the men in this study, sex with migrant women in Singapore is never regarded as a product of serious romantic love. Instead, when discussing their sexual encounters, these men described their sexuality in terms of erotic desire as well as engagement of sexual intercourse. The participants believed that sex was a necessary part of their lives, whether they were single or married. It is considered part of their "labor-selling" life (*chiwit khai raeng*) abroad. Many of the participants repeatedly used the phrases "men's business" (*rueang khong phuchai*) or "things that all men know by heart" (*khong baep ni phuchai thuk khon ru kan*) when referring to matters of sex and their sexual urges. Sex was commonly assumed among them to be a psychological and biological need and they believed that all healthy men possess sexual fantasies, desires, and urges. Sommai, age forty-eight, bluntly stated, "Taking a look at some good sensual female figures on the street, I wished I could have sex with them. These young ladies' figures are damn sexy. Their busts and bottoms are so 'killable' (*pen ta kha thae*)."

The term "killing" is Thai slang used by men to describe a man's desire to have sex with a female object of his fantasy.[3] It is a term that objectifies women as desirable sexual beings. In this sense, a woman is dehumanized and reduced to a non-human object of men's sexual desire (*khong*). The same term—"*khong*" (thing)—is also generally used to refer to desirable, feminine bodies and also a woman's vagina. Women who are identified as *khong* are usually sex workers, call girls, or bar girls. For most Thai men, to have sex with women of their choice is equivalent to releasing their sexual desire to "kill things." Women who are identified as *khong* are often labeled "naughty" girls, such as prostitutes, call girls, and bar girls.

Ideal sexual partners. The Thai men I spoke with expressed a strong desire to have sex with women of other nationalities. For them, having sex with foreign women was one of the most rewarding parts of their transient migrant life in Singapore. Songwut, age forty-six, acknowledged that "it is always in the back of every worker's mind. It is a man's profit in life (*kamrai chiwit*) to have sexual encounters with girls from another country." Sex is fundamental in their transient, mostly short-term intimacies. Weera, age thirty-seven, who regards himself as a true playboy or a womanizer (*suea phuying*) commented, "I have lost count of how many Filipina and Indonesian partners I have had sex with in my seven years of employment in Singapore." Anon, age forty-three, also confirmed that having sex with women from other nationalities was a "good experience, but we cannot take the relationships seriously because we are married. We have wives and kids back home."[4]

Among the different national groups preferred by the men were Chinese-Singaporeans, mainland Chinese, Indonesian, Filipinas, Malays, Indians, and Thais. Sommai liked Chinese girls' "good figures and fair skin" but also Indian and Malay girls' "larger breasts," whereas Chatchai desired "Indian girls' fair skin, pretty dreamy eyes, and large chest" but their "rather strong body odor" turned him off.[5] Chinese-Singaporean women were more the object of the men's fantasies than realistic partners. Weera explained that Thai men prefer them because of their "fair skin and curvy figures." He explained further:

However, it is almost impossible to have sex with Chinese-Singaporean women. We know from their look that they regard foreign workers as very low. We are dirt in their eyes. They look down on us. Besides, it is against Singapore's law for foreign workers to establish relationships with local women. If the women report sexual molestation, harassment, or rape to the police, we are in danger. Singaporean police always protect their citizens and the laws here are very strict. We can easily be put in jail or deported. It is too risky for us. We have to be extremely careful dealing with the Singaporeans. We sometimes have to restrain ourselves from gazing or looking at them too obviously.

Chatchai, age forty-one, who had spent years working as a factory worker in Taiwan before coming to Singapore, agreed:

Singaporean women look down on us, unlike the Taiwanese girls who are friendlier to foreign workers. I was upset when I offered them my seat on the bus or the MRT [train] and they ignored my hospitality. I know they look down on us, but failing to acknowledge our good will is rather painful for us. They are too suspicious of us and regard themselves as above us.

Women from mainland China who work as sex workers in the red-light district of Geylang are more realistic partners for the Thai workers. They are preferred because they are young and have good figures. They fit an idealized image of beauty shared by men in contemporary Thailand, namely "fair skinned, pretty, Chinese-looking, and busty" (*khao, suai, muai, uem*). The downside of approaching Chinese girls for sex is that they demand higher fees for their services (80–120 Singapore dollars per service). To them, sex is business. By contrast, women from Indonesia, the Philippines, or Thailand provide intimate companionship and friendship without the expectation of payment.

The majority of the focus group participants agreed that Indonesian and Filipina domestic workers were their most realistic and approachable choices as foreign sexual partners in Singapore. Jetsada, age forty-three, preferred Indonesian and Filipina women because they have "strong legs" and "compact breasts."[6] Songwut, who had already had four Filipina and two Indonesian domestic workers as lovers in Singapore, commented:

They are by far most similar to Thai girls both in their appearances and manners. They have good hearts and are ready to embrace us as lovers and friends. They are not sex workers. They do not demand money. We are more comfortable having relationships with them.

Like most of the men in this study, Songwut had another incentive for engaging in relationships with Indonesian and Filipina girls. He loved practicing his spoken English with them. Bunmee, age thirty-two, said his English improved dramatically since he began seeing his Filipina girlfriend: "She taught me a lot and I have expanded my grammatical and conversational skills." Bunmee's efforts to improve his English have paid off; he was one of my top students in my evening English classes for overseas Thai workers. Chaiwat, age twenty-eight, who studied English with me briefly, would consult me (mostly via telephone) when he had problems understanding the English-language text messages (SMS) he received on his mobile phone from his Malaysian and Indonesian girlfriends.

Thai migrant workers regard Filipina and Indonesian domestic workers as ideal sex partners, despite their ethno-religious and cultural differences. The men I spoke with believed that the migrant women share their sexual fantasies and urges. They consider foreign domestic workers to be sexually mature women removed from their husbands and lovers. As live-in domestic workers they are closely supervised by their employers. Their work seems endless and more tiring than men working on a construction site. Songwut, who has had relationships with several Filipina domestic workers, expressed his sympathy towards these women:

They earn a very low monthly income (250–300 dollars for Indonesians and 300–350 for Filipinas). Some maids have to work from early morning until almost midnight. Some are not given enough food to eat or do not have days off at all. As they are isolated from their fellow maids, they need someone to talk to. They need friends. They talk and make friends via SMS messaging or hand-phones. When they are allowed to go out on Sundays, it is common to see them hanging out with friends or boyfriends.

Weera added:

> Female workers want to have sex just like us; sometimes they are more
> sexually active than us [male workers]. They work very hard and need
> somebody to share their frustration, loneliness, and hardship. Sex is
> a common part of their life when they are off duty. I can catch their
> inner feelings from the ways they look at men.[7]

Weera went on to characterize Filipina and Indonesian domestic workers as generally "open and easy-going." For him,

> the Indonesians are more sincere and committed lovers in comparison
> with the Filipina. An Indonesian woman says, "you may undress me,
> even if you do not pay me" (*mai chai ko kae*). Love, sincerity, and loyalty
> mean more to her than money. For the Filipina, money comes first.
> "Show me the money, or you can never undress me" (*mai chai, mai kae*).[8]

Most of the Thai women the men encountered in Singapore were sex
workers (*phuying ha ngoen*) in the Golden Mile Complex or Geyland, or
were women who traveled to Singapore on social visit passes to "sell sex"
(*khai borikan thang phet*) in the mobile, jungle brothels near the men's
dormitories. Thai women who come to work in Geylang brothels legally
as entertainers are known as "home-stationed girls" (*dek ban*). Some
women from Thailand who come to Singapore on short-visit passes are
tradeswomen (*mae kha*) who are ready to offer sexual services to the
workers. Many young Thai women also work in the beer bars and karaoke
pubs as waitresses (*dek soep* or *sao cheer beer*) with the real intention of
making money from temporary sex work.

When the men spoke of their liaisons with Thai women, there was no
excitement or admiration in their voices or eyes. Perhaps these women
seem too familiar or remind the men of their wives or girlfriends back
home. One notable exception to this lack of interest in Thai women was
Pornchai, age thirty-nine, who came to Singapore as a divorcee and had
had many Thai girlfriends in the seven years he was away from home. He
maintained:

I always love and wish to preserve Thainess (*anurak khwam pen Thai*). I think Thai women are the best for me. We come from similar cultural backgrounds. We get along with each other well. I rarely look at foreign girls.

Pornchai met his fiancé, who came to Singapore from Chiang Rai in northern Thailand. This couple is one of many examples of how men and women from Thailand's different regions have become sexual partners and have established long-term relationships. Anon noted from his twenty-two years of experience working in Singapore that

northern Thai girls tend to get along well with Isan men. I do not know why. I met many northern Thai couples [both of whom were from northern Thailand] who ended up with broken relationships. They quarreled quite often. Maybe Isan men are more cool-hearted (*chai yen*) [i.e., calm, even keel, non-confrontational]. Or maybe there are simply too many Isan workers here.

None of the men mentioned having sexual relationships with women from South Asian countries, such as Bangladesh, India, or Sri Lanka, who are regarded as *khaek* women—*khaek* being a Thai racialized and ethnocultural construction of the people of South Asian, Indo-Malay, Persian, and Middle Eastern origins. Although there are some sex workers from these countries in Geylang, they were not selected by the Thai workers because they prefer women with fairer skin color, skinnier shapes, and more familiar body odor. Totally absent from the men's accounts of their sexual partners were Caucasian women (*sao farang* or *phuying farang*). Although there are some white women, mainly from Eastern European countries, who provide sex-for-sale services in Singapore (Lim 2004), they target customers with high purchasing power, and never foreign construction workers. The Thai workers' marginalized lifestyles and work patterns, along with linguistic barriers, make it almost impossible for them to have any social encounters with Caucasian women. There were no intimate relationships among them.

Homosexuality. Homosexuality was not a preferred sexual practice by the Thai workers. However, it does not imply that homosexuality does not exist among them. Several men pointed out that they had witnessed homosexual practices among their fellow workers in their dormitories, both Thai and foreign. They clearly distinguished gay men (*ke*) from transvestites (*kathoei*, *tut*, or *taeo*). The former is a man who prefers to have sex with male partners, while the latter is a male who cross-dresses, wears makeup, and adopts female manners. There are a small number of Thai gays and transvestites working as construction workers in Singapore. Chatchai, age forty-one, claimed that he witnessed a pair of Thai gay lovers in one of the hostels for foreign workers. They hung out together, went out together, cooked and ate together, and expressed some possessive gestures (*hueng*) when a partner gets too close to another man. The "gay queen" (receptive partner) usually gave his "gay king" (sexually-active partner) some money and other gifts.[9]

Chaiwat, age twenty-eight, and Somchai, age thirty-five, were once approached at the Golden Mile Complex by a Singaporean gay man who spoke some broken Thai language. He offered them free music and movie VCDs. He also gave them his mobile phone number and offered fifty dollars as an incentive for them to meet him. They managed to get together for beer, but Chaiwat and Somchai said they were too reluctant to go out on the town with him. They were grateful for what he had offered, but swore they never considered the possibility of having a sexual relationship with a gay man.[10]

Patterns of Migrant Sexual Intimacy

Complicated and delicate webs of human agency lie behind all intimate practices. The Thai workers I spoke with emphasized much more their mutual, intimate relationships with women than purchasable sex. Their accounts point to migrant sexual intimacies that do not necessarily belong to the categories of casual or commercial sex or relationships. I do not use these terms because they do not correspond to the complex realities of sexual practice among the men I studied.

In their conversations about sex, the men revealed a number of established patterns of intimacy, including paid sexual encounters and one-night stands, as well as short- and long-term relationships. Thai workers employ complex friendship networks to get to know their sexual partners. They use a number of different channels to meet women: SMS messaging networks; telephone conversations; meeting in person via friends or acquaintances on Sundays and during social events; and meeting in workplaces or spots where migrants gather, such as construction sites (for construction workers), residential areas (for domestic workers), or places like Little India, Lucky Plaza, and Golden Mile Complex. Most initial contact begins with one introducing oneself and stating a friendly purpose. "I want to be your friend" or "I need someone to talk to" are popular expressions used by Thai workers in their first-time conversations.

Temporary sexual encounters. Thai workers engage in temporary sexual relationships through two distinct methods. One involves dating a female partner, such as an Indonesian or Filipina domestic worker, which can often lead to sex in a rented hotel room in Geylang. Many couples decide to terminate their relationship after the first few sexual encounters. The men I spoke with insisted, however, that their female domestic worker friends were not prostitutes. Sex between them was enacted by mutual consent. As one Thai worker explained, "It would definitely disappoint her if you offer her money after sex. You have to be careful." Thai men also could have temporary sexual encounters by visiting sex workers in Geylang or in the jungle brothels near their residences. Usually after payday, workers engaged in one-night stands or purchased sexual intimacy with women (e.g., bar hostesses, karaoke girls, or tradeswomen) in the Golden Mile Complex. Thawon, age twenty-nine, insisted that "younger guys pay lots of money for sex. They usually do it when they are drunk." Songwut agreed and added, "Alcohol stimulates sexual lust. When you are drunk, an ordinary-looking girl becomes a sex diva. You are ready to take her to bed at any cost. Sometimes they fight over girls." In Geylang's brothels and open-space lanes, men can choose women of various nationalities, age, and physical features. The fees range from 35 to 200 Singapore dollars per night, including the cost of the hotel room.[11]

Short-term affairs. The men agreed that it takes time to establish mutual relationships with Indonesian and Filipina domestic workers. Developing a friendship requires continued follow-ups. SMS messaging and daily chats are very important if one wants to get to know one's potential partner more closely. Songwut said:

I use many phone cards each month. I had to make phone calls to my [Filipina] girlfriend every day before our first date that led eventually to sex. SMS messaging helped me save money as it is a much cheaper way to communicate. We talked about our daily lives and what each of us had been up to. She shared with me her work situation and how her employers treated her. I also told her my story. We felt connected. Our daily chitchats always lifted our spirits. We got to know each other more and more as we began to trust each other. In the later stage of our relationship, we decided to go out with each other on Sundays. We went to Lucky Plaza, movie houses, or tourist spots. Of course, we ended up at love motels in Geylang many times.

Short-term relationships between Thai workers and foreign domestic workers usually lasted a few months. Going out together as a couple for a few months is rather realistic for foreign workers who hold only one-year work permits as non-residents of Singapore. Romance in a migrant's life is usually difficult to sustain over the long term. Weera, the most experienced lover among the participants, explained that lovers break up for a number of reasons:

They argue over things, like the girl going out with another man or vice versa or the lovers have had enough of each other sexually. Money is not a big deal because each side has separate incomes. Many women, like men, have more than one potential partner. Some girls I went out with just sent me a message to thank me, said goodbye, and wished me luck. I did not feel any heartbreak because I knew the nature of our relationship. Sometimes one of us was sent home as our employers terminated our contracts, and therefore our romance automatically ended. Sometimes, if either party fails to respond to SMS messaging or phone calls, we have no way of continuing our romance. Breaking up the relationship is quite easy. We all understand that our relationships in Singapore are just temporary and makeshift. We can't get too serious with girls here.[12]

Long-term lovers. Any relationship extending beyond a year between Thai men and Thai women or foreign women in Singapore can be regarded as a long-term commitment. Longer relationships are considered unusual for foreigners who make their living in transit. Very few couples entered into international or interracial marriages.[13] Even where they are possible, they are not necessarily desired. Thawon found it would be possible to marry an Indonesian domestic worker. His Singaporean employer promised to sponsor the marriage because he wanted to keep a model worker like Thawon in his company. However, Thawon refused:

> The girl is quite good-looking and has worked in Singapore for three or four years. I liked her a lot, but she is a Muslim. I am Buddhist. She does not speak Thai. I do not speak Indonesian. I do not think my marriage would be a happy one. We are so different.[14]

Long-term relationships are more likely to develop between Thai workers and Thai women who work as cashiers, store clerks, bar girls, sex workers, or who are divorced or estranged housewives in Singapore. The single participants explained that ultimately they would marry Thai women. As Chaiwat, age twenty-eight, said:

> I am rather serious with love and life. I think my realistic choice of a future bride is a Thai woman. Filipina, Indonesian, or Singaporean girls are not for me. They are good and pretty, but I know where I stand. We are quite different.[15]

Their long-term relationship usually follows the Thai cultural pattern at home, which develops based on deeper trust and commitment. They share the money they have earned and plan their future together. Some couples even invested their money together by buying land, a house, or some property in Thailand.

Stepping into an intimate relationship. Like most relationships, the first step to initiating an intimate relationship is to get to know each other. The men learned from each other various ways of hooking up with women. Some of the men used the term "courting" (*chip sao*) to describe their interactions with women. Meeting women depends on a combination of factors, including the location of the man's workplace, free time, appearance, courage, and luck. The men who worked in residential areas were more likely to get to know domestic workers in the same building complex, while men in supervisory positions had a better chance of moving around and had some more spare time to strike up conversations with women. For example, Anon took advantage of his position as a supervisor to attract the attention of foreign domestic workers. When he rode his bicycle between construction sites to oversee the workers under him, he would talk to domestic workers who took their employer's children to playgrounds or who ran errands for their employers at the neighborhood supermarket. He liked the person-to-person approach and gradually established friendships with women through these meetings. According to Anon, the neighborhood supermarket is one of the best spots to meet the domestic workers, who shop on a daily basis. "You can help her carry her basket or push her shopping cart while engaging her in conversation. If the girl is interested in you, she will respond to you positively. You can ask her out when she has a day off."[16]

Despite their limited English and the regulations that govern their mobility, the men had a number of common "tricks" that they used to attract the attention of women they fancied. Songwut revealed the secret of his success in approaching Indonesian and Filipina domestic workers:

> I become overtly friendly to the girl I am interested in as I try to befriend her. The most important thing is to know her name and mobile phone number. In some situations, I used to write my number on a small piece of paper and drop it her way. I also saw some fellow workers and their girls exchange phone numbers via hand-signals from a distance, for example, from different buildings or floors. The mobile number is the best way to get to know a girl.[17]

After obtaining a woman's mobile number, the next step is to keep in touch via phone calls and SMS messaging. Weera described the intensive use of mobile phones to court women as "courtship through media" (*chip sao phan sue*).[18] For many, the mobile phone is their lifeline, allowing them to talk to their families back home as well as maintain social networks with fellow workers, and of course, to talk to their lovers on a daily basis. Migrant romance and sexuality require an investment of money as well as a fun-loving attitude. In recognition of this fact, the men are willing to spend money to top up their girlfriends' phones. Songwut said:

> The girl usually asks for one phone card or two from us. We have to understand that she earns less than we do. Besides, giving her phone cards shows our willingness to be her friend and our generosity. You

cannot be stingy if you wish to win a girl over. You can give her the card's PIN number via daily chats. Or you can give it to her in person when you go out together. I think giving phone cards to the girl of your choice is a worthy investment. Normally, girls from Indonesia or the Philippines whom I went out with do not ask for anything else. They do not have sex with us for money. You have to respect them and treat them well. They are your girlfriends, not prostitutes.

Courtship thus begins once the man has the woman's mobile number. As Chaiwat explained, it was quite common for Filipina and Indonesian domestic workers to exchange their mobile numbers with male workers:

They begin with SMS messaging. If the correspondence goes well and both sides like each other, this will follow up with chats on their mobile phones. SMS is used intensively because it is cheaper than making phone calls. Everything begins from there.[19]

However, some older Thai workers explained that they did not enjoy using SMS messaging because their written English skills are limited. They prefer phone conversations in which they can hear the woman's voice and simultaneously react to her. One of them commented, "It is a totally different feeling. I feel better talking to the girl I am interested in. It is much better than composing, sending, or responding to mere messages."

The Thai workers claimed that they had to talk or correspond with women via SMS messaging several times a day. They had to maintain contact on a regular basis in order to show their genuine interest in establishing a friendly or romantic relationship. Despite the obvious language barriers, the Thai workers tried their best to attract the women's attention. Weera shared a few tips:

Besides common issues like your job and other personal particulars, the most commonly asked question is whether you are married. In my early days in Singapore, I simply lied. I was quite lonely in Singapore and I had to look for a girlfriend. I wanted somebody I could talk to and lift my spirit at the end of a day's hard work. I was much younger then so I could still do such things. Nowadays, I am getting older. When I am asked if I am married, my answer is almost always, "yes," but I am still available for a girlfriend. My wife is away in Thailand. I want to keep it straight. I find it quite effective. Many Indonesian and Filipino girls are in the same situation. Most are married, but like us, they wish to have sexual partners or foreign boyfriends. They too have their husbands and children back home. If we are mature enough, we have to be open and straight.

The third step in establishing an intimate relationship is going out together. The men usually took their girlfriends to popular migrant spots like the Golden Mile, Little India, or Lucky Plaza, or Singaporean tourist attractions such as Sentosa Island, the Orchard Road shopping malls, or movie houses. Many women prefer to go out in a group on their first date. They wish to get to know one another before entering into a deeper relationship. Networks of friends help introduce couples during initial meetings.

The next step in the courtship ritual is initiating sexual relations. The men all clearly stated that sex is the prime reason for having a foreign girlfriend. They believe that the girls also have similar desires. Many of the men mentioned learning English and getting to know foreign friends as important as well, but sex is the most exciting and rewarding part of a relationship for them. Generally, couples do not have sex on their first date. Chaiwat, for example, exchanged messages and chatted with his Indonesian girlfriend (*sao Indo*) for weeks before meeting her in person. They finally met at Eunos MRT station and later ended up in a Geylang hotel room. Although they talked on the phone many times afterwards, they have never managed to get together again. The rules also vary from girlfriend to girlfriend. Weera revealed that

no sex on the first date is the rule for Filipina partners. It usually applies to the Indonesian girls, too. Guys have to be patient, especially when your date is an inexperienced young girl. I had sex with two virgins from the Philippines. In each case, it took me over a year. You have to build up trust. The Filipina girls are rather romantic and serious about love. However, each relationship is different. Each girl I date has her own personality. I have had sex with many girls after just a few outings together. Some look forward to long-term engagements, others just want to have fun.

As Chaiwat's experience suggests, the chance to have sex is also subject to a confluence of circumstances. Indeed, as Bunmee pointed out, "sex is possible if the couple finds themselves the right opportunity (*okat*), place (*sathanthi*), and time (*wela*)." The men use a variety of places as temporary "love nests, including the homes of their girlfriends' employers.[20] Songwut took his Filipina lover to a dark corner of the neighborhood park on one of their nighttime dates. However, most participants admitted that Geylang's numerous and cheap hotels, where rooms can be rented by the hour for 10–15 Singapore dollars, were their popular destinations. Some hotels offered a special rate of 20 dollars for three hours. For those able to stay overnight, the cost ranges from 30 to 45 or 48 dollars per room, depending on the room's condition and facilities, according to Weera.[21] Chatchai confirmed that "if you have money, you can stay in a luxury, air-con room with proper towels, soap, shampoo, and purified drinking water. Beware of bedbugs, lice, or mosquitoes, if you prefer a cheap one."

Experienced lovers like Anon, Thawon, Songwut, and Weera agreed that men should know when, where, and how to act when they take their girlfriends to a Geylang hotel. In particular, they should show some signs of unfamiliarity with the place. Instead of taking the lead, they should allow the girl to reveal what she knows. For instance, Songwut said:

> You should show some signs that you too are a rather innocent guy. I sometimes pretend I do not know how to use an electronic card key to open the door and ask my girlfriend to help. However, every guy should always have condoms handy. This will save both sides. Sex without using a condom is harmful in all accounts. Your girlfriend could be pregnant. Both of you might contact some disease. Using condoms also shows that you are willing to save her and honor the relationship with her.

All the participants, except Bunmee, used condoms when they had sexual intercourse with their girlfriends. Bunmee said it was uncomfortable to use condom, but if his girlfriend insisted on it, he had no choice but to acquiesce. The men felt that it was important that the man impress his lover during their first sexual encounter. Weera claimed that men should be prepared to satisfy their sexual partners:

In bed, young, single, and married women are quite different. I prefer experienced, mature women as they know how to satisfy their lover. They are very good. A virgin girl is not tasty (*bo saep*), despite the fact that she is in better shape. Men have to be aware that women tend to be ready for multiple orgasms. They can be ready for the next round, while most men tend to finish after the first shot. A good lover should be careful enough to satisfy and care for his partner. You cannot just act like "bam, bam, thank you, ma'am," and then proceed to take a bath and dress up to get ready to leave after intercourse. Your girlfriend wants to be held or caressed. She loves to have your attention and wants to stay in bed with you for a while.

The fifth step in cultivating intimate relationships is to maintain the relationship after the first sexual encounter. It is important that the man impresses his lover during their first encounter, so that sex leads to more sex. Having affairs with girlfriends requires different approaches compared to buying sex from sex workers. A good lover has to be careful and know how to handle the relationship smoothly, as Weera revealed:

Most Indonesian and Filipina girls I slept with cried after our first sexual encounter. Some said, "I should not have slept with you. Our relationship went too far. We are more than friends now. Before, I was not an easy girl who always had sex with men I went out with." From my side, I would give her my best, sweet hug and say, "Calm down. Don't cry. Don't be sad. I am a gentleman and responsible for what I did. You can trust me." I know it is girls' touching side. I have to show her my side, too. I assure her that I am a gentleman as well as a good lover.

The final step is ending the relationship, which involves either a mutual or non-consensual breakup or separation. Lovers usually part ways, given their non-resident, transient status in Singapore. Very few cases end up in marriage or some form of co-habitation after one's employment contract ends. The men accepted that their relationships with foreign girlfriends gradually came to an end after spending time together over a period of a few months. In fact, the men were keen to keep their relationships with foreign lovers short-lived. For them, the migrant romance is for fun (*sanuk*), is an exotic, new experience (*prasopkan mai*), and is temporary (*chua khrao*).

The Thai workers agreed that male sexual patterns and processes have their own characteristics, which are heavily embedded in and conditioned by their lives as migrant workers. Their sexual experiences, as they understand them, take place under the unusual context of their transient life. Migrant workers have assumed patterns and processes of migrant sexuality with their own distinctive flavors. Migrant romance and sexuality require an investment of money as well as a fun-loving attitude. Jetsada insisted that he had never been interested in going out with foreign women. He is married and faithful to his wife. He had a few chances to be with girls but chose not to. His fellow workers always accused him of not being man enough:

> There was an Indonesian girl working in an apartment near my worksite. She expressed interest in me and sent me some signals, for example giving me her mobile phone number via a friend. One day, she came to see me at a building corner. I cannot speak English well, but she really wanted to go out with me. She even held me tight and kissed me on the mouth. I simply couldn't respond to her. She left disappointed. I had to run away and throw up. My mind is always with my wife and family. I can't betray them.

Conclusion

Cross-border sex involving migrant workers is a rather complicated human experience. Migrant workers, both men and women, buy and sell sex. However, it is not always one-time, commercial, or casual sex, as widely suggested in the literature. I argue that cross-border sex must be understood as migrant sexual encounters that are complexly perceived and practiced by men and women as gendered beings. It has distinctive features, patterns, and processes that are embedded in and conditioned by transient employment and migrant livelihood situations.

Migrant sexuality has its particular characteristics and patterns, which are different from other forms of transient sexual intimacy, such as tourist and high-class sex-for-sale businesses. The stories that the Thai workers in Singapore shared show that within the context of transnational labor migration, male and female workers do not view sex as a reproductive mechanism. It is completely removed from the domestic domains of family and home. Migrant sexuality involves sexual relationships and initiatives mainly between men and women as foreign migrant workers, whose lives "selling their labor" have brought them to an intersecting transient destination within a highly regulated labor marketplace such as Singapore. Men and women meet in the transient labor market and develop social and emotional bonds that reflect a relationship between two marginalized souls in the broader socioeconomic spectrum of a global city like Singapore.

The Thai workers agreed that migrant sex constitutes an important aspect of the private life of border-crossing workers. It is primarily considered a pleasure-oriented activity, with certain degrees of freedom from moral, religious, or familial restraints. Their responsibility as married men is to work hard to earn and send money back home while keeping in touch with their families via regular phone calls. They believe that as mature men in transient situations, they are entitled to go out and have fun. Migrant sex is among the many activities open to them during their free time, especially at night and on Sundays when they are free from job assignments and allowed to get together in some migrant public spaces. Other migrant activities for Thai workers in Singapore include games and gambling, playing music and sports, reading, and taking educational courses, such as computer training, English as a foreign language or for obtaining high school certificates through non-formal education or college degrees from Sukhothai Thammathirat Open University. Going out with foreign domestic workers and seeking sex are only part of their private life away from home.

Migrant men as well as women are potentially active sex-seekers. Migrant sexuality is a highly mutual and reciprocal enterprise. The Thai workers' narratives show that men as well as women are willing to establish relationships and pursue sexual pleasure with partners of their choice. They are aware of immigration, legal, and economic regulations and sanctions imposed by Singapore's authorities and employers. However, they have learned to adjust and live within the limited freedom, rights, and resources they are allowed to possess. The intensive use of mobile phones, their creativity in using the English language, their communicative skills, and the permission to have a day off on Sundays are among the valuable resources and rights which foreign workers have enjoyed in the Singaporean context.

The narratives about male migrant sexuality express the Thai workers' constructed selfhoods vis-à-vis the foreignness that immediately surrounds them and Singapore's state-controlled multiculturalism. The stories of their private life are told with a migrant, masculine sensibility. They were shared among themselves (and now, directly to audiences reading this book) and express their unique sense of what it means to be contract workers who live and lead transient, laborious lives away from home over extended periods of time. Unlike death and tragedy in labor migration contexts (see chapter 6), migrant sex stories are often told and shared in common, joyful moods. When Thai workers talk and discuss their sexual desires and experiences, the sense of socioeconomic inferiority is consciously removed from the masculine selfhood. They often position themselves as successful tricksters, lovers, or womanizers, who "somehow anticipate the coming freedom" (Foucault 1980, 6). Stories are fun to tell, especially parts involving their fellow workers' or somebody else's affairs. Embarrassment and shame are turned into jokes that generate laughter. Success and failure are converted into lessons and wisdom. Of course, joyful emotion is shared with pride. In other words, migrant sexuality constitutes channels to express masculine sensitivity, which is strangely meaningful in the laborious and backbreaking everyday life of Thai workers in Singapore.

Most importantly, migrant sexuality is usually situated within heavily gendered narratives. The Thai workers seemed to caution that their accounts should be understood from a male, working-class, mature person's perspective. Accounts of the workers' sexual encounters in a foreign country must be read against their own contextual backdrops and the gender identities of the storytellers. Their narrative accounts display their private life realities as much as their sexual fantasies, biases, frustration, and imagination. Their agency as storyteller-actors from rural Thai working-class backgrounds is heavily present throughout. However, these narratives must be countered by their status as highly marginalized, low-wage earners in the eyes of Singapore society. They constitute only a portion of the armies of male foreign workers from countries like Bangladesh, China, India, Myanmar, and so on. Their active engagement with Indonesian or Filipina domestic workers also pales in comparison to similar initiatives adopted by other foreign men in Singapore. Workers from other countries too have actively developed relationships with foreign women in transit in Singapore.

The patterns and processes of migrant sexual intimacy show some distinctive transient sexual practices, which are rather different from casual or commercial sex encounters between Western or Asian men from economically developed countries and local Southeast Asian female sex workers, or between local men and local sex workers. The men in this study offer some insights regarding the highly transient contexts in which both migrant men and women are potential and active sex-seekers. Sex within the context of transnational labor migration is not necessarily characterized by buying or selling patterns. It represents a complex form of social relationship among men and women in their migrant transient life. In the case of Thai workers in Singapore, their sexual practices primarily involve women in transit from multinational and multi-ethnocultural backgrounds. In the context of Singapore, Thai migrant workers from different national origins are likely to be drawn closer to each other rather than to the local citizens. Due to the strict enforcement of immigration laws as well as certain socioeconomic and ethnocultural differences and certain negative attitudes of the local population toward foreign workers, Singapore is a place of impossibility for migrant workers to develop relationships with local women.

The narratives of these men's private lives depict transient foreign workers engaging in sexual relationships with transient foreign women. As low-skilled foreign workers, they meet, get to know each other, and get together through their migrant social networks in a labor marketplace like Singapore. Sex forms part of their leisure social life in their overseas labor migration. It is a temporary relationship in which both male and female actors are deeply cognizant of its uncertain, short-lived destiny.

Chapter 6

Death, Tragedy, and Ghosts

In this chapter, I place the deaths and other tragic tales of transnational migrant workers at center stage. I view the tragedies suffered by migrant workers as one of the most powerful "signs and sites" (Tadiar 1997, 153) for de-mystifying and disclosing the other side of the dominant discourse, a discourse where transnational labor migration is seen primarily as a source of economic and social remittance (see Stahl and Arnold 1986; Stark and Lucas 1988; Levitt 1998b).

Despite widespread knowledge that "migrants are particularly vulnerable to exploitation" (Allen 2003, 1) and that "overseas contract workers often relate lives of loneliness, deprivation, and abuse" (Rafael 2000, 210),[1] studies on Southeast Asian transnational labor migration seem to have neglected the mortality rates of onsite working-age adult subjects, whether they are legal or illegal migrant workers. A number of studies focusing on migrant workers' rights, abuses, and social exclusion began to appear in the early 2000s (see Sen and Koray 2000; Sellek 2001; Yamanaka 2004). Other than a handful of reports and studies (Mills 1995; Tadiar 1997; Human Rights Watch 2000; Rafael 2000), the deaths and other tragedies of migrant workers in the Southeast Asian context seem to be, by and large, uncharted in studies of transnational labor migration in the region, which have focused mainly on the productive bodies of migrant workers and on transnational labor migration as primarily an economic enterprise, with some cultural and political consequences for both the sending and receiving countries (Supang, Germershausen, and Beesey 2000; Supang et al. 2001a; Ananta and Arifin 2004; Parnwell 2005).[2]

Thai migrant workers have endured death and other tragedies throughout their three-decade-long history of inter-ASEAN transnational migration. An unusually large number of Thai workers in Singapore have experienced tragic deaths, with causes ranging from sudden unexplained nocturnal death syndrome (SUNDS) and worksite accidents to murder and suicide. The stories behind these deaths and tragedies expose the strenuous lives of underclass foreign laborers in Singapore. On a more general scale, they represent reflexive accounts of the human costs of transnational labor migration, and they should shape our understanding of the processes involved in it. For semiskilled and unskilled foreign migrant workers who earn their wages through "working lives in transit," transnational labor migration can be a risky route that leads to a gold mine or to the graveyard. Not all journeys undertaken by overseas migrant workers end up as triumphant individual ventures where the self is transformed in a "rite of a successful homecoming" (Aguilar 1999, 103).

Death and tragedies involving migrant workers must be given a significant place in studies on transnational labor migration. Migrant workers' deaths, especially the "tragic, unnecessary, and entirely preventable [ones]" (Ng 2004b), are symbolic and material reminders of the cruelties of transnational labor exploitation; they unveil the dark and disturbing side of "transnationalism from below" (Smith and Guarnizo 1998). Death within the context of transnational labor migration critically exposes the untold and underrepresented life stories of ill-fated migrant workers and other sojourners who, suddenly displaced from their home villages, find themselves "subjected to discrimination and social exclusion in their places of destination" (Allen 2003, 6). In this light, I believe that the bodies of dead migrant workers tell tales that demand anthropological analysis.

Death and Other Tragedies in Singapore's Labor Market

Each life lost may deprive one family of a husband and a breadwinner, a son, a brother, a friend. (Ng 2004a)

Singapore is a nation that was built by migrant workers from multiple origins, and generations of them have remained the island nation's most important asset.[3] Since the late 1970s, Singapore has become one of the hubs for migrant workers from Southeast Asia (Low 1995; Rahman 2003; Yeoh and Willis 2005). For those from Thailand, Singapore is the most stable and steadily growing labor market in the region (Supang and Germershausen 2000, 2). Recently, Ng Eng Hen, acting minister for manpower and minister of state for education, claimed that "we have about 80,000 professionals for a workforce of two million, and they make up about 9 percent of the total professionals, managers, and executives in our workforce. The Ministry of Trade and Industry estimates that they contributed 37 percent of GDP."[4] Notably absent from this comment is an acknowledgement of the contributions by unskilled and semiskilled workers. These contributions cannot be underestimated. *The Sunday Times* (Li 2004) reported that "there are over 500,000 work-permit holders [in Singapore], 135,000 of whom are construction workers . . . Foreign workers make up about 12 percent of Singapore's population of four million." In 2000, there were approximately 612,200 foreign workers out of the country's 2,094,800 total labor force, compared to only 20,828 out of its 659,892 total labor force in 1970.[5]

Recognizing that Singapore's fast-growing economy needs to be sustained by input from foreign workers, the government has carefully managed imported labor as "an economic asset" based on market demand and supply (Wong 2000). Singapore's labor management policy is open to migrant workers with professional skills, but rather strict with unskilled and semiskilled workers in the construction, shipbuilding, ship-repair, and other menial labor-intensive industries. Huang and Yeoh (2003, 80) have pointed out that Singapore's policy "has remained firmly committed to ensuring that unskilled and low-skilled foreign workers are managed as a temporary and controlled phenomenon through a series of measures, key among which are the work permit system, the dependency ceiling (which regulates the proportion of foreign to local workers), and the foreign worker levy."[6]

These measures have allowed Singapore to exploit the surplus of labor found in global migratory flows to sustain its economic growth, even as the working-age local population enjoys a healthy rate of employment and a high quality of life. These measures are also instrumental in ensuring that migrant workers end up in low-skilled, low-wage jobs that are inherently risky and dangerous.

Accidents at work and other work-related injuries. Singapore, through the Ministry of Manpower (MOM), has taken seriously the promotion of safety at worksites.[7] Nonetheless, the dangers faced by workers in 3D jobs are underlined by the statistics. There was an average of 167 fatal and 14,999 non-fatal accidents in Singapore per year from 2000 to 2004 (see table 1).

Table 1. Work-related accidents in Singapore, 2000–2004

Year	Fatal	Non-Fatal	Total
2000	204	15,623	15,827
2001	199	14,893	15,092
2002	141	15,194	15,335
2003	135	14,169	14,304
2004	156	15,118	15,274
Total:	835	74,997	75,832
Average:	167	14,999.4	15,166.4

Source: Ministry of Manpower.

A number of these work-related accidents took place in Singapore's major industries, such as marine, construction, shipbuilding and repair, as well as on various factory sites. Table 2 shows the total number of industrial accidents from 1998 to 2003. This official record shows an average of 3,679 industrial accidents and 67.5 deaths per year in these industries. Although the Ministry of Manpower's official statistics do not give details concerning the age, gender, or nationalities of the workers involved, the numbers nevertheless show how prone workers are to accidents.

Information on the places where these work-related accidents occur and the persons involved can be traced in media reports. In 2004, there were three major tragic accidents: the collapse of Nicoll Highway on April 20, killing four workers; the collapse of the steel latticework at the Fusionpolis construction site that killed two and injured twenty-nine workers on April 29; and a flash fire on board a crude oil tanker at a Keppel shipyard that claimed the lives of seven workers (five Indians and two Malaysians) on May 28. From January to June 2004, a total of forty-six workers lost their lives in factories and construction sites (see Ng 2004b). In early 2005 alone, *The Straits Times* reported on January 26, "Explosion at Linde Gas factory in Tuas Basin Link. A twenty-two-year-old technician, a China national, suffered serious head injuries and later died;" on February 12, "Three Thai workers died while spray painting walls under a road bridge at Choa Kang Way;" and on February 23, "Explosion at warehouse of Hong Huat Hung, a chemical company, in Tuas. Two died and two others were injured." All of these fatal accidents involved foreign workers.

Table 2. Total number of industrial accidents in Singapore's major industries (shipbuilding and repair, construction, and factories), 1998–2003

Year	No. of Accidents	Fatal Cases/Persons
1998	4,247	91
1999	3,953	69
2000	3,517	74
2001	3,790	52
2002	3,388	64
2003	3,179	55
Total:	22,074	405
Average:	3,679	67.5

Source: Ministry of Manpower (Electric New Paper 2005).

In fairness, Singapore has a world-class workplace safety profile. As measured by the number of fatal accidents, "Singapore's safety record [based on a report by the International Labor Organization] is comparable to that of the USA, France, and Canada but lags behind the UK and Sweden" (Ng 2004a). Singapore's safety record has improved through the years. "The overall numbers have been coming down over the years from 4,222 cases [of accidents] in 1997 to 3,179 cases in 2003 . . . [and] the number of fatal accidents has fallen by more than half from 1993 to 2003. There were 72 deaths in 1997 and 31 in 2003, or 0.3 fatal accidents per 1,000 employees in 1997 compared to 0.2 in 2003" (Ng 2004a). The Ministry of Manpower also reports that the occupational health situation continues to improve and that the "medical and industrial hygiene surveillance activities indicate that noise and chemical exposure levels in workplaces remain satisfactory" (Ministry of Manpower 2005).

Deaths of Thai Workers in Singapore

Rain or shine, Thais never took shelter. They work all the time. On the
dark side, they drank a lot. When they drank anything could happen.
I witnessed drunken Thais killing one another in brawls. They often fought
over women. (Lee Kwan Ho, cited in Wuth Nontarit 1996)[8]

Among the fifty thousand members of the Thai community in
Singapore, death is a regular occurrence. Yet it has mostly gone unnoticed
by the public.[9] In media reports, deaths of Thai workers appear to be
sporadic, unfortunate, and unexpected events, but most workers I
interviewed accepted the possibility of death or injury to be a fact of
their daily life. Death and injuries are everyday topics that they discuss
with their friends, overhear, and read about, watch, witness, and maybe
even experience themselves on their worksites.[10] At least one Thai died
every week in the eight year period between 1997 and 2004. Table 3 shows
that in those eight years, 435 Thai nationals died in Singapore, an average
of 54.3 per year.

Table 3. Certificates of Death Issued by the Royal Thai Embassy in
Singapore, 1997–2004

Year	Male	Female	Total
1997	103	4	107
1998	74	5	79
1999	47	5	52
2000	45	8	53
2001	38	3	41
2002	35	10	45
2003	22	14	36
2004	19	3	22
Total:	383	52	435
Average:	47.8	6.5	54.3

Source: The Royal Thai Embassy, Singapore (2005a).

Most of the Thai migrant workers who died in Singapore were male.
This implies a key population characteristic of Thai migrant workers in

Singapore. There are only a small number of Thai women working as domestic workers or engaged in small businesses in Singapore. Some are married to Singaporean men and have settled in Singapore. As can be seen in table 4, the top five causes of death among Thai nationals were heart failure, accident, illness, suicide, and murder. These five causes of death account for more than 98 percent of the total number of deaths during the period 1997–2004.

Table 4. Causes of Death among Thai Subjects in Singapore, 1997–2004

	Heart Failure	Accident	Illness	Suicide	Murder	Death Penalty	Other	Total
1997	70	12	12	3	6	3	1	107
1998	50	13	3	7	6	0	0	79
1999	27	9	9	3	4	0	0	52
2000	16	12	12	6	7	0	0	53
2001	19	6	7	8	1	0	0	41
2002	18	11	12	3	0	1	0	45
2003	10	6	10	4	3	3	0	36
2004	11	4	4	3	0	0	0	22
Total:	221	73	69	37	27	7	1	435
Average:	27.6	9.1	8.6	4.6	3.3	0.8	0.1	54.3

Source: The Royal Thai Embassy in Singapore (2005a).

The deaths of Thai migrant workers can be seen as the consequence of border-transgressing acts (Thailand–Malaysia–Singapore borders), poor self-adjustment in displaced situations, or engagement in high-risk jobs and other dangerous activities in Singapore. While it is still unclear whether deaths by heart failure and sudden unexplained nocturnal death syndrome (SUNDS) stem from working conditions or genetic and sleep abnormalities, other causes (accidents, illnesses, suicide, and murder) show that the lives of Thai workers in Singapore are very stressful, highly risky, and unusually vulnerable.

Also, the lives of Thai workers seem to be surrounded by a crime-infested subculture. This is reflected in the number of Thais in Singapore who seek refuge in the Thai embassy because they have lost their passports or are without proper travel papers. They are categorized as "persons abroad in need of urgent help" (*bukkhon tok thuk dai yak nai tai daen*). The absence of such papers usually means that those involved are in trouble, either from involvement in crime (e.g., prostitution, drugs) or from working in Singapore illegally. Table 5 shows that 5,936 Thai nationals, or an average of more than 989 persons per year between 1999 and 2004, were classified as displaced and required certificates of identity.

Table 5. Certificates of Identity Issued by the Royal Thai Embassy, 1999–2004

Year	No. of Issued Certificates of Identity
1999	1,627
2000	1,936
2001	973
2002	628
2003	469
2004	303
Total:	5,936
Average:	989.33

Source: The Royal Thai Embassy in Singapore (2005b).

Furthermore, in 1996, *The Straits Times* reported that Thai gangsters slipped into Singapore to work illegally, gamble, extort money, and commit other crimes, often against other Thais. They were known as heavy drinkers. They also fought over Hat Yai prostitutes who snuck into Singapore fortnightly. Some Thai workers on construction sites reportedly take "amphetamines or some other drugs when they feel exhausted or when they feel despair" (cited in Supara 2002). The consequences of this crime-infested subculture are disturbingly evident in the number of Thais that have been executed in Singapore. In June 2002, the Thai embassy reported that "twenty-one Thais have been executed (by hanging) and two others are waiting execution" (ibid.).

Mysterious death stories. Of all the causes of death suffered by Thai workers in Singapore, sudden unexplained nocturnal death syndrome (SUNDS) is perhaps the most controversial one. At the peak of its incidence in the early 1990s, SUNDS caused some political strain between Thailand and Singapore. Thai politicians and officials commented that the Singapore government and Singaporean employers failed to provide proper accommodations and overworked Thai workers to death. SUNDS epitomizes the politically sensitive history of Thailand's labor migration to Singapore; it also reflects a sense of the traumatic suffering of the Thai population in Singapore.

SUNDS, known as *rok lai tai* by the Thais, *bangungot* by the Tagalog-speaking people of the Philippines, or *tsob tsuang* by the Hmong of Vietnam (Tan 2002), refers to a nightmarish death, usually of a healthy young male without any history of illness who dies suddenly in his sleep. The causes for this sudden death have largely remained mysterious to the medical community. When SUNDS claimed hundreds of lives of Thai construction workers in Singapore in the early 1990s, teams of medical researchers offered different findings. A researcher from Mahidol University in Bangkok stated that "a genetic disorder . . . or an abnormality of the X chromosome, stress, excessive work, and the use of drugs" caused SUNDS (*Bangkok Post* 1993 and June 11, 1994), while a study by Chao Tze Cheng, a SUNDS specialist from Singapore's Institute of Science and Forensic Medicine, suggested that "the death has nothing to do with the health and living conditions of Thai workers because most of those who die are young healthy men. The only thing they need is psychological support. They should also be warned not to overwork and to eat clean food" (*Bangkok Post*, September 17, 1994). Other findings proposed a link between SUNDS and a significantly low level of potassium and vitamin B1 in the workers' blood as the possible cause of this tragic death (*Straits Times* 1990). The *Straits Times* (1997) listed possible causes of SUNDS, based on findings from the study by Chao Tze Cheng, as follows: ventricular fibrillation—a change in the heartbeat and blood pressure; a potassium and vitamin B1 deficiency; sleep abnormalities; psycho-social stress; and genetic factors.

SUNDS has been one of the major causes of death among healthy, working-age Thai construction and factory workers in Singapore since the late 1980s. It is reported that SUNDS killed 407 Thai workers between May 1982 and July 1994. The annual incidence rate varied from eleven cases in 1982 to fifty-nine cases in 1993, with an average of about twenty-eight cases per year. There were forty-two reported cases of SUNDS between January and July 1994 (*Bangkok Post*, September 26, 1994). Most of the workers died within two to four months of arriving on the island (*Bangkok Post*, June 11, 1994).[11] Reports by Thailand's Ministry of Public Health in the late 1980s and early 1990s indicated that around "600 Thai workers had died in similar circumstances in the Middle East. Similar deaths have also been reported among Indochinese refugees in the United States, Japan, and the Philippines" (Erlanger 1990).

In 1990, Singapore repatriated 9,300 illegal Thai workers just after a spate of SUNDS-suspected death among Thai workers. Vattana Assavahem, Thailand's then deputy minister of interior, remarked that "I could not stand seeing 30,000 workers being used as slaves" (*Bangkok Post* 1990). His controversial comment on Thai workers' accommodations in Singapore in which he stated "my pet dogs live better" was quoted by *The New York Times* (Erlanger 1990). Other outspoken Thai politicians echoed Vattana's view. After visiting Singapore in 1990, Krasae Chanawongse, a Thai politician and former medical doctor as well as a winner of the prestigious Ramon Magsaysay Award, wrote a short article in a Thai-language newspaper in which he stated that Thai workers had been treated as though "they are not our fellow human beings." After returning to Thailand from a visit to Singapore in 1994, Sawai Phrammanee, then permanent secretary of the Ministry for Labor and Social Welfare, said, "prisoners in Thailand have better living conditions than Thai workers in Singapore" (*Bangkok Post*, September 17, 1994).

SUNDS has not dominated media headlines since the late 1990s. However, this does not mean that the mysterious syndrome has completely vanished. The lives of Thai workers are still at risk of SUNDS. Later statistics compiled by the Thai embassy in Singapore indicated that between 1997 and 2004, a record of 221 Thai workers—an average of 27.6 persons per year—died due to "heart failure" (see table 3). This number is unusually high as it is unlikely that such a large number of healthy workers suffer actual heart problems on a regular basis. It may indicate that the

SUNDS death rate is very persistent and comparable to the average of twenty-eight cases per year in the early 1990s (*Bangkok Post*, September 26, 1994). With less media coverage to provoke the government's attention, SUNDS seems to be out of the limelight. In reality, it has continued to pose a threat to the lives of working-age men from Thailand employed in Singapore's construction and marine industries.

Men Who Live Dangerously in Singapore

I am poor. I have lots of debt back home. My wife and children do not have much to eat. Therefore, I decided to come to Singapore. I wish to earn more income here, although I have to work very hard. I am a man and the leader of the family. I alone should bear the hardships. (Ruangdet, age thirty-five, construction worker from Khon Kaen, northeastern Thailand)[12]

Thai migrant workers on construction sites and in factories and farms throughout the city are men who make their living on 3D jobs and live their lives dangerously. These men's lives and work have some particular characteristics that directly and indirectly contribute to injuries or the eventual loss of their lives.

Thai migrant workers' lives are basically grounded in the nature of their menial 3D jobs. Although they generally work in construction, there are specific categories and assignments that require special skills and experience, such as cement and form work, structure and platform building, electricity, carpentry, underground and open drainage system work, pipe work and maintenance, painting, road work and other civil works projects, and various kinds of factory work. Many workers assured me that Thai workers are generally "jacks of all trades," who are gifted with multiple skills and good at on-the-job training. They have also gained a reputation for working diligently, especially outdoors. These characteristics may be derived from their agricultural background and the fact that many of them are veteran workers who have spent years in industrialized areas of Thailand and overseas countries.

Most of the workers I interviewed had their own definitions and descriptions of what 3D jobs meant to them, but a widely accepted ranking of the top-three 3D jobs was: (1) pipeline construction and maintenance, (2) underground and open drainage systems, and (3) underground railway systems. Some workers mentioned the danger of working with chemical and toxic substances. These were the most unwanted and physically demanding jobs, which they wished they could avoid. Besides very strict supervision from the foremen, engineers and contractors, these jobs completely exhausted them. It exposed them to waste (including human waste), mud and dust, and noise. Sometimes they were required to work below ground where oxygen was not sufficient. All of this had undesirable effects on their health and safety.[13]

Working long hours is the next hazardous condition contributing to the deterioration of workers' health. Although this varies from company to company, most Thai workers I interviewed work from 8 a.m. to 7 p.m., six days a week. This means they worked between sixty and seventy hours a week (excluding overtime), far beyond the forty-four hour standard legal work week set in Singapore's Employment Act (cited in US State Department 2005, 34) and the average of fifty hours per week in the construction industry (Ofori n.d., 17, table 10). These workers have one day off on Sundays, but some companies require them to work a half-day on Sundays. Given their short contracts (one to two years) and low wages (23 Singapore dollars per day), most workers are rather grateful and willing to work overtime. Sometimes their work ends as late as 10 p.m. or midnight. Many workers told me that they needed overtime work in order to pay off their debts and support families back home. Usually they are more than happy to work on public holidays, as long as the company owners or contractors (thao kae) pay double time (*dai kha chang song raeng*).

Most of the workers' accommodations are crowded and some have serious hygiene problems.[14] Thai workers usually live in container-like, makeshift housing on construction sites or dormitories. The lucky ones share apartment rooms in HDB flats provided by their employers. In any case, their accommodations are below standard. There can be up to five to ten persons sharing a room, a kitchen, and a bathroom. One middle-class Thai woman working for a Bangkok-based Christian church in Singapore provided this account of workers' onsite accommodations: "I visited one construction site, where forty persons lived in a small room not more than twenty square meters, with one toilet. They cooked, ate, slept, and got dressed there" (cited in Supara 2002). Two dormitories for foreign workers I visited in the Jurong East and Amakeng areas in early 2005 confirm this observation. Workers spent their time away from the construction sites amidst dirty work-clothes, kitchens, and bathrooms.[15]

Thai workers are exposed to dangers even in their leisure time during off-work activities (Pattana 2005a). Away from their routine menial jobs, Thai migrant workers enjoy an excessively masculine lifestyle, especially on Sundays at the Golden Mile Complex on Beach Road and at restaurants and bars in the nearby Geylang area, Singapore's red-light district.

Haunted by the Ghosts of Overseas Migrant Workers

Statistics cannot match the tragedies. (Bose 2003)

Death, as illustrated in the case of Thai migrant workers in Singapore, epitomizes the tragic end of a journey into the international labor market. For the relatives and loved ones left behind, it is a painful and shocking form of homecoming. For government officials, it is an especially awkward and difficult time as they deal with the dead migrant's relatives or the dead migrant's remains, if they are unclaimed.

Due to high costs, almost all of the dead bodies of Thai overseas workers are cremated abroad and their ashes are "remitted" home. In Thailand, the return of these "officially processed and channeled" ashes or bodies of dead migrant workers from countries like Brunei, Israel, Japan, Taiwan, and Singapore usually corresponds with the appearance of "ghosts." In late October 2004, for example, Thai Rath, one of the most widely circulated Thai dailies, reported that the ghosts of nameless overseas migrant workers haunted the officials at the Ministry of Foreign Affairs (MFA) in Bangkok. The ashes of both identified and unidentified dead workers abroad were mailed home to the Office of the Protection of Thai Nationality. When the boxes of ashes had been accumulated, the officials experienced some eerily mysterious events, such as the smell of burning incense and decaying corpses, the appearance of moving shadows, and the sounds of walking or running steps. At other times, officials reported seeing "ghosts" dressed like fishermen, in old clothes and wearing a pair of slippers.

While these reports sound much like typical Thai ghost stories, they contain grains of sociocultural and political significance. One way of understanding the "haunting" effect of these "ghosts" is to situate not just the workers' lives but also their deaths and how they are treated after they die in the economically and socially marginalized situations they endure. The fact that these ill-fated migrant workers died suddenly away from home and in most cases without proper funerals or ritual procedures underlines their having "no rights in life, no dignity in death" (*Straits Times* 2005). This becomes especially poignant when framed within the Thai cultural cosmology where bad and violent deaths (*tai hong*), such as those suffered by Thai migrant workers, give birth to dangerous and resentful ghosts (*phi tai hong*) that are determined to exact revenge from those who owe them.

Within the political arena, the "ghosts" of Thai migrant workers symbolically lodge their complaints against the Thai state's problematic handling of transnational labor affairs by "haunting" (through their appearance before certain officials) and "threatening" (through the smell of rotten corpses and incense burning) immigration officials at their workplace. The ghosts of Thai migrant workers appear to direct their resentfulness to the government officials who were supposed to protect them when they were alive. In their death, the ghosts of transnational labor migrants "speak to" Thai state authorities about the hardships and difficulties they suffered as overseas migrant workers, and they symbolically protest the officials' indifference and shortcomings in saving their lives. These "ghost" stories then could be thought of as dramatic tales in which the dead migrant workers "speak" for those who are alive.

Disturbing Tragedies

"Migrants make contributions to community development" (Levitt and Neberg-Sorensen 2004, 8), but at what cost and at whose expense? Thai migrant workers in Singapore remitted more than 220 million Singapore dollars back to Thailand between 2001 and 2003; most of these remittances (203 million) were generated by construction workers (Office of Labor Affairs 2004). However, a large number of them risked their lives to support their families and their country's economic development.

In contrast to popular perceptions, death and injuries among Thai migrant workers in Singapore are regular occurrences. They are inevitable consequences of these workers' everyday life away from home and represent the cruelest punishment workers have to pay for their highly risky journeys. The "haunting effects" of the ghosts of dead workers manifest in a number of ways. For instance, deaths and tragic injuries in both numerical and narrative forms command powerfully disturbing images. These images invoke deeply sensitive sentiments and grievances from relevant parties, whether they are the dead's family members, relatives, and friends, or government officials and politicians. Personal grief can easily be turned into national mourning and political outcries. These images can also provoke a strong sense of nationalism that can go beyond the boundaries of reason and lead to an international "war of words." The deaths and injuries among workers can potentially initiate the destructive side of "transnationalism from below." Such images draw the "boundaries of participation" (Harper 1997, 261) for the constructed and imagined communities of transnational migrants and those who are left behind.

Deaths and tragic injuries also disrupt the seemingly well-established orders of transnational flows of capital, manpower, technology, and information because they materially and symbolically represent the cruelest and most brutal forms of exploitation. They counterbalance the popular perception that international labor migration can lead to a pot of gold. Also, they certainly, as Hollifield (2000, 138) argues, "provoke a sense of crisis," particularly in the sending country. Many times, the deaths of migrant workers have created international tensions, similar to what happened between Thailand and Singapore in the early 1990s. Deaths and other tragedies can also engender sensitive debates at home, especially among politicians. In March 1996, for example, when five Thai workers were executed by Singapore authorities for killing a Myanmar national and two Indians in a series of gang raids at construction sites in 1992 and 1993 (Lee 1996), a Thai politician commented that "the government is to blame for its ignorance towards Thai workers in Singapore" (*Bangkok Post*, March 15, 1996).

Further, the deaths and other tragedies suffered by migrant workers provoke "transnational shame" (Aguilar 1999) among the living, especially among fellow citizens. Rafael (2000), in referring to the death of Flor Contemplacion, a Filipino domestic worker who was hanged by Singapore authorities in 1995, writes:

Confronted by disfigured corpses, the living find themselves in the midst of deaths out of place. The dead appear to be not quite dead and so threaten to blur the line that separates them from the living. Mourning the dead, the living are drawn to identify with their history of degradation, taking on the shame that is written on each corpse's visage. (Rafael 2000, 222)

Reactions to the deaths of migrant workers in Thailand are not as dramatic and controversial as the Philippines. The status of Thai overseas workers is nothing close to the Philippines where migrant workers are deemed to be national heroes or heroines. In Thailand, they are simply known as *nak rop setthakit*, or economic warriors, who sometimes are looked down upon when they line up wearing their companies' jackets for their departing flights at Don Muang International Airport. Thai migrant workers leave and return to their home country quietly because their relatives cannot afford to see them off or welcome them home. Of course, when some of them die and their ashes are sent home, they are met silently and indifferently by the officials. This explains why the "ghosts" of overseas workers are angry, resentful, and outraged, especially against the authorities of the state.

While deaths within the context of transnational labor migration have produced and circulated "haunting" effects at home, these have not deterred potential and veteran workers from searching abroad for a better living. The myth of foreign labor markets as "gold mines" has always outplayed the realities of displacement, hardship, and marginalization. Poor and impoverished villagers have their own strong reasons for migrating to earn a living. In this way, Thai workers are like their Filipino counterparts, for whom

to go abroad is to find one's fortune (*palad*) as well as to take risks (*magbakasakali*). One seeks to convert the products of one's labor into gifts with which to endow one's kin at home, thereby gaining their respect and recognition. At the same time, one also risks uncertain conditions and the prospect of becoming alienated abroad and at home. (Rafael 2000, 210)[16]

Conclusion

While it is not my primary intention to criticize or draw recommendations for the relevant authorities in Thailand and Singapore, an immediate implication from the statistics and narratives of the deaths and injuries suffered by Thai migrant workers is that the parties involved need to work harder to improve these workers' welfare, health, and employment situations. The lives and rights of migrant workers must be respected. Their lives cannot be left unguarded in the hands of individual job placement agents and employers. In both sending and receiving countries, governmental and non-governmental (or civil) organizations, and other parties involved could play their part in providing support to those working in the transnational labor market. Overseas workers need to be well-prepared prior to their trip to their destination country, especially in regard to the quality of life they should expect both on and off their worksites, which should be scrutinized and monitored on a regular basis. In Thailand, for example, the worker recruits' medical records should be thoroughly examined and detailed information concerning migrant life and work overseas should be sufficiently distributed. In Singapore, channels and mechanisms to enforce related laws and regulations for supervising agents, employers, and workers need to be strengthened.

International scholars working on transnational labor migration in Southeast Asia somehow appear to lag behind their colleagues studying other regions of the world in terms of applying engaged academic criticism to issues pertinent to the deaths and tragedies of migrant workers. As has been done here, taking a close look at how and why migrant workers suffer unfortunate deaths and tragedies would contribute significantly to studies of overseas migrant workers' legal and human rights. The statistics of death and injuries of the workers could serve as indices to capture how far and how well each host country has managed its transnational migrant labor force. These statistics must be taken into consideration when formulating and implementing relevant labor management policies at both national and international levels. The stories behind fatal tragedies will further our understanding of the human side of what seemingly appears to be a predominantly economic enterprise. Future studies should advance transnational labor migration as an emerging field of study by taking a balanced view of the dialectical interplay between human agency and structural forces in specific labor migration settings.

Deaths and injuries may result from various causes, but what they have in common is that they stand as harsh and critical reminders of migrant workers' vulnerability to exploitation. While their job placement agents, employers, and government authorities simply consider them "economic assets," "labor commodities," or "human inputs," workers pay the highest price—their own lives—to sustain their countries' economic growth and progress.

From the transnational social space, we have witnessed how the "ghosts" of transnational migrant workers speak out against the inhumane and exploitative practices shaped by the transnational economic development paradigm.

Chapter 7

Conclusion

Thai-Isan transnational migrant laborers in Singapore generally view their bare life as *lakhon chiwit* (lit., a real-life drama).[1] Life as a migrant worker is full of dramatic episodes, ranging from suffering, disappointment, and sadness to contentment and happiness. Their status as contract guest workers makes their life truly transient. These men are uprooted and displaced from their homes and their families as they travel to work in unfamiliar foreign environments. Whatever life and work experiences a migrant worker has to encounter during his contract overseas very much resembles an everyday-life drama. It is the migrant worker who performs his role in transnational settings, thereby initiating the poetics and politics of being a transnational actor who tries to keep a foot in both worlds. Thai workers have embraced transnationalism through diverse sets of activities and real life episodes that often expose the critical bareness of migrant life away from home.

The transnational world is a theater of dreams and sensibilities. Most Thai workers I met could be described as strong performers of the "poetics of manhood" (Herzfeld 1985) during their transnational employment in Singapore. The poetic sensibility of these men is particularly evident when they drink and listen to their favorite *lukthung* and *molam* folk music. Drinking and listening to music are two major domains of everyday life. In their spare time, especially at night when they are free from the gaze of supervising authorities, they drink alcohol, sing karaoke songs, chat with friends, or listen to music. Drinking and music are effective stimulants, mediating and inducing the workers to transcend their harsh laborious reality and to move into a masculine world of imagination and recollection. Familiar musical rhythms and lyrics tell stories "about themselves to themselves" (Geertz 1973) and for themselves. One Sunday afternoon in late 2005, I asked Wit, a young worker from Udon Thani, what his favorite song was. He replied, *"Siang khaen, siang khluen"* (The sound of *khaen*, the sound of the sea) by Mike Phiromphon. The song tells of the emotional reflexivity of a tired and lonely young Isan man working on a fishing fleet in the deep sea. In his private time, he plays the *khaen*, a traditional Thai-Lao musical instrument—a gift from his father. Wit explained:

> I feel my life is exactly like what the lyrics say. An Isan worker is away from home, at sea. The haunting sound of the *khaen* is so deep in the heart and soul of most Isan people. You can be emotional and cry easily when you are alone in the world and listen to the *khaen* melody. The lyrics tell of a scene of life in transit, of a lonely *khaen* player who is releasing his longing for home and for his loved ones through the sound of his music. A young man of the Isan rice fields wishes to surrender his labor in exchange for money. He begs the guardian spirit of the sea for plentiful catches of fish and for protective power, so that he can earn some money and go home safely to the people and the place to which he belongs.[2]

The song is deeply emotional and sad. In private moments, many Thai workers lament their life paths to transnational migrant employment. For Wit, the song speaks about the countless journeys of Isan workers into transnational employment and brings some migrant predicaments and human sensibility back to the audience. The lyrics are full of symbolism: *khaen*, fish, the sea, and the young seafarer. These all are metaphors related to transnational labor migration.[3] The young fisherman from the rice fields, or the hinterlands of Isan, travels the world to engage in overseas employment. With him he has a *khaen* and the skills to play the instrument that his father gave him. His life and fate are highly uncertain and depend very much on other people's mercy, market fluctuations (sea waves), and the fertility of the sea. His goal is to help his employer catch fish in exchange for wages. The sea can be read as the endless and boundless space of transnational fields. A young worker from the Thai countryside is deemed both powerless and marginal. In the theater of real life, his strength, besides from his youthful body, lies in the self-realization that his parents and family have always given him full moral support. He continues to comfort and encourage himself to soldier on. He has pinned his hopes on the knowledge that there is always light at the end of tunnel. He looks forward to the end of his long-suffering, difficult days, wishing to overcome the loneliness of the sea and fast-forward to the glorious moment of homecoming and reunion with his family.

Singapore and the Contexts of Migrant Bareness

The state of Singapore has created and facilitated certain forms of migrant intimacy while limiting certain other patterns of transnational practices. Despite its vigorous self-branding as a global city, Singapore as a transnational destination for Thai workers appears to be strangely paradoxical. While Singapore is the most stable labor market in the region for workers from Thailand and elsewhere and provides an accountable, competitive, profitable labor market where workers can earn good wages, it is far from what workers would call an "adopted home." The "impossibilities of transnational intimacy" are highly conditioned and constrained by the particularities of Singapore as a sovereign state and as a multiracial and multicultural society.

Singapore provides no opportunity for permanent settlement to unskilled foreign workers—let alone citizenship. Its small geographical area, strict immigration policies, and effective control over its labor market make it impossible for these workers to settle down on a permanent basis. Unlike in the United States (Levitt 2001; Parrenas 2001a) and Europe (Faist 2004; Salih 2003), long-term stay and chances for cultural intimacy are limited, unless individual workers acquire more advanced skills and secure appropriate work papers with a better paying job. Many Thai workers I met also told me that Singapore is too expensive to live in. A worker's salary, with no other earnings or resources, is not sufficient to survive in Singapore. In addition, most foreign workers in Singapore have limited opportunities to interact with ordinary Singaporeans beyond their workplaces and assigned residential areas. Indeed, overseas migrant workers in the construction industry and domestic employment are viewed from a distance with some suspicious and stereotypical judgments by the local population. Since there is no official plan of inclusion of foreign workers into the mainstream of population in Singapore, working-class guest workers, especially Thai workers, have found themselves with just two viable options in which to live their transnational lives. They can either develop bonds and ties among fellow compatriot workers or extend their social networks to migrant workers of different national origins—this is how workers from Thailand experience transnationalism in Singapore.

Homecomings and the Bare Life

The question of returning home looms large in every worker's mind. Home is where they hang both head and heart. Home is the ultimate destination where they wish to end their transnational labor journeys and return to their familiar personal and social intimacies. Thai workers of all means wish to go home once they believe they have earned enough money. Homecoming scenarios are different for different workers from Thailand. Although they may involve personal choices, these scenarios tell us something about how migrant workers view their attachment to home and what their homecoming means to them.

Wirat, a close informant of mine at FTWA, hopes to return home once he completes his undergraduate degree in political science. He has been working as an electrician in Singapore for seven years while enrolled in a long-distance course at Thailand's Sukhothai Thammathirat Open University. Such courses are popular for workers with higher pay, and most of them are young enough to study given that they have fewer familial and financial burdens. Wirat's father is also a migrant worker in Singapore, but he has an estranged relation with him. After Wirat finished his term serving in the Royal Thai Air Force when he was in his mid-twenties, he came to Singapore with the aim of helping his mother and younger sisters. He has virtually achieved all his obligations to his family as he has regularly sent remittances to them over the years. While volunteering at Thailand's Office of Labor Affairs in Singapore, he became a self-taught computer technician and trainer. He fixes computers and trains his fellow workers in basic computer knowledge. He plans to say goodbye to Singapore within the next few years. He once told me that

> Singapore is a good place to work and earn some money, but it is not my home. I want to go home and run for public office in my home village in Udon Thani. My university degree, plus my work and life experience in Singapore, should be a plus for me. I wish to help improve the quality

of life of my fellow villagers. I am still young and I wish very much to have my own family soon.[4]

Some Thai workers I met in Singapore are devout Buddhists. They usually have some background serving the Buddhist Sangha at home. They know how to practice Buddhist meditation and recite certain texts on their own. They read publications by famous abbots, listen to and watch dhamma talk sessions on VCDs, and usually carry with them blessed amulets for spiritual protection while on their "labor-selling" missions in Singapore. Surin, a twenty-nine-year-old carpenter from Buri Ram, is one such Buddhist worker. He grew up in a monastery with a well-known forest-dwelling abbot in his hometown. His father sent him to live with the abbot and learn how to behave as a young school boy. Although he came to work in Singapore to help his family financially, his dream has always been to wear the yellow robes and serve as Buddha's disciple. His fellow workers and people around him have always known Surin's life destiny. He wishes to return home once his work contract expires. He cannot wait for his ordination. He wants to spend some time in the forest-dwelling Buddhist tradition and wishes to pursue his Buddhist studies in India. His friends always wish him well because such an other-worldly aspiration is very rare among the more worldly-attached Thai workers in Singapore.

Thana's and Surasak's homecomings offer two contrasting scenarios of how these reunions can pan out. Unlike Surin, both are married men. Thana was a foreman when we met in 2006. He earned a very good salary but spent heavily on drink and going out with girls. He earned some extra income from his moneylending business. It was illegal, but he borrowed money from a well-to-do friend and lent it out to needy workers. He charged 20 percent interest per month. His life took a twisted turn when he met Oy in a pub at the Golden Mile Complex. They dated and developed an intimate relationship. His friends tried to remind him that Oy was a veteran sex worker who could easily peel him off. Thana was in love as he was a romantic and sensitive man. He refused to heed his friends' warnings. Instead, he believed Oy was a sincere lover. Thana told his friends that "Oy is the first lady I slept with in Singapore without wearing a condom. This girl is for real."[5] Thana's life took a disastrous turn. Most of his salary went to the girl, who traveled back and forth between Thailand and Singapore as she was on a short-term social visit visa. She became Thana's dependent in Singapore and she knew the tricks to ask for more money from him. Thana went broke and was in trouble with his moneylending business. His life was threatened by an influential creditor. He returned home as a lovelorn worker with heavy debt. His wife and children in Udon Thani, whom he neglected over the years, deserted him. Thana was one of the losers in this episode of transnational labor migration.

Some episodes of transnational life and pleasure can, however, be carried out and effectively monitored from a distance. I met Surasak in my Sunday English classes. He worked as a safety supervisor for a construction firm in Woodland. Surasak is a talented singer and is well-liked by girls. He entered the karaoke competitions that FTWA volunteers and I organized every May Day. He ended up as a finalist twice and took home some prize money and trophies. Surasak was in his early thirties and married with a child when I met him. He came from a rural village in Nong Bua Lamphu Province, but his wife and her relatives had been migrant workers in Bangkok for years. He borrowed some money from his wife's side to sponsor his overseas employment in Singapore. Surasak has always lived a migrant life on the thin line between being a faithful, committed family man and a fun lover who was ready to exploit his personal freedom in Singapore. However, his wife was very determined to keep Surasak in check from afar. Each week they spent a lot of money on prepaid telephone cards. Surasak's friends all know that his wife is very jealous and what they consider a "henpecking woman." She once threw away a gift from Surasak after she learned he bought it for her on the advice of a Thai girl he met in Singapore. She demanded Surasak return home as soon as his current contract expired. Surasak told me when I joined a small picnic he organized as a farewell to his friends that "my wife said she does not care whether I earn a hundred thousand baht a month in Singapore. She ultimately wants me to go home."

"Did you pay off all the debts you owed for your overseas job here?" I asked.

"That should be no problem since we borrowed it from my wife's parents. I have sent them remittances every month over the past few years," replied Surasak in his usual gentle but playful manner.

What is your plan once you return home?" I asked.

"I will help my wife's family and her brothers who sell snacks to school children in Bangkok. I did it before and made some good money."

Accounts from these Thai workers indicate that their bare life as transnational migrant laborers always takes place in between the two points of coming and departing—an undeniable truth for every migrant worker. Transnational migrant life always spans these two destinations, each with its own intimate ties and networks of interaction. For Wirat, Surin, Thana, and Surasak, returning home is inevitable and expected. Their trips home seem far from being bitterly estranged and ambivalent returns, as Constable (1999) describes in the case of Filipina domestic workers coming home from Hong Kong. For Thai workers, home is explicitly located at the opposite end of the host country. As fathers or sons, their reunions with families and home villages are not as complicated as returning mothers who had to leave behind their children to take care of other people's children. With their wives and parents taking care of their children, "care deficit" and "care crisis" (Parrenas 2002, 39), which trouble most households with migrant mothers in the Philippines and elsewhere, do not disturb most male workers' homecomings. However, reuniting and re-embedding oneself back into one's familial ties and textures are complicated matters. As indicated in many popular song lyrics, ex-overseas workers have encountered difficulties resulting from their extended absence, the mishandling of remittances, and personal intimacies. The issues involving returning migrant workers need more informed discussion and investigation.

Episodes of *lakhon chiwit* always involve dramatic twists and turns, especially for poor migrant workers who have soaked themselves in the sweat and tears of the mobile theater of transnational labor migration. The immediate task at hand is to carry out work and earn a salary. In the meantime, they have to survive the bare life. The lucky ones make successful homecoming trips alive and richer. The not-so-lucky ones return home in debt. The most tragic and unlucky ones return home in coffins or as cremated ashes.

Notes

Chapter 1 Introduction

1. Interview with a Thai labor councilor, January 14, 2005.

2. I am indebted to Vineeta Sinha (Department of Sociology, National University of Singapore) for pointing this out to me in our personal communication. She writes that "I do feel quite strongly that there has been an 'over-reading' and 'over-analysis' of Singapore as a highly urban space, where the world of official bureaucratic rationality, discipline and over-regulation are dominant frames. If one looks at the city outside these frames, a different world appears—and one which is more meaningful, either in enabling or obscuring the business of day-to-day living" (personal communication, October 15, 2005).

Chapter 2 The Lyrics of a Laborious Life

An earlier version of this chapter was published in *Inter-Asia Cultural Studies* 10, no. 3 (2009).

1. *Phleng lukthung* is a popular Thai music genre whose songs often reflect the daily hardships of rural life in Thailand.

2. *Molam* (*mo* = specialist/skilled person; *lam* = to sing/singer) refers to a traditional music genre of the Thai-Lao speaking people. This type of folk music is found in northeastern Thailand, Laos, and some Thai-Lao speaking communities overseas.

3. *Phleng phuea chiwit*, literally "songs for life," emerged as a musical genre of protest in Thailand during the country's political turbulence of the 1970s. Influenced by Western country music and adopted by student and activist movements in the 1960s, *phleng phuea chiwit* inspired public protests against Thailand's right-wing government in the 1970s. This genre of music was popular on university and teachers' college campuses throughout the country. It acquired its revolutionary leanings when student leaders and

leftist activists joined the Communist Party of Thailand (CPT) following the massacre of students on Thammasat University campus on October 6, 1976. *Phleng phuea chiwit* grew out of the student and social movements in the 1970s and developed closely with contemporary grassroots social movements and drew members of working and middle classes both in rural and urban areas. By the early 1980s, it had become an established popular genre after amnesty was given to former CPT members. This music genre stormed the country's music industry with a hybridity of Western and traditional/regional music sources. Its subject content mirrors the hardship, injustice, and social problems faced by ordinary people since then. Leading *phleng phuea chiwit* bands include Caravan, Carabao, Khon Dan Khwian, Su Su, Marijuana, and individual artists like Phongthep Kradonchamnan, Phongsit Khamphi, and the like (Wong 1995, 1998). Wong (1998, 98) argues that *phleng phuea chiwit* is seen as an emerging genre that bridges "the field (*thung*) and the city (*krung*), [and] denotes a musical landscape and class as well as metaphoric realms." She cites Caravan and Carabao as the founders of this popular genre. More comprehensive studies on this genre are crucially needed.

4. By using the term "popular music," I refer to the three major Thai music genres: *lukthung*, *molam*, and *phleng phuea chiwit*. For generations, these genres have constituted the voice-culture of rural and urban working-class people in Thailand, especially that of emerging migrant workers. Miller (1998, 333) notes that "everyday life in modern Thailand is seemingly dominated by popular culture. Popular music is heard throughout the country—in hotels and restaurants, on the radio, on temporary stages in remote villages, on cassette tapes, and in music videos."

5. Musical commodities in the form of VCDs, DVDs, tape cassettes, song books, and images of well-known singers' are available everywhere in the world where Thai diasporic communities exist (e.g., Australia, Brunei, Europe, Japan, Malaysia, Singapore, the Middle East, Israel, Taiwan, and the US). In Singapore, within the Golden Mile Complex on Beach Road, several large stores display and sell popular music for Thai migrant workers. They offer virtually every musical genre produced and consumed at home, plus movies and duplicated copies of TV drama series. Although both copyrighted master and pirated copies are available, Thai customers prefer to buy the latter, which are much cheaper. Curiously, Singapore, which is famous for its law enforcement, allows the commercial piracy of intellectual property.

6. Internal migrant workers as a social class were given considerable attention in the literature, arts, and music of Thai Marxism in the 1950s and 1960s. Novels by Kulap Saipradit (a.k.a. Sriburapha) and essays and poems by Jit Phumisak are among key examples (Reynolds 1987). The song entitled *"Siang khruan khong kammakon"* (Voices of Thai workers) was composed

by Jit Phumisak to celebrate May Day in 1957 while he was imprisoned in Bangkok. It laments how workers were unfairly treated by the feudal (*sakdina*) and bourgeois (kradumphi) classes and urges them to stand up, unite, and fight for justice, rights, and freedom in the name of class struggle. The song, alongside other writings by Jit Phumisak and other leftist public intellectuals in the 1950s, was very influential to the student and activist movements of the 1970s. The song also inspired the birth of the *phleng phuea chiwit* movement during the same period.

7. Rural migrants are also drawn to employment in Bangkok because of the city's urban mystique as "a place of boundless novelty and excitement" (Mills 1999a, 128).

8. One of many popular Thai sayings that reflect the excitement experienced by migrants from the countryside newly arrived in Bangkok in the early days is "*ban nok tuen krung*" (lit., a country bumpkin is shocked by the might of the city). Mills (1999a, 109) observes that "Bangkok itself comes as a near-physical shock to many newcomers: the size, the noise, the pace may be overwhelming to the uninitiated. Migrants' urban sojourns begin as a visceral encounter with a chaotic, sprawling urban giant."

9. This quote originally referred to the cultural nostalgia of overseas Chinese migrating to America. The full sentence reads: "The overseas Chinese respect 'Chinese culture' most when they are comfortably removed from it" (Chang 1999, 137).

10. Indeed, the term "labor migration" does not have a place in the Thai vernacular language. In Thai official and academic discourses, it is roughly translated as *kan yai thin raeng ngan* or *kan opphayop raeng ngan*. These terms are more expressive of economic or political refugees than of migrants and labor migration. The terms are not used in everyday language. In the Isan dialect, people are familiar with either *pai nok* (to go abroad) or *pai het ngan mueang nok/tang prathet* (lit., to go and work abroad), but never *kan yai thin raeng ngan kham chat* (transnational labor migration).

11. Mills (1999a, 134) discovered a similar expression in a labor-sending village in Thailand's province of Mahasarakham. One of her informants said, "In the city there's money; in the village there's none." It reflects Isan villagers' common perception that one can only seek wealth and better opportunities and experience modernity outside one's own locality.

12. According to the *Merip Reports* ("Letter from Bangkok" 1984, 26), "in 1975, around 1,000 Thai workers left for Bahrain and Saudi Arabia; by 1982, 108,520 workers, over one-third of all Thailand's expatriate workforce, had left for 11 different countries in the Middle East region. Their remittances, totaling over US450 million, amounted to the equivalent of half the foreign

exchange brought into Thailand by its foreign visitors and exceeded revenues from the country's main commodity exports, except rice and tapioca."

13. My informants explained that almost all of them had worked in Bangkok since their early teens, and more than 70 percent were veteran workers with years of experience in several overseas countries such as Saudi Arabia, Libya, Bahrain, Taiwan, Brunei, Japan, and Israel. It is typical for young boys and girls from the region to leave home to seek employment in Bangkok soon after they finish the compulsory six years of school. They usually begin in domestic and service jobs because of their young age, and then proceed to factory jobs when they are eighteen years old. Their biggest life challenge occurs when they want to leave the country to work overseas since it requires a large investment, generally generated from family savings and assets. The decision to seek overseas employment usually is one made by the family, especially parents and spouses (Fieldnotes, September 22 and October 28, 2004).

14. I am grateful to Achan Suriya Smutkupt, a retired, Chiang Mai-based Thai anthropologist and my mentor, for bringing this point to my attention.

15. Phongthep Kradonchamnan (1990) produced the megahit "Tangke" (Isan fishermen). A large number of young men from Isan find employment in the fishing industry in Thailand's eastern and southern provinces. The musician Mike Phiromphon (2002d) also tells of the daunting and lonely life of young men from the hinterland of Isan working on fishing fleets amid the sea and the sky in *"Siang khaen, siang khluen"* (The sound of *khaen*, the sound of the sea).

16. GMM Grammy's major collections of *lukthung* hits dedicated to migrant workers include *Lukthung raeng chai raeng ngan* ("Lukthung collections intended to delight workers' spirits"), released in 2003, and *Wan chai raeng ngan* ("Collections of lukthung love songs dedicated to workers") from 2005.

17. Accounts of Thailand's legal loopholes, corrupt government officials and politicians, and notorious job-placement agencies are well-known. From the boom times of labor exportation to the Middle East to the present heyday of labor migration to East Asian countries like Taiwan, Singapore, and Brunei, the same old cases of middlemen cheating or taking advantage of Thai workers (e.g., the overcharging of job-placement fees) have featured regularly in news stories in the local press.

18. Fieldnote, July 14, 2004.

19. Supang Chantavanich et al. (2001b), citing Germany's *Statistik Bundesamt*, note that there were 23,870 Thai women and 4,576 men living and working in Germany in 1996. The majority of Thai women migrated to and settled in European countries through interracial matchmaking and

marriages. Some of them ended up as sex workers and prostitutes. Ratana Tosakul Boonmathya (2005) shows a large number of Isan women marrying European men in countries like France, Germany, Switzerland, and the Netherlands. Suphaphim (2004, 38) reports her experience encountering groups of Thai female workers from rural northeastern and northern Thailand working in textile factories owned by Indochinese settlers in France. Workers have to pay as much as 100,000 baht (US2,500) for airfare and job-placement fees, but they can earn up to 70,000–80,000 baht (US1,780–2,040) per month.

20. Given the cultural conservativism and the preference for men in public and political domains of Thai society, as well as the dominance of male composers in the *lukthung-molam* industry, it is not surprising that there are an overwhelming number of messages in Thai popular music restricting female sexuality and mobility in the modern world. Lukthung songs and lam lyrics are usually written from men's perspective by men. Yet, Adorno (1962, 31) reminds us that the composer/producer of popular music has his own predicament: "He must write something impressive enough to be remembered and at the same time well-known enough to be banal."

21. The message in this song contrasts starkly with research on *phanraya farang* (wives of *farang* men) by Ratana Tosakul Boonmythya (2005), who argues that these *farangs'* wives have strong commitments to their parents, relatives, and the cultural roots of their village traditions.

22. While the Thai workers in Singapore that I interviewed insisted that adultery and its tragic consequences are partly rumors and tales in villages across the region, one of my informants shared with me two "factual" accounts. The first one was about his own cousin from Udon Thani who for years worked in a factory job in Taiwan. Against goodwill caution from his parents, he completely trusted his wife and sent her monthly remittances. His wife "put a pair of buffalo horns on his head" by using his remittance to live with her policeman lover. The husband came back to a broken home and spent months recovering from his heart-breaking sorrow and resentment. He now drives a lorry for a company in the provincial town. In the second account, a man from Nong Khai did not realize his wife's betrayal until he came back from abroad without forewarning. He took his wife to the bank to withdraw his remittance, so that he could buy a brand-new pick-up truck. On the way to the bank, his wife asked him to wait for a while because she wanted to quickly drop by to see a friend. The husband waited and waited only to soon learn that his wife had gone to commit suicide by throwing herself into the Mekong River as a way to escape her shameful behavior of being unfaithful to him (Fieldnote, February 29, 2006).

23. In this respect, remittances are assigned dual functions: economic and sociocultural. Remittances help feed mouths and foster lives at home.

The purchasing power of remittances also brings "social face" (*na ta*) and honor to the families left behind. It reinforces emotional and personal bonds between the sender and the receiver. Kittisak Chaichana's (2005) song "I deposit my heart into the remittance envelope I send to my mother" (*Fak chai sai song*) reveals the tender feelings of a migrant son toward his mother back home when he sends his wages wrapped up with love and care for his mother. One overseas migrant worker in Singapore told me that "the moment I remit money to my parents is always the proudest moment in my life." This worker and his friends regularly send money (*song ngoen*) home once or twice a month.

24. A long epic story about *sao Taiwan* (a wife of an Isan man working in Taiwan) was performed during a *molam rueang* (storytelling molam) by Khana Nokyung Thong (1998[?]). The wife's handling of her husband's remittance, a love affair, and tensions from her husband's relatives are the dramatic themes of the performance.

25. *Lam toei* is the name of the Isan *lam* style and is noted for its "faster-paced and metrical" pattern (Miller 1998, 325). *Lam toei* is widely adopted as a compromised musical pattern between *lam* and *lukthung* music genres. Among the pioneers of modern *molam*, Phonsak Songsaeng (1986a[?]) made a wide impact with this musical style in the mid-1980s with his megahit album *Sao chan kang kop* ("A disgraceful girl named Chan").

26. Mills (1995) discusses the widespread fear and tension in Isan villages in the early 1990s created by the mysterious death syndrome and attacks by a ghost of a widow's husband.

27. In his famous essay "Popular Music," Adorno (1962, 21) writes that "the concept of popular music is both murky and self-evident. We all know what happens to us when we absentmindedly turn on the radio, and this knowledge seems to relieve us of reflecting on it." I adopt Adorno's characterization of European-American popular music as "murky and self-evident." This characterization fits well with Thailand's popular musical enterprise, especially the country's series of song hits.

28. Fieldnote, August 17, 2004.

Chapter 3 Village Transnationalism

An earlier version of this chapter appeared in *ARI Working Paper Series* No. 71 (Asia Research Institute, Singapore 2006).

1. In her book *The Transnational Villagers*, Levitt (2001) studies Dominicans living in Boston who maintain close connections with family and politics in the Dominican Republic. She explores how ordinary people can continue to keep a foot in two worlds and create communities that span borders. While

I share the "village" metaphor in my own work, the "villages" I study are situated in a totally different world. Since Isan workers from Buddhist villages in northeastern Thailand will never be allowed to settle in Singapore, my study is more concerned with how resources, knowledge, and skills acquired and brought from the Thai countryside are turned into limited cultural and symbolic capital and transborder identities during temporary stays abroad.

2. Interview with Sorachai, September 12, 2004.

3. In 2004, the currency exchange rates were roughly 1 Singapore dollar to 24 baht; 1 US dollar to 39 baht.

4. Jones and Tieng Pardthaisong (1999, 32–46) discuss the dominant role of commercial agencies that act as intermediaries between workers and foreign employers, as well as the overall recruitment and job placement processes practiced in Thailand in the mid-1990s. In 1995, private agencies typically charged a fee of 1,800 US dollars per person to locate a construction job in Singapore (ibid., 41, table 5). Wong (2000, 73) mentions the market rate of 1,250 US dollars (about 50,000 baht) per head as the recruitment fee in 1995. While the rate for a renewed work permit holder has been roughly stable over the past ten years, in 2004 each first-time worker had to pay up to 2,500 US dollars (Interview, December 19, 2004).

5. Tony, the owner and operator of a major remittance service outlet at the Golden Mile Complex, estimates that an average Thai migrant worker sends money home two to three times a month, with each transaction totaling around 500 Singapore dollars (307 US dollars; 12,000 baht) in most cases (Interview, May 8, 2005). Another long-time operator of a remittance service in the Golden Mile Complex said most Thai workers send home an average of 500 Singapore dollars per month (Fieldnote, September 17, 2005). My interview data show that the Thai workers in my study remitted an average of only 150 US dollars once a month to their families. Even though they are paid weekly (250–300 Singapore dollars; 156–187 US dollars), Thai migrant workers prefer to save and send home a single larger sum of money. It is considered a kind of prestige for families to have a regular monthly remittance from a family member similar to government officials and other office workers (Interview, May 9, 2005).

6. Article 5(2) of Singapore's Employment of Foreign Workers Act (chapter 91A) states that "no foreign worker shall be in the employment of an employer without a valid work permit."

7. For years, foreign workers of different national origins in Singapore have maintained their own popular places for social gathering during off-duty hours. The Indian and Bangladeshi communities, for example, have their favorite spot in Little India, the Filipina domestic workers occupy Lucky Plaza

and a nearby park on Orchard Road, the Indonesians visit City Plaza near Kan Tong, and the Thais gather at the Golden Mile Complex on Beach Road. These meeting spots seem to be products of self-designed and self-controlled ethnocultural sanctuaries or enclaved zones, since Singapore's iron-clad legal, economic, and cultural regulations have insistently denied or ruled out the possibility of integrating or assimilating foreign workers into its geopolitical and cultural bodies. Unskilled contract workers of foreign origin have been dealt with in "an economically efficient manner" (cited in Wong 2000, 64). In other words, all means are used to guard against contact with the local community and to keep foreign workers as outcast "others" whose labor on 3D jobs is valued only insofar as it helps fuel economic growth and maintains social well-being and a high quality of life.

8. By negatively portraying the Golden Mile, it is easy to stigmatize the place. And, to be fair, the mall is far from a lawless place. Apart from frequent inspections by the local police, the complex has established its own regulations. During its peak hours, usually on Sunday afternoons, the Golden Mile management repeatedly plays recorded messages in both Thai and English through its public address system such as: "Welcome all our customers and visitors to the Golden Mile. Please listen to an announcement and give us your cooperation. First, do not smoke in the Golden Mile Complex because it is an air-conditioned area. In case of an offense, a fine of one thousand dollars will be imposed. Second, do not sit on or litter the floor. Please drop the rubbish in the bin. Third, do not urinate on the stairs, at the building's corners, or in the parking lots. Please use the public toilet. Fourth, do not disturb or bother other people. Do not quarrel or put up a fight in the Golden Mile area. And do not drink too much as you will lose control of yourself. With best wishes from the Golden Mile management. Thank you" (Fieldnote, January 15, 2005). Here I translate and quote the Thai-language version of this public announcement. It provides a specific and extensive message aimed at keeping order and disciplining the crowd of Thai customers who apparently are indifferent to the message. The English version is rather brief and less persuasive. It does not incur a sense of serious warning or threat. Rather, it simply makes the announcement: "Do not smoke. Do not litter. Thank you and happy shopping at the Golden Mile" (Fieldnote, January 15, 2005). As Thai workers do not speak English, the English-language address is intended for English-speaking Singaporeans and other international customers and visitors that are more cooperative and well-behaved. These messages suggest that the Thai workers are troublemakers, but nonetheless, for business reasons, their wild and unsophisticated behavior can be tolerated. This reflects the attitude of the Singaporean government and society toward Thai and other foreign workers.

9. Interview with Thakur Phanit, Thailand's ambassador to Singapore, September 4, 2004.

10. The Housing and Development Board (HDB) is a Singaporean government agency that is in charge of planning and overseeing the country's residential apartments and housing units.

11. Thai worker's diary #7, January 21, 2005.

12. Ibid.

13. Thai worker's diary #1, January 28, 2005.

14. Thai worker's diary #12, January 28, 2005.

15. Interview, July 25, 2004. In his diary, Naruchai, age thirty-two, wrote, "I am glad that we have the center for my fellow workers from Thailand at the Golden Mile. It is the place for us, no matter how far away it is located. I try my best to be there. Most of my friends meet there every week. If we renamed it "Thai Town," it would be cool!" (Thai worker's diary, January 16, 2005).

16. Son, age twenty-four, a young worker from Sakon Nakhon, told me that he and his friends were arrested by the police as they were walking back to the foreign workers' dormitory when one of the residents got suspicious of them and called the police. They were fortunate since they had their work permits with them (Interview, January 16, 2004). Many workers I interviewed during their visits to the Kallang Riverside Park complained that some residents threw water bottles or yelled at them when they walked into the residential housing, even though they had permission and had followed proper procedures (Interview with Son, November 21, 2004). Prasit, age thirty-three, and Thosaporn, age forty-one, both veteran migrant workers who previously worked in Taiwan and Brunei before coming to Singapore, commented that Singaporeans are generally not generous and helpful (*mai mi nam chai*). They come from different ethnic, linguistic, and cultural backgrounds. They are rather individualistic. The job placement agents always take advantage of foreign workers. Taiwanese employers are much more generous and pay respect to their foreign employees, according to interviews with Prasit and Thosaporn, February 8, 2004.

17. Eric Thompson (personal communication, January 2005) brought to my attention that the mobile phone, which is extremely popular among foreign workers in Singapore, is used to offset these workers' limited physical mobility as they are usually confined to their construction sites, employers' homes, and foreign workers' dormitories. Thanks to its affordable price, the mobile phone allows foreign workers of all nationalities to maintain social networks both in Singapore and in their home countries. Culturally and physically handicapped as they do not speak English (except workers from

countries like the Philippines and India) and living and working away from their friends, lovers, families and relatives, the mobile phone is not only a wireless technology and fashion, but also has multiple psychosocial, economic, and cultural functions. More importantly, it empowers migrant workers to communicate in their own language at those times when they might feel a sense of power and control over their lives, despite it lasting only a short temporary moment and, of course, at some personal expense.

18. Interview, March 6, 2005.

19. Ibid.

20. Interview with Chai, February 20, 2005.

21. Fieldnote, February 13, 2005.

22. Field documents, January and March, 2005.

23. Many ordinary Thai-Isan construction workers make 23 Singapore dollars per day, plus any over-time earnings (3–5 dollars per hour). They work six days a week. Most of them earn less than 700 dollars per month. Some veteran and skilled workers (i.e., crane operators, electricians, carpenters, etc.) usually earn up to 1,000 per month. Therefore, if one makes a donation of 500 dollars, he is considered very generous. It means he donates more than 50 percent of his monthly earnings to the *pha pa* merit making activities. As a result, he would be unable to remit money to his family that month.

24. Interview with Panya, February 20, 2005.

25. Interview with Pornchai, March 6, 2005.

26. Fieldnote, January 16, 2005. I use the XE.com Currency Convert available at http://www.xe.com. As of February 2005, one Singapore dollar was equivalent to sixty cents in US dollars or twenty-four Thai baht.

27. Fieldnote, February 9, 2005.

28. Fieldnotes, February 9 and March 6, 2005.

29. Thailand is currently the king of Southeast Asian football despite some reports of poor management, corruption, and power struggles in running the Football Association of Thailand. It has won six consecutive gold medals at the bi-annual Southeast Asian (SEA) Games since 1993. Its national team also won three out of five Tiger Cups—in 1996, 2000, and 2002. The SEA Games are billed as the official Southeast Asian championship. Since the late 1990s up until the present, leading Thai football players have come to play professional football in Singapore's professional football league. It should be noted that football, due to its overwhelming popularity at the grass-root level, has become a major rival to Thai and international-style boxing. It is also used by politicians, high military officials, and bureaucrats as a political tool to gain popular support. The government under the leadership of Thaksin Shinawatra

consistently exploited the country's passion for this sport to achieve its political gains by supporting heavily publicized projects like a proposal to buy partial shares in famous English premier league football clubs (which ultimately failed), street football tournaments, and even a VIP league among politicians and officials working in different ministries and departments.

30. The original idea to organize an official competitive football tournament among workers in Singapore reflects the populist politics under the Thaksin Shinawatra regime. In the name of promoting health and well-being, popular team sports such as football and mass-participatory aerobic dance were organized nationwide. In 2001, the Ministry of Labor Affairs established the popular "Labor Cup" among workers from different factories and corporations in Bangkok and its suburbs.

31. Fieldnote, November 27, 2004.

32. Interview with Yutthana, November 28, 2004.

33. There are a number of Christian churches, including the Thai True Way, that work with Thai migrant workers in Singapore. The Bangkok-based Thai Chen-Li Church, for example, hosts non-formal education classes, which have enrolled a number of worker-students for years. With some support from local churches in Singapore, these churches aim to convert workers to Christianity. However, some workers I interviewed told me that only a small group of workers join these churches for purely religious reasons. "As I am a Buddhist, it is hard to force myself to accept God. I do not want to lie to them, so I have to distance myself from them." Others felt that they did not like the way the preachers imposed on them something alien to their previous religious faith and belief (Interviews, June 12, 2004).

34. Fieldnote, December 19, 2004.

35. Interview with Som, December 19, 2004.

36. Interview with Yutthana, December 19, 2004.

37. Fieldnotes, November 28, 2004 and February 27, 2005.

38. Interview with Yutthana, February 27, 2005.

39. The concept of *kin khao pa* is a traditional Thai-Isan custom of going trekking to hunt game, gather wild food, and picnic in a forest, as a change from having meals at home on the farm or other rural sites. It is a trip away from and beyond home villages as Kampoon Boontawee (1976) demonstrated in his classic novel *Luk Isan* (Child of the Northeast).

40. Fieldnote, September 19, 2004.

41. In his diary, Chatri wrote "besides sports like football and *sepak takraw*, my friends and I go fishing and gather fruits in the forests" (Thai worker's diary #4, January 16, 2005).

42. Sompong, age twenty-three, noted that "as we are unskilled construction workers, earning only 23 dollars per day and having to pay 200–300 per month for food, our trips to the forest gives us not only fun, but also our favorite wild food, like bamboo shoots, edible leaves, fruits, and fish. We can save our hard-earned salary, too" (Thai worker's diary #16, February 2, 2005).

43. Wisit's life story is a prime example of how Thai-Isan men use their physical labor as a commodity in the international labor market. Age forty-five and a veteran worker from Udon Thani, Wisit had endured significant hardship working in Singapore as a plumper fixing toilets in schools and houses for more than two years. He said, "I carried out the dirtiest job in the world. Sometimes, shit, urine, and human waste spilled all over my body from head to toe. I even swallowed it a number of times. My Singaporean boss just gave me an order and left. I had to carry out the job on my own. Sometimes, I had lunch without washing or cleaning at all." As a migrant worker in Singapore's capitalist transnationalization movement, Wisit was able to leave the "dirtiest job in the world" and become an electrician with a new company. He has endured and survived the harsh realities away from home for almost a decade now.

44. See note 5.

45. Kai, age thirty-two, a veteran factory worker from Khon Kaen, once made the comment to me that because of Singapore's strict regulations, male Thai workers' lives in Singapore centered only on a few items: "carrying out their daily job, then visiting the Golden Mile, getting drunk, womanizing, and gambling when they are free" (Interview with Kai, September 12, 2004).

Chapter 4 State, Intimacy, and Desire

An earlier version of this chapter was published in *Gender, Place & Culture: A Journal of Feminist Geography* 2, no. 6 (2008).

1. Askew and Cohen (2004, 96) describe Thailand's lower southern region as a permissive space for Malaysian and male Singaporean tourists "to engage in forms of sexual and recreational behaviour with a freedom and abandon impossible in their own countries." I apply this concept to the case of sexual intimacies between foreign sex workers and transient overseas workers in Singapore. Although the sex-for-sale industry is heavily regulated in Singapore, there are zones, places, and channels that are somehow implicitly and explicitly permitted (Brazil, 2004; Lim, 2004).

2. The Employment of Foreign Workers Act governs the employment of foreign workforces as economic assets whereas the Immigration Act ensures the legal flows of people and goods in and out of the country.

3. Indeed, Singaporean authorities (e.g., Ministry of Manpower) are highly circumspect regarding the number of foreign workers in the country. No officially released data is available. Most cited figures are estimates. Li (2004) quotes 500,000 as an estimated total number of foreign workers in Singapore. Rahman (2006) reports that of the 620,000 foreign workers reported in the local press, 540,000 were work permit holders and the remaining 80,000 were employment pass holders.

4. See http://www.mom.gov.sg/NR/rdonlyres/2F03CDE4-3B1A-43DE-893 3-4ABC638A5458/7612/WPSPassConditions.pdf, retrieved June 26, 2006. I am grateful to Teo You Yenn, my colleague at the Asia Research Institute, National University of Singapore, for bringing this document to my attention.

5. For major works on the history of prostitution, Chinese migrant laborers, and Singapore's colonial past, see Dobbs (2003); Warren (2003a, 2003b); Yeoh (2003b).

6. Appadurai (1999, 464) defines global ethnoscapes as "the landscape of persons who make up the shifting world in which we live: tourists, immigrants, refugees, exiles, guest workers, and other moving groups and persons constitute an essential feature of the world and appear to affect the politics of and between nations to a hitherto unprecedented degree."

7. For many years, the Royal Thai Embassy and the Office of Thai Labor Affairs in Singapore have sponsored a series of healthcare and educational activities for Thai workers at the Golden Mile Complex. Efforts by these organizations not only help foreign workers adjust to their work environments in Singapore, but also educate them on how to properly manage social life on and off worksites.

8. Fieldnote, September 12, 2004.

9. Fieldnote, October 17, 2005.

10. Ibid.

11. Ibid. One cross-border sex worker from Thailand was interviewed by a Thai journalist who visited Singapore's famous nightlife district at Orchard Tower. She explained to the journalist that young, single Thai women working as sex workers are encouraged to have Chinese-Singaporean boyfriends. "It helps when we are asked by other Thais. I just tell them that I am married to a Singaporean man and have a family here, [otherwise I will be looked down upon or suspected of working as a sex worker]" (*Manager Online*, February 5, 2003).

12. Fieldnote, August 1, 2004.

13. Ibid.

14. Fieldnote, August 12, 2004.

15. Fieldnote, September 27, 2004.

16. Fieldnote, November 21, 2004.

17. Fieldnote, September 27, 2004.

18. Ibid.

Chapter 5 Male Workers Talking Sex

An earlier version of this chapter was published in *Man and Masculinities in Southeast Asia*, edited by Michele Ford and Lenore Lyons (Routledge 2012).

1. The focus group participants comprised Thai-Lao Isan-speaking Buddhists from the northeastern Thai provinces of Nong Khai, Khon Kaen, Udon Thani, Buri Ram, Phetchabun, Sakon Nakhon, and Surin. I consider Phetchabun to be an extended part of Thailand's northeastern region due to its close geographical and ethnocultural connections to the rest of Isan's nineteen provinces. The participants' average age was 37.75 (the oldest was forty-eight years old; the youngest was twenty-eight years old). All of them had some basic education but none of them were college graduates. The majority of them were married with one or two children and several of them were single or divorced. All of them had passed Singapore's standard skills tests for construction workers and had an average of nearly ten years of employment in Singapore. Many of them had worked overseas in countries such as Brunei, Qatar and Taiwan, and had first come to Singapore in the 1990s. Their average monthly earnings were 22,750 baht (35,000 was the highest monthly income; 10,000 was the lowest). All of the participants had regularly remitted portions of their income back home to their families, averaging approximately 13,000 per month. To protect their privacy and identity, pseudonyms have been used for all participants.

2. All participant quotes in this chapter are based on the author's fieldnotes taken during the course of the October 2006 focus group discussion, unless otherwise indicated.

3. Aside from the Thai-Lao/Thai-Isan term for sexual intercourse (*si*), I also frequently heard female vendors use the terms "*kha*" (lit., to kill) or "*kha khong*" (to kill a thing). Sexually explicit language usually features in everyday conversation between male Thai-Isan workers and tradeswomen in the Kallang Riverside Park. One of my informants boldly told me that "these *mae kha* sell either their goods (*khai khong*) or their virginity (*khai hi*)" (Fieldnote, September 27, 2004).

4. Fieldnote by Suriya Smutkupt, October 28, 2006.

5. Ibid.

6. Ibid.

7. Similarly, a Filipina domestic worker employed in Singapore stated, "It's human to have sexual urges. Sometimes you get lonely here in Singapore. So you find a foreign boyfriend, whether Singaporean, Bangladeshi, or Indian" (*Electric New Paper*, September 19, 2005).

8. Fieldnote by Suriya Smutkupt, October 28, 2006. A Malay Singaporean taxi driver in his late forties had a similar account. He told me that "the Indonesians are the most sincere lovers and are less demanding. They honor their male partners. They do not demand money, but rather accept whatever is given to them by their lovers. The Filipina are the most romantic lovers. They are serious and faithful once they have committed themselves to their lovers. They demand both love and money. The Thais are the most money-oriented lovers. You have to show them money first. They can be the most loveable ladies in your life, when you supply them with enough money."

9. Sommai shared an account of his one-time, casual oral sex encounter with a Singaporean gay man: Many years ago when I was a driver for my company in Tuas [in western Singapore], I was approached by a gay man at the truck-stop in a gas station. As I did not speak English, he showed me a series of homosexual pornographic illustrations. He offered me 200 dollars in exchange for one oral sex session. It was good money, so I accepted it. He gave me the oral sex of my life. He sucked me dry and really enjoyed himself, while it was quite painful for me. I tried to push him away, but he insisted on finishing his 200 dollars' worth of business. I was totally exhausted. I used the money to buy some whisky for my friends. They asked where I got the money. I told them I got it from a girl.

10. Fieldnote by Suriya Smutkupt, November 28, 2005.

11. Fieldnote by Suriya Smuktkupt, October 28, 2006.

12. Ibid.

13. One of my informants, Bunmee, reported that he heard of a Roi Et worker who married a Filipina domestic worker in Singapore and took her home to settle in Thailand. This appears to be a rather uncommon situation, however.

14. Fieldnote by Suriya Smutkupt, October 28, 2006.

15. Fieldnote by Suriya Smutkupt, August 27, 2006.

16. Ibid.

17. Fieldnote by author, November 28, 2005.

18. Fieldnote by Suriya Smutkupt, October 28, 2006.

19. Fieldnote by author, November 28, 2005.

20. Fieldnote by Suriya Smutkupt, October 28, 2006.

21. Ibid.

Chapter 6 Death, Tragedy, and Ghosts

An earlier version of this chapter was published in *Asian Migrations: Sojourning, Displacement, Homecoming and Other Travels*, edited by Beatriz D. Lorente et al. (Asia Research Institute, National University of Singapore, 2005).

1. Bridget Lew, an NGO activist who runs a refuge center for foreign workers in Singapore, describes the characteristics and mentalities of foreign workers in Singapore as those of semiskilled or unskilled foreign workers who "are very vulnerable. They don't know their rights. And they constantly fear being listed or repatriated by their employers. Their greatest fear is losing their jobs" (*Straits Times* 2004).

2. My observation is informed by my reading of selected sociological and anthropological overviews of transnational labor migration. Yeoh and Willis (2005, 269), for example, note that while the studies of skilled, professional workers in the past twenty years have been "recognized from an economic perspective, much less has been researched from a social and cultural angle." Hollifield (2000, 141) demonstrates that major concerns in this field of study deal with "the ability or inability of a state to control its border... [and] whether international migration in the late twentieth century poses a dramatic threat to the sovereignty and integrity of nation-states." A number of sociologists of migration ask the following questions: Why does migration occur and how is it sustained over time? What happens to migrants in the receiving societies and what are the economic, social, and political consequences of their presence (Heisler 2000, 77)? Scholars working on "transnationalism from below" raise issues concerning "how this process [of transnationalization at the grassroots level] affects power relations, cultural constructions, economic interactions, and more generally, social organization at the level of locality" (Guarnizo and Smith 1998, 6).

3. Chiew (1995, 485) argues that "the presence of foreign labor in Singapore is not a recent phenomenon but has been a part of Singaporean society over the past 175 years.... Singapore's society was founded by immigrants."

4. See Ministry of Manpower, Singapore, http://www.mom.gov.sg/MOM/CDA/0,1858,3669-----178_2001~3278_2004---4973----,00.html, accessed June 10, 2005.

5. The percentage of foreign to domestic workers in Singapore has grown steadily, from 3.2 in 1970 to 7.4 percent in 1980, and from 16.1 in 1990 to 29.2 percent in 2000 (see Huang and Yeoh 2003, 80, table 1). *Country Reports on Human Rights Practice, 2004* compiled by the US State Department (2005, 34) states that "because of a domestic labor shortage, approximately 600,000 foreign workers [in Singapore] were employed legally, constituting about 30

percent of the total work force. There were no reliable estimates of the number of foreigners working illegally."

6. In addition to measures for controlling and managing its labor market, Singapore's borders are tightly guarded and policed against illegal migrants. Attempts to enter Singapore's territories by land and sea are frequently reported in the media. On June 13, 2005, three Bangladeshi men, aged twenty to twenty-five, were caught as they swam from Johor, Malaysia toward Singapore at 3:40 a.m. There were seventy-four cases of illegal immigrants trying to enter Singapore by sea from January to mid-June 2005 (ChannelNewsAsia.com 2005).

7. Worksite accidents are a major concern of Singapore's Ministry of Manpower. In the first half of 2004, it was reported that forty-six workers died in factories and on construction sites, seventeen more than during the same period the previous year. See "Accidents at Worksites and Factories Claim 46 Lives in First Half of 2004," *Channel News Asia*, July 22, 2004, http://www.channelnewsasia.com/stories/singaporelocalnews/view/97073/1/.html, accessed May 3, 2004. See also, "3 Thai Workers Found Dead at Worksite," *The Straits Times Interactive*, February 13, 2005, http://www.straitstimes.asia1.com/sub/storyprintfriendly/0,5578,300580-1108331940,0, accessed February 14, 2005.

8. This characterization of Thais is a personal observation by Lee Kwan Ho, an overseer at a construction site in Singapore.

9. Other controversial cases are the death and abuse of foreign domestic workers in Singapore, especially those coming from Indonesia and the Philippines. Statistics released by the Indonesian embassy in Singapore show that between 1999 and 2003, a total of eighty-nine Indonesian foreign domestic workers were killed either from falling from high-rise flats while doing house chores, or committing suicide due to work-related and other pressures, or as a result of abuse by their employers. Of the eighty-nine deaths, fifty-one were accidents, twenty-five were suicides, and another thirteen cases are still being investigated (G. Sim 2003; *Straits Times* 2004).

10. Interviews, February 8 and September 12, 2004.

11. I compare these records with a study by Chao Tze Cheng of Singapore's Institute of Science and Forensic Medicine, who was the first to bring this matter to the attention of the Thai embassy in Singapore. The study shows that "from May 1982 to December 1990, 235 Thais died in this sudden and unexplained way. Another 317 died between 1991 and 1996" (*Straits Times* 1997).

12. Fieldnote, September 12, 2004.

13. Fieldnotes, January 22 and February 8, 2004.

14. Sim (2005b) reported a dispute concerning a "dirty and unsafe" workers' dormitory in Tuas, housing more than three hundred Bangladeshi and Indian workers. The workers went on strike by refusing to leave their dormitory to go to work. They complained that the dormitory's common areas, such as the corridors, kitchen, and toilets, were filthy. The management charged each worker 93 Singapore dollars per month.

15. Fieldnotes, February 22 and May 17, 2005.

16. Under such highly risky and uncertain conditions as the SARS epidemic in Hong Kong in 2003, for example, Jaroonsri, a Thai domestic worker there, firmly insisted that "I can't give up. I need money to support my family. It's hard to find a well-paid job like this in Thailand" (cited in Chayada 2003). Somsak, a migrant worker from Nakhon Ratchasima who had worked in Singapore for eight years, announced proudly that "when I send money home, it's one of the happiest moments of my life here" (cited in Supara 2002).

Chapter 7 Conclusion

1. This is poignantly captured in Mike Phiromphon's (2001b) song by the title "*Lakhon chiwit*" on his album *Ruam hit khon su chiwit chut thi* 1 [Collection of song hits for the fighters in the endeavors to make a living, vol. 1], released by GMM Grammy.

2. Fieldnote, November 22, 2005.

3. The role of music in shaping workers' transborder identities is worth deeper exploration.

4. Fieldnote, September 16, 2006.

5. Fieldnote, June 8, 2006.

References

Books and Articles

Adorno, Theodore W. 1962. *Introduction to the Sociology of Music*. Translated by E. B. Ashton. New York: The Seabury Press.

Agamben, Giorgio. 1993. *The Coming Community*. Translated by Michael Hardt. Minneapolis: University of Minnesota Press.

—. 1998. *Homo Sacer: Sovereign Power and Bare Life*. Translated by Daniel Heller-Roazen. Stanford: Stanford University Press.

—. 2005. *State of Exception*. Translated by Kevin Attell. Chicago: University of Chicago Press.

Aguilar, Filomeno V., Jr. 1999. "Ritual Passage and the Reconstruction of Selfhood in International Labour Migration." *Sojourn* 14 (1): 98–139.

—, ed. 2002. *Filipinos in Global Migrations: At Home in the World?* Quezon City: Philippine Migration Research Network and Philippine Social Science Council.

Agustin, Laura. 2006. "The Disappearing of a Migration Category: Migrants Who Sell Sex." *Journal of Ethnic and Migration Studies* 32: 29–48.

Allen, James. 2003. "Voices of Migrants in Asia: A Panorama of Perspectives." Paper presented at the Regional Conference on Migration, Development, and Pro-Poor Policy Choices in Asia, organized by the Refugee and Migratory Movements Research Unit, Bangladesh, and the Department for International Development, UK, June 22–24.

Amit, Vered, ed. 2000. *Constructing the Field: Ethnographic Fieldwork in the Contemporary World*. London: Routledge.

Ananta, Aris, and Evi Nurvidya Arifin, eds. 2004. *International Migration in Southeast Asia*. Singapore: Institute of Southeast Asian Studies.

Appadurai, Arjun. 1993. "Disjuncture and Difference in the Global Cultural Economy." In *The Phantom Public Sphere*, edited by Bruce Robbins, 269–95. Minneapolis: University of Minnesota Press.

——————. 1999. "Global Ethnoscapes: Notes and Queries for a Transnational Anthropology." In *Migration, Diasporas and Transnationalism*, edited by Steven Vertovec and Robin Cohen, 463–83. Cheltenham, UK: Edward Elgar Publishing.

Appadurai, Arjun, and Carol A. Breckenridge. 1989. "On Moving Targets." *Public Culture* 2: i–iv.

Askew, Marc, and Erik Cohen. 2004. "Pilgrimage and Prostitution: Contrasting Modes of Border Tourism in Lower South Thailand." *Tourism Recreation Research* 29: 89–104.

Atkinson, Paul. 1990. *The Ethnographic Imagination: Textual Constructions of Reality*. London: Routledge.

Ayal, Eliezer B. 1992. "Thailand's Development: The Role of Bangkok." *Pacific Affairs* 65(3): 353–67.

Bales, Kevin. 2002. "Because She Looks Like a Child." In Ehrenreich and Hochschild 2002, 207–29.

Besio, Kathryn. 2005. "Telling Stories to Hear Autoethnography: Researching Women's Lives in Northern Pakistan." *Gender, Place and Culture* 12: 317–31.

Bottomley, Gillian. 1992. *From Another Place: Migration and the Politics of Culture*. Melbourne: Cambridge University Press.

Bourdieu, Pierre. 1977. *Outline of a Theory of Practice*. Translated by Richard Nice. Cambridge: Cambridge University Press.

——————. 1990. *The Logic of Practice*. Translated by Richard Nice. Stanford: Stanford University Press.

Brazil, David. 2004. *No Money, No Honey: A Candid Look at Sex-for-Sale in Singapore*. 5th ed. Singapore: Angsana Books.

Castles, Stephen, and Mark J. Miller. 1998. *The Age of Migration: International Population Movements in the Modern World*. 2nd ed. London: Macmillian Press.

Chang, Gordon H. 1999. "Writing the History of Chinese Immigrant to America." *The South Atlantic Quarterly* 98(1/2): 135–42.

Channel New Asia. 2004. "Accidents at Worksites and Factories Claim 46 Lives in the First Half of 2004," July 22.

Charuwan Thammawat. 1997. *Phumpanya molam ek: khwam rungrot khong adit lae panha khong molam nai patchuban* [The wisdom of top *molam* singers: the prosperity of the past and the problems of *molam* in the present]. Mahasarakham, Thailand: Faculty of Humanities and Social Sciences, Mahasarakham University.

Chayada Roongsamai. 2003. "An Added Job Risk." *Bangkok Post*, May 18.

Chia, Tze Yong. 2002/2003. "Listen to the Thais Speak: The Case of Golden Mile Complex." B.Soc.Sci honors thesis, Department of Geography, National University of Singapore.

Chiew Seen Kong. 1995. "Citizens and Foreign Labour in Singapore." In *Crossing Borders: Transmigration in Asia Pacific*, edited by J. H. Ong, K. B. Chan, and S. B. Chew, 472–86. Singapore: Prentice Hall.

Chitraporn Vanaspong. 2002. "A Portrait of the Lady: The Portrayal of Thailand and Its Prostitutes in the International Media." In Thorbek and Bandana 2002, 139–55.

Clifford, James. 1997. *Routes: Travel and Translation in the Late Twentieth Century*. Cambridge, MA: Harvard University Press.

Cohen, Christine. 1996. "Diasporas and the Nation-State: From Victims to Challengers." *International Affairs* 72(3): 507–20.

Connell, John, and Chris Gibson. 2004. "Cultural Industry Production in Remote Places: Indigenous Popular Music in Australia." In *Cultural Industries and the Production of Culture*, edited by D. Power and A. J. Scott, 243–58. London and New York: Routledge.

Connell, Robert W. 1995. *Masculinities*. Berkeley: University of California Press.

———. 1998. "Masculinities and Globalization." *Men and Masculinities* 1(1): 3–23.

———. 2000. *The Men and the Boys*. Berkeley: University of California Press.

Connell, Robert W. and James Messerschmidt. 2005. "Hegemonic Masculinity: Rethinking the Concept." *Gender and Society* 19(6): 829–59.

Constable, Nicole. 1997. *Maid to Order in Hong Kong: Stories of Filipina Workers*. Ithaca, New York: Cornell University Press.

———. 1999. "At Home but Not at Home: Filipina Narratives of Ambivalent Returns." *Cultural Anthropology* 14(2): 203–28.

———. 2005. *Guest People: Hakka Identity in China and Abroad*. Seattle: University of Washington Press.

Curran, Sara R. "Agency, Accountability, and Embedded Relations: What's Love Got to Do With It?" *Journal of Marriage and Family* 64(3): 577–84.

Curran, Sara R., Filiz Garip, Chang Y. Chung, and Kanchana Tangchonlatip. 2005. "Gendered Migrant Social Capital: Evidence from Thailand." *Social Forces*. 84(1): 225–56.

Dararat Mettarikanon. 2003. *Kanmueang song fang Khong* [The politics on both sides of the Mekong River]. Bangkok: Matichon.

Darwin, Muhadjir, Anna Marie Wattie, and Susi Eja Yuarsi, eds. 2003. *Living on the Edges: Cross-Border Mobility and Sexual Exploitation in the Greater Southeast Asia Sub-Region*. Yogyakarta: Center for Population and Policy Studies, Gadjahmada University.

Dashefsky, Arnold, and Bernard Lazerwitz. 1983. "The Role of Religious Identification in North American Migration to Israel." *Journal for the Scientific Study of Religion* 22(3): 263–75.

Day, Lincoln H., and Ahnet Icduygu. 1998. "The Effect of International Migration on Religious Observance and Attitudes in Turkey." *Journal for the Scientific Study of Religion* 37(4): 596–607.

Derks, Annuska. 2000. *Combating Trafficking in South-East Asia: A Review of Policy and Programme Responses*. Geneva: International Organization for Migration.

Dobbs, Stephen. 2003. *The Singapore River: A Social History 1819–2002*. Singapore: Singapore University Press.

Donaldson, Mike, Raymond Hibbins, Richard Howson, and Bob Pease, eds. 2009. *Migrant Men: Critical Studies of Masculinities and the Migration Experience*. New York: Routledge.

Duara, Prasenjit. 1997. "Transnationalism and the Predicament of Sovereignty: China, 1900–1945. *The American Historical Review* 102(4):1030–1551.

Ehrenreich, Barbara, and Arlie Russell Hochschild, eds. 2002. *Global Woman: Nannies, Maids, and Sex Workers in the New Economy*. New York: Metropolitan Books.

Elmhirst, Rebecca, and Ratna Saptari, eds. 2004. *Labour in Southeast Asia: Local Processes in a Globalized World*. London: RoutledgeCurzon.

Employment of Foreign Workers Act. Singapore: Ministry of Manpower, January 1, 1991. http://www.mom.gov.sg/NRrdonlyres/2F03CDE4–3B1A-43DE-8933-34ABC638A5458/7612/WPSPassConditions.pdf, accessed June 26, 2006.

Erlanger, Steven. 1990. "Singapore Journal: 'Nightmare Death" Fells Thais and Nations Bicker." *New York Times*, May 8.

Ewing-Chow, Michael. 2001. "Singapore: Legal Issues Relating to Thai Migrant Workers." In Supang Chantavanich et al. 2001a, 223–36.

Faist, Thomas. 2000. "Transnationalization in International Migration: Implications for the Study of Citizenship and Culture." *Ethnic and Racial Studies* 23(2): 189–222.

———. 2004. "The Border-Crossing Expansion of Social Space: Concepts, Questions, and Topics." In *Transnational Social Spaces: Agents, Networks and Institutions*, edited by Thomas Faist and Eyup Ozveren, 1–34. Aldershot: Ashgate Publishing.

Foucault, Michel. 1977. *Discipline and Punish: The Birth of the Prison*. London: Allen Lane.

———. 1980. *The History of Sexuality. Vol. 1, An Introduction*. Translated by Robert Hurley. New York: Vintage Books.

Fuller, Theodore D., Paul Lightfoot, and Peerasit Kamnuansilpa. 1985. "Toward Migration Management: A Field Experiment in Thailand." *Economic Development and Cultural Change* 33(3): 601–21.

Gardner, Katy. 1995. *Global Migrants, Local Lives: Travel and Transformation in Rural Bangladesh*. Oxford: Clarendon Press.

Geertz, Clifford. 1973. *The Interpretation of Cultures*. New York: Basic Books.

Giddens, Anthony. 1979. *Central Problems in Social Theory: Action, Structure and Contradiction in Social Analysis*. Berkeley: University of California Press.

—————. 1992. *The Transformation of Intimacy: Sexuality, Love, and Eroticism in Modern Societies*. Cambridge, UK: Polity Press.

Gold, Raymond L. 2005. "Roles in Sociological Field Observations." In Pole 2005, 93–101.

Guarnizo, Luis, and Michael P. Smith. 1998. "The Locations of Transnationalism." In *Transnationalism from Below*. Vol. 6., edited by Luis Guarnizo and Michael P. Smith, 3–34. New Brunswick, New Jersey: Transactions Publishers.

Harper, T. N. 1997. "Globalism and the Pursuit of Authenticity: The Making of a Diasporic Public Sphere in Singapore." *Sojourn* 12(2): 261–92.

Hayes, Michael. 2004. "Capitalism and Cultural Relative: The Thai Pop Industry, Capitalism and Western Cultural Values." In *Refashioning Pop Music in Asia*, edited by Allen Chun, Ned Rossiter, and Brian Shoesmith, 17–31. London and New York: RoutledgeCurzon.

Heisler, Barbara Schmitter. 2000. "The Sociology of Immigration: From Assimilation to Segmented Integration, from the American Experience to the Global Arena." In *Migration Theory: Talking Across Disciplines*, edited by Caroline B. Brettell, James F. Hollifield, 77–96. London: Routledge.

Heng, Geraldine, and Janadas Devan. 1995. "'State Fatherhood': The Politics of Nationalism, Sexuality and Race in Singapore." In Ong and Peletz 1995, 195–215.

Herzfeld, Michael. 1985. *The Poetics of Manhood: Contest and Identity in a Cretan Mountain Village*. Princeton, New Jersey: Princeton University Press.

—————. 1997. *Cultural Intimacy: Social Poetics in the Nation-State*. New York: Routledge.

Hewison, Kevin. 2006. "Thai Workers in Hong Kong." In Hewison and Young 2006, 90–109.

Hewison, Kevin, and Ken Young, eds. 2006. *Transnational Migration and Work in Asia*. London: Routledge.

—————. 2006. "Introduction: Globalization and Migrant Workers in Asia." In Hewison and Young 2006, 1–11.

Hochschild, Arlie Russell. 1983. *The Managed Heart: Commercialization of Human Feeling*. Berkeley: University of California Press.

Hollifield, James F. 2000. "The Politics of International Migration: How Can We Bring the State Back In?" In *Migration Theory: Talking Across Disciplines*, edited by Caroline B. Brettell and James F. Hollifield, 137–85. New York: Routledge.

Huang, Shirlena, and Brenda S. A. Yeoh. 2003. "The Difference Gender Makes: State Policy and Contract Migrant Workers in Singapore." *Asian and Pacific Migration Journal* 12: 75–97.

Hugo, Graeme. 2004. "International Migration in Southeast Asia since World War II." In Ananta and Arifin 2004, 28–70.

Hui, Weng-Tat. 1997. "Regionalization, Economic Restructuring and Labour Migration in Singapore." *International Migration* 35: 100–20.

Human Rights Watch. 2000. *Owed Justice: Thai Women Trafficked into Debt Bondage in Japan.* New York: Human Rights Watch.

Iyer, Avanti, Theresa W. Devasahayam, and Brenda S. A. Yeoh. 2004. "A Clean Bill of Health: Filipinas as Domestic Workers in Singapore." *Asian and Pacific Migration Journal* 13: 11–38.

Jackson, Peter, Philip Crang, and Claire Dwyer, eds. 2004. *Transnational Spaces.* London: Routledge.

Jones, Huw, and Tieng Pardthaisong. 1999. "The Commodification of International Migration: Findings from Thailand." *Journal of Economic and Social Geography/ Tijdschrift voor Economische en Sociale Geografie* 90(1): 32–46.

Kampoon Boontawee. 1976. *Luk Isan* [Child of the Northeast]. Bangkok: Bannakit.

Kandel, William, and Douglas S. Massey. 2002. "The Culture of Mexican Migration: A Theoretical and Empirical Analysis." *Social Forces* 80(3): 981–1004.

Kearney, Michael. 1986. "From the Invisible Hand to Visible Feet: Anthropological Studies of Migration and Development." *Annual Review of Anthropology* 15: 331–61.

————. 1995. "The Local and the Global: The Anthropology of Globalization and Transnationalism." *Annual Review of Anthropology* 24: 547–65.

Kempadoo, Kamala. 1998. "Introduction: Globalizing Sex Workers' Rights." In Kempadoo and Doezma 1998, 1–28.

————, ed. 2005. *Trafficking and Prostitution Reconsidered: New Perspectives on Migration, Sex Work, and Human Rights.* Boulder: Paradigm Publishers.

Kempadoo, Kamala, and Jo Doezma, eds. 1998. *Global Sex Workers: Rights, Resistance, and Redefinition.* New York: Routledge.

Keyes, Charles F. 1967. "Isan: Regionalism in Northeast Thailand." Data Paper 65, Cornell University, Department of Asian Studies, Southeast Asia Program.

————. 1983. "The Observer Observed: Changing Identities of Ethnographers in a Northeastern Thai Village." In *Fieldwork: The Human Experiences*, edited by Robert Lawless, Vinson H. Sutlive, Jr., and Mario D. Zamora, 169–94. New York: Gordon and Breach.

————. 1984. "Mother or Mistress but Never a Monk: Buddhist Notions of Female Gender in Rural Thailand." *American Ethnologist* 11(2): 223–41.

————. 1986. "Ambiguous Gender: Male Initiation in a Buddhist Society." In *New Perspectives on Religion and Gender*, edited by Caroline Bynum, Stevan Harrell, and Paula Richman, 66–96. Boston: Beacon Press.

—. 2002. "Migrants and Protestors: 'Development' in Northeastern Thailand." Keynote Address. Presented at the 8th International Conference on Thai Studies. Nakhon Phanom, Thailand.

—. n.d. "Persistence of the Village as a Viable Community in a Post-Development World: Reflections on Rural Northeastern Thailand with Reference to Cambodia." Unpublished manuscript. Department of Anthropology, University of Washington.

Khondker, Habibul Haque. 2003. "A Tale of Two Communities: Bangladeshis in Singapore." In *Approaching Transnationalisms: Studies on Transnational Societies, Multicultural Contacts, and Imaginings of Home*, edited by Brenda S. A. Yeoh, Michael W. Charney, and Tong Chee Kiong, 321–36. Dordrecht, Netherlands: Kluwer Academic Publishers.

Kirsch, A. Thomas. 1966. "Development and Mobility among the Phu Thai of Northeast Thailand." *Asian Survey* 6(7): 370–78.

—. 1982. "Buddhism, Sex-Roles and Thai Society." In *Women of Southeast Asia*, edited by Penny van Esterik, 16–41. Center for Southeast Asian Studies Occasional Paper 9, Northern Illinois University.

Kleinman, Arthur, Veena Das, and Margaret Lock, eds. 1997. *Social Suffering*. Berkeley: University of California Press.

Kondo, Dorinne K. 1990. *Crafting Selves: Power, Gender, and Discourses of Identity in a Japanese Workplace*. Chicago: University of Chicago Press.

Kong, Lily. 1993. "Negotiating Conceptions of 'Sacred Space': A Case Study of Religious Buildings in Singapore." *Transactions of the Institute of British Geographers* 18(3): 342–58.

Kuo, E. C. Y, and J. S. T. Quah. 1988. *Religion in Singapore: Report of a National Survey*. Singapore: Ministry of National Development.

Laclau, Ernesto. 2007. "Bare Life or Social Indeterminacy." In *Giorgio Agamben: Sovereignty and Life*, edited by Mathew Calarco and Steven DeCaroli, 11–22. Stanford: Stanford University Press.

"Letter from Bangkok." 1984. *MERIP Reports, No. 123: Migrant Workers in the Middle East*, 26.

Levitt, Peggy. 1998a "Local-Level Global Religion: The Case of US–Dominican Migration." *Journal for the Scientific Study of Religion* 37(1): 74–89.

—. 1998b. "Social Remittances: Migration Driven Local-Level Forms of Cultural Diffusion." *International Migration Review* 32(4): 926–48.

—. 2001. *The Transnational Villagers*. Berkeley: University of California Press.

Levitt, Peggy, and Ninna Nyberg-Sorensen. 2004. "The Transnational Turn in Migration Studies." *Global Migration Perspectives* 6. Geneva: Global Commission on International Migration, http://www.gcim.org, accessed March 23, 2005.

Li, Xueying. 2004. "Think Foreign Workers Dislike Us? You Will Be Surprised." *Sunday Times*, September 5.

Lim, Gerrie. 2004. *Invisible Trade: High-Class Sex for Sale in Singapore*. Singapore: Monsoon Books.

Lorente, Beatriz P., Nicola Piper, Shen Hsiu-Hua, and Brenda S. A. Yeoh, eds. 2005. *Asian Migrations: Sojourning, Displacement, Homecoming and Other Travels*. Singapore: Asia Research Institute, National University of Singapore.

Low, Linda. 1995. "Population Movement in the Asia Pacific Region: Singapore Perspective." *International Migration Review* 29: 745–64.

Mahler, Sarah J., and Patricia Pessar. 2001. "Gendered Geographies of Power: Analyzing Gender across Transnational Spaces." *Identities: Global Studies in Culture and Power* 7: 441–59.

Marigold, J. A. 1995. "Narratives of Masculinity and Transnational Migration: Filipino Workers in the Middle East." In Ong and Peletz 1995, 274–98.

McCargo, Duncan, and Krisdawan Hongladarom. 2004. "Contesting Isan-ness: Discourses of Politics and Identity in Northeast Thailand." *Asian Ethnicity* 5(2): 219–34.

Meaker, Linda. 2002. "A Social Response to Transnational Prostitution in Queensland, Australia." In Thorbek and Bandana 2002, 59–68.

Miller, Terry E. 1998. "Thailand." In Miller and Williams 1998, 218–334.

Miller, Terry E., and Sean Williams, eds. 1998. *The Garland Encyclopedia of World Music*. Vol. 4, *Southeast Asia*. New York: Garland Publishing.

—————. "The Impact of Modernization on Traditional Music." In Miller and Williams 1998, 113–43.

Mills, Mary Beth. 1995. "Attack of the Widow Ghosts: Gender, Death, and Modernity in Northeast Thailand." In Ong and Peletz 1995, 244–73.

—————. 1997. "Contesting the Margins of Modernity: Women, Migration, and Consumption in Thailand." *American Ethnologist* 24(1): 37–61.

—————. 1999a. *Thai Women in the Global Labor Force: Consuming Desires, Contested Selves*. New Brunswick: Rutgers University Press.

—————. 1999b. "Migrant Labor Takes a Holiday: Reworking Modernity and Marginality in Contemporary Thailand." *Critique of Anthropology* 19(1): 31–51.

—————. 2003. "Gender and Inequality in the Global Labor Force." *Annual Review of Anthropology* 32: 41–62.

Ministry of Foreign Affairs, Royal Thai Embassy, Singapore. 2004. "Khomun Kan Lueaktang Nok Ratcha-anachak" [Information for Overseas Voters Concerning the Election]. August 16.

—————. 2005. "Sathiti kan ok bai moranabat" [Statistics on Death Certificates Issued by the Royal Thai Embassy in Singapore]. Unpublished report.

Ministry of Information and the Arts, Singapore. 1992. *The Need for the Maintenance of the Religious Harmony Act*. Singapore: Ministry of Information and the Arts.

Ministry of Labor Affairs, Thailand. 2006. *Sathanakan lae khwam tongkan raeng ngan Thai nai tang prathet 2548–2549* [labor situations and international demands of Thai workers 2005–2006]. Bangkok: Ministry of Labor Affairs.

Ministry of Manpower, Singapore. n.d. http://www.mom.gov.sg/MOM/CDA_PopUp/1,1135,4023--------6996----,00.html, accessed June 10, 2005.

Monzini, Paola. 2005. *Sex Traffic: Prostitution, Crime and Exploitation*. London: Zed Books.

Morris, Desmond. 1997. *Intimate Behaviour*. New York: Kodansha International.

Murray, Alison. 1998. "Debt-Bondage and Trafficking: Don't Believe the Hype." In Kempadoo and Doezma 1998, 51–64.

————. 2001. *Pink Fits: Sex, Subculture and Discourses in the Asia-Pacific*. Victoria, Australia: Monash Asia Institute, Monash University Press.

Myers, Scott M. 2000. "The Impact of Religious Involvement on Migration." *Social Forces* 79(2): 755–83.

Naficy, Hamid. 2001. *An Accented Cinema: Exilic and Diasporic Filmmaking*. Princeton, New Jersey: Princeton University Press.

New Oxford American Dictionary, The. 2001. New York: Oxford University Press.

Ng Eng Hen. 2004a. "Opening Address." Global Workforce Summit. Ritz Carton Hotel, Singapore, http://www.mom.gov.sg/MOM/CDA/0,1858,3669-----178_2001~3278_2004---4973----,00.html, accessed January 17, 2005.

————. 2004a. *Singapore Yearbook of Manpower Statistics*. Singapore: Ministry of Manpower.

Nidhi Eoseewong. 1995. *Pha khaoma, pha sin, kangkeng nai* [Wrap-around loincloths, female tube skirts, and underwear]. Bangkok: Samnak Phim Matichon.

Noulmook Sutdhibhasilp. 2002. "Migrant Sex-Workers in Canada." In Thorbek and Bandana 2002, 173–92.

Office of Labour Affairs, Royal Thai Embassy, Singapore. 2004. "Sathanakan Raeng-ngan Nai Prathet Singapore" [The labor situation in Singapore]. Technical Report.

Ofori, George. n.d. "Foreign Construction Workers in Singapore." Working Paper. Unpublished manuscript.

Ong, Aihwa. 1999. *Flexible Citizenship: The Cultural Logics of Transnationality*. Durham: Duke University Press.

Ong, Aihwa, and Michael G. Peletz, eds. 1995. *Bewitching Women, Pious Men: Gender and Body Politics in Southeast Asia*. Berkeley: University of California Press.

Osella, Filippo, and Caroline Osella. 2000a. *Social Mobility in Kerala: Modernity and Identity in Conflict.* London: Pluto Press.

————. 2000b. "Migration, Money and Masculinity in Kerala." *The Journal of the Royal Anthropological Institute* 6: 117–33.

Ottenberg, Simon. 1990. "Thirty Years of Fieldnotes: Changing Relationship to the Text." In *Fieldnotes: The Making of Anthropology*, edited by Roger Sanjek, 139–60. Ithaca, New York: Cornell University Press.

Parnwell, Michael J. G. 2005. "Developmental Implications of Transnational Migration in Southeast Asia." Paper presented at the Asia-Europe Foundation Conference "Contemporary Migrations in Asia and Europe: Exploring Transnationalism, Development and Multiple Linkages," organized by Scalabrini Migration Center, Manila, Philippines, January 12–13.

Parrenas, Rhacel Salazar. 2001a. *Servants of Globalization: Women, Migration and Domestic Work.* Stanford: Stanford University Press.

————. 2001b. "Mothering from a Distance: Emotions, Gender, and Intergenerational Relations in Filipino Transnational Families." *Feminist Studies* 27(2): 361–90.

————. 2002. "The Care Crisis in the Philippines: Children and Transnational Families in the New Global Economy." In Ehrenreich and Hochschild 2002, 39–54.

————. 2005. *Children of Global Migration: Transnational Families and Gendered Woes.* Stanford, California: Stanford University Press.

Pasuk Phongpaichit and Chris Baker. 2002. *Thailand: Economy and Politics.* 2nd ed. New York: Oxford University Press.

Pataya Ruenkaew. 2002. "The Transnational Prostitution of Thai Women to Germany: A Variety of Transnational Labour Migration?" In Thorbek and Bandana 2002, 69–85.

Pattana Kitiarsa. 2003. *Lives of Hunting Dogs: Rethinking Thai Masculinities through an Ethnography of Muay Thai.* Nakhon Ratchasima, Thailand: Suranaree University of Technology.

————. 2005a. "Village Transnationalism: Transborder Identities among Thai-Isan Migrant Workers in Singapore." Paper presented at the Annual Meeting of the Association for Asian Studies (Panel No. 122: Permeable Borders), organized by the Association for Asian Studies (AAS), Chicago, Illinois, USA, March 31–April 6.

————. 2005b. "Village Transnationalism: Transborder Identities among Thai-Isan Workers in Singapore." Paper presented at the 9th International Conference on Thai Studies, organized by the Center for Southeast Asian Studies, Northern Illinois University, DeKalb, Illinois, April 3. Also presented at the International Conference on Transborder Issues in the Greater Mekong

Region, organized by the Faculty of Liberal Arts, Ubon Ratchathani University, Thailand, June 30.

————. 2005c. "The Ghost of Transnational Labor Migration: Death and Other Tragedies of Thai Workers in Singapore." In *Asian Migrations: Sojourning, Homecoming and Other Travels*, edited by Beatriz P. Lorente, Nicola Piper, Shen Hsiu-Hua, and Brenda S. A. Yeoh, 194–220. Singapore: Asia Research Institute, National University of Singapore.

————. 2006a. "Sex in Overseas Labor Migration: Informalizing Economy, Traveling Biographies, and Transient Intimacies among Thai Migrant Workers in Singapore." Paper presented at the International Workshop on Sexuality and Migration in Asia, organized by Asia Research Institute, National University of Singapore, April 10–11.

————. 2006b. "The Romance of Overseas Migrant Workers: Popular Music and the Transformation of Cultural Intimacies in Northeastern Thailand." Paper presented at the AAS Annual Meeting, San Francisco, California, USA, April 6–9.

————. 2006c. "Village Transnationalism: Transborder Identities among Isan-Thai Migrant Workers in Singapore." ARI Working Paper Series 71 (November), Asia Research Institute, National University of Singapore, http://www.ari.nus.edu.sg/docs/wps/wps06_071.pdf.

————. 2006d. "Headnotes, Heartnotes and Persuasive Ethnography of Thai Migrant Workers in Singapore" *International Sociology Association E-Bulletin* 5: 87–99. Reprinted in *Journal of the Mekong Society, Khon Kaen University* 3(1): 53–71.

————. 2006e. "My Wife Is Not Here With Me: The Private Life of Thai Workmen in Singapore." Focus Group Report, Asia Research Institute, National University of Singapore.

Penporn Tirasawat. 1978. "Economic and Housing Adjustment of Migrants in Greater Bangkok." *International Migration Review* 12(1): 93–103.

Phaibun Phaeng-ngoen. 1991. *Klon lam: Phumpanya khong Isan* [Poetical texts of *lam*: The wisdom of Isan]. Bangkok: Samnak Phim Odeon Store.

Pimpawan Boonmongkon, Philip Guest, Amporn Marddent, and Steve Sanders. 2003. "From Trafficking to Sex Work: Burmese Migrants in Thailand." In *Living on the Edges: Cross-Border Mobility and Sexual Exploitation in the Greater Southeast Asia Sub-Region*, edited by Muhadjir Darwin, Anna Marie Wattie, and Susi Eja Yuarsi, 163–229. Yogyakarta: Center for Population and Policy Studies, Gadjahmada University.

Piper, Nicola. 2006. "Economic Migration and the Transnationalisation of the Rights of Foreign Workers: A Concept Note." ARI Working Paper Series 58 (February), Asia Research Institute, National University of Singapore, http://www.ari.nus.edu.sg/pub/wps.htm.

Pole, Christopher, ed. 2005. *Fieldwork*. Vol. 2. London: SAGE Publications.

Porntipa Atipas. 2001. "The Regional Economic Crisis and the Migration of Thai Workers to Singapore." In Supang et al. 2001a, 129–170.

Prapairat Ranataloan Mix. 2002. "Four Cases from Hamburg." In Thorbek and Bandana 2002, 86–99.

Pratt, Geraldine, and Brenda Yeoh. 2003. "Transnational (Counter) Topographies." *Gender, Place and Culture: A Journal of Feminist Geography* 10(2): 159–66.

Rafael, Vicente L., and Itty Abraham. 1997. "Introduction." *Sojourn* 12(1):145–52.

————. 2000. *White Love and Other Events in Filipino History*. Duram, North Carolina: Duke University Press.

Rahman, Md. Mizanur. 2006. "Foreign Manpower in Singapore: Classes, Policies and Management." ARI Working Paper Series 57 (February), Asia Research Institute, National University of Singapore, http://www.nus.ari.edu.sg/pub/wps.htm.

Rahman, Md. Mizanur and Lian Kwen Fee. 2005. "Bangladeshi Migrant Workers in Singapore: The View from Inside." *Asia-Pacific Population Journal* 20: 63–89.

Ratana Tosakul Boonmathya. 2005. "Women, Transnational Migration, and Cross-Cultural Marriages: Experiences of '*Phanrayaa-farang*' from Rural Northeastern Thailand." Paper presented at the AAS Annual Meeting, Chicago, Illinois, March 31–April 3. Also presented at the 9th International Conference on Thai Studies, Northern Illinois University, DeKalb, April 3–6.

Reynolds, Craig J. 1987. *Thai Radical Discourse: The Real Face of Thai Feudalism Today*. Ithaca, New York: Southeast Asia Program, Cornell University.

————. 2006. *Seditious Histories: Contesting Thai and Southeast Asian Pasts*. Seattle: University of Washington Press.

Rigg, Jonathan. 1989. *International Contract Labor Migration and the Village Economy: The Case of Tambon Don Han, Northeastern Thailand*. Honolulu: East-West Population Institute.

Salih, Ruba. 2003. *Gender in Transnationalism: Home, Longing and Belonging among Moroccan Migrant Women*. London: Routledge.

Sanders, Teela. 2006. "Researching Sex Work: Dynamics, Difficulties and Decisions." In *The SAGE Handbook of Fieldwork*, edited by Dick Hobbs and Richard Wright, 201–21. London: SAGE Publications.

Sangha, and Executive Committee, Palelai Buddhist Temple. 2007. *Phra Maha Chedi Dhammasathit at Palelai*. Singapore: Palelai Buddhist Temple.

Saranya Bunnak and Soawapha Bunmusik. 1985. *Raeng ngan Thai nai Singapore* [Thai laborers in Singapore]. Bangkok: Samakhom Sakhomsat Haeng Prathet Thai.

Sassen, Saskia. 1991. *The Global City: New York, London, Tokyo*. Princeton, New Jersey: Princeton University Press.

—————. 1994. "The Informal Economy: Between New Developments and Old Regulations." *The Yale Law Journal* 103: 2294–2304.

—————. 2002. "Global Cities and Survival Circuits." In Ehrenreich and Hochschild 2004, 254–74.

Schiller, Nina Glick, Linda Basch, and Cristina Szanton Blanc. 1995. "From Immigrant to Transmigrant: Theorizing Transnational Migration." *Anthropological Quarterly* 68(1): 48–63.

—————. 1994. *Nations Unbound: Transnational Projects, Postcolonial Predicaments and Deterritorialized Nation-States*. New York: Gordon and Breach.

—————, eds. 1998. *Towards a Transnational Perspective on Migration: Race, Class, Ethnicity and Nationalism Reconsidered*. New York: New York Academy of Sciences.

Scott, James C. 1976. *The Moral Economy of the Peasant: Rebellion and Subsistence in Southeast Asia*. New Haven: Yale University Press.

Sellek, Yoko. 2001. *Migrant Labor in Japan*. New York: Palgrave.

Sen, Faruk, and Sedef Koray. 2000. "Migrant Workers' Rights." *Human Rights: Concepts and Standards*, edited by Janusz Symonides, 327–41. Aldershot, Hampshire: Ashgate Publishing Limited.

Shaffir, William. 2005. "Managing a Convincing Self-Presentation: Some Personal Reflections on Entering the Field." In Pole 2005, 22–37.

Silvey, Rachel. 2004. "Power, Difference and Mobility: Feminist Advances in Migration Studies." *Progress in Human Geography* 28: 490–506.

Sim, Chi Yin. 2005. "Saved by Secret Calls." *The Electric New Paper*, May 31.

Sim, Glenys. 2003. "66 People Flushed out of Forest Hideout." *Straits Times*, September 25.

Singapore Department of Statistics. 2001. *Population Census 2000*. Singapore: Department of Statistics.

Singapore Health Promotion Board. 2003. *The Manual for Foreign Workers in Singapore*. Singapore: Health Promotion Board.

Smith, Michael Peter. 2001. *Transnational Urbanism: Locating Globalization*. Malden, MA: Blackwell.

Smith, Michael Peter, and Luis Guarnizo, eds. 1998. *Transnationalism from Below: Comparative Urban and Community Research*. New Brunswick, New Jersey: Transaction Publishers.

Sorensen, Ninna Nyberg, and Finn Stepputat. 2001. "Narrations of Authority and Mobility." *Identities: Global Studies in Culture and Power* 8: 313–42.

Sowell, Thomas. 1996. *Migrations and Cultures: A World View*. New York: Basic Books.

Stahl, Charles W., and Fred Arnold. 1986. "Overseas Workers' Remittances in Asian Development." *International Migration Review* 20(4): 899–925.

Stark, Oded and R. E. B. Lucas. 1988. "Migration, Remittances and the Family." *Economic Development and Cultural Change* 36: 465–81.

Stern, Aaron. 1998. *Thailand's Migration Situation and Its Relations with APEC Members and Other Countries in Southeast Asia.* Bangkok: Asian Research Center for Migration, Institute of Asian Studies, Chulalongkorn University.

Stocking, George W., Jr., ed. 1983. *Observers Observed: Essays on Ethnographic Fieldwork.* Madison, Wisconsin: University of Wisconsin Press.

Suchada Thaweesit. 2006. "Unfolding Cross-Ethno Sexual Intimacies of Thai Men: A Research Proposal." Unpublished manuscript.

Sullivan, Gerard, S. Gunasekaran, and Sununta Siengthai. 1992. "Labour Migration and Policy Formation in a Newly Industrialized Country: A Case Study of Illegal Thai Workers in Singapore." *ASEAN Economic Bulletin* 9(1): 75–76.

Supang Chantavanich. 1999. "Thailand's Responses to Transnational Migration during Economic Growth and Economic Downturn." *Sojourn* 14(1): 159–77.

Supang Chantavanich, Andreas Germershausen, and Allan Beesey, eds. 2000. *Thai Migrant Workers in East and Southeast Asia 1996–1997.* Bangkok: Asia Research Center for Migration, Institute of Asian Studies, Chulalongkorn University.

Supang Chantavanich, Andreas Germershausen, Chiaki Ito, Samarn Laodumrongchai, Jiraporn Chotipanich and Sajin Prachason. 2001a. *Thai Migrant Workers in East and Southeast Asia: The Prospects of Thailand's Migration Policy in Light of the Regional Economic Recession and Conditions in Destination Countries.* Bangkok: Asia Research Center for Migration, Institute of Asian Studies, Chulalongkorn University.

Supang Chantavanich, Suteera Nittayananta, Prapairat Ratanaolan-Mix, and Pataya Ruenkaew. Translated by Aaron Stern. 2001b. *The Migration of Thai Women to Germany: Causes, Living Conditions and Impacts for Thailand and Germany.* Bangkok: Asian Research Center for Migration, Institute of Asian Studies, Chulalongkorn University.

Supara Janchitfah. 2002. "Passports to Pain." *Bangkok Post*, June 30.

Suphaphim [pseud.]. 2004. "Chao Thai nai Farangset" [Thai people in France]. *Matichon Sutsapda* [Matichon Weekly], August 13–19.

Suriya Smutkupt and Pattana Kitiarsa. 1996. "Khon chai khop: Chiwit lae chumchon khong raeng ngan kham chat Thai nai Yipun" [The marginal people: The lives and communities of transnational Thai laborers in Japan]. In *Manutsaya witthaya kap lokaphiwat: Ruam botkhwam* [Anthropology and globalization: Thai experiences]. Nakhon Ratchasima, Thailand: Suranaree University of Technology.

Swearer, Donald K. 1995. *The Buddhist World of Southeast Asia.* New York: State University of New York Press.

Tadiar, Neferti Xina. 1997. "Domestic Bodies of the Philippines." *Soujourn* 12(2): 153–91.

Tamney, Joseph B., and Linda Hsueh-Ling Chiang. 2002. *Modernization, Globalization, and Confucianism in Chinese Societies*. Westport, Connecticut: Praeger.

Tan, K. Y. L. 2002. "The Legal and Institutional Framework and Issues of Multiculturalism in Singapore." In *Beyond Rituals and Riot: Ethnic Pluralism and Social Cohesion in Singapore*, edited by Lai Ah Eng, 98–113. Singapore: Eastern University Press.

Thai Sangha Samatca (Singapore). 2006. *Samatca Night: 6th Anniversary*. Singapore: Internal Printers.

Thak Chaloemtiarana. 2007. *Thailand: The Politics of Despotic Paternalism*. Chiang Mai: Silkworm Books.

Thorbek, Susanne, and Bandana Pattanaik, eds. 2002. *Transnational Prostitution: Changing Global Patterns*. London: Zed Books.

Toh, Ruby. 1993. *Foreign Workers in Singapore*. SILS Information Series. Singapore: Singapore Institute of Labor Studies.

Troung, Than Dam. 1990. *Sex, Money and Morality: Prostitution and Tourism in Southeast Asia*. London, Zed Books.

Ubonrat Siriyuvasak. 1990. "Commercialising the Sound of the People: *Pleng Luktoong* and the Thai Pop Music Industry." *Popular Music* 9(1): 61–77.

US State Department. 2005. *Country Reports on Human Rights Practices 2004*. Washington, DC: US State Department.

Warren, James F. 2003a. *Ah Ku and Karayuki-san: Prostitution in Singapore, 1870–1940*. Reprint, Singapore: Singapore University Press. First published 1993 by Oxford University Press.

————. 2003b. *Rickshaw Coolie: A People's History of Singapore, 1880–1940*. Singapore: Singapore University Press. First published 1986.

Watenabe, Satoko. 1998. "From Thailand to Japan: Migrant Sex Workers as Autonomous Subjects." In Kempadoo and Doezema 1998, 114–23.

Wee, Vivienne. 1976. "Buddhism in Singapore." Department of Sociology, National University of Singapore (mimeograph).

————. 1997. "Buddhism in Singapore." In *Understanding Singapore Society*, edited by Ong Jin Hui, Tong Chee Kiong, and Tan Ern Ser, 130–62. Singapore: Times Academic Press.

Willis, Katie, Brenda S. A. Yeoh, and S. M. Abdul Khader Fakhri. 2004. "Introduction: Transnationalism as a Challenge to the Nation." In Yeoh and Willis 2004, 1–15.

Wilson, Ara. 2004. *The Intimate Economies of Bangkok: Tomboys, Tycoons, and Avon Ladies in the Global City*. Berkeley: University of California Press.

Wolcott, Harry F. 2005. "Fieldwork: The Basic Arts." In Pole 2005, 102–29.

Wong, Deborah. 1995. "Thai Cassettes and Their Covers: Two Case Histories."

In *Asian Popular Culture*, edited by John Lent, 43–59. Boulder, Colorado: Westview Press.

—————. 1997. "Transience and Settlement: Singapore's Foreign Labor Policy." *Asian and Pacific Migration Journal* 6: 135–67.

—————. 1998. "Popular Music and Cultural Politics: Thailand." In Miller and Williams 1998, 95–112.

—————. 2000. "Men Who Built Singapore: Thai Workers in the Construction Industry." In *Thai Migrant Workers in East and Southeast Asia 1996–1997*, edited by Supang Chantavanich, Andreas Germershausen, and Allan Beesey, 58–107. Bangkok: Asia Research Center for Migration, Institute of Asian Studies, Chulalongkorn University.

—————. 2004. *Speak It Louder: Asian Americans Making Music.* New York: Routledge.

Wong, Yuen Lee. 1986. "Thai Buddhism in Singapore." Honors thesis, Department of Sociology, National University of Singapore.

Wuth Nontarit. 1996. "Alcohol Brings Downfall of Thai Workers." *Bangkok Post*, April 10.

Yamanaka, Keiko. 2004. "Citizenship and Differential Exclusion of Immigrants in Japan", in Yeoh and Willis 2004, 67–92.

Yang, Fenggang, and Helen Rose Ebaugh. 2000. "Religion and Ethnicity among New Immigrants: The Impact of Majority/Minority Status in Home and Host Countries." *Journal for the Scientific Study of Religion* 40(3): 367–78.

Yang, Xiushi. 1994. "A Sensitivity Analysis of Repeat Migration in the Study of Migrant Adjustment: The Case of Bangkok." *Demography* 31(4): 585–92.

Yao, Souchou. 2007. *Singapore: The State and the Culture of Excess.* London: Routledge.

Yeh, Christine. 1995. *Foreign Workers in Singapore.* SILS Information Series. Singapore: Singapore Institute of Labor Studies.

Yeoh, Brenda S. A. 2003a. "Approaching Transnationalism." In *Approaching Transnationalism: Studies on Transnational Societies, Multicultural Contacts, and Imaginings of Home*, edited by Brenda S. A. Yeoh, Michael W. Charney, and Tong Chee Kiong, 1–12. Dordrecht, Netherlands: Kluwer Academic Publishers.

—————. 2003b. *Contesting Space in Colonial Singapore: Power Relations and the Urban Built Environment.* Singapore: Singapore University Press.

—————. 2004. "Migration, International Labour and Multicultural Policies in Singapore." ARI Working Paper Series 19 (February), http://www.ari.nus.sg/pub/wps.htm, accessed October 10, 2006.

—————. 2006. "Bifurcated Labour: The Unequal Incorporation of Transmigrants in Singapore." *Journal of Economic and Social Geography/Tijdschrift voor Economische en Sociale Geografie* 97(1): 26–37.

Yeoh, Brenda S. A., Michael W. Charney, and Tong Chee Kiong. 2003. "Approaching Transnationalisms." In *Approaching Transnationalisms: Studies on Transnational Societies, Multicultural Contacts, and Imaginings of Home*, edited by Brenda S. A. Yeoh, Michael W. Charney, and Tong Chee Kiong, 1–12. Dordrecht, Netherlands: Kluwer Academic Publishers.

Yeoh, Brenda S. A., and Shirlena Huang. 1998. "Negotiating Public Space: Strategies and Styles of Migrant Female Domestic Workers in Singapore." *Urban Studies* 35(3): 583–602.

Yeoh, Brenda S. A., Shirlena Huang, and Joaquin Gonzalez III. 1999. "Migrant Female Domestic Workers: Debating the Economic, Social and Political Impacts in Singapore." *International Migration Review* 33(1): 114–36.

Yeoh, Brenda S. A., and Katie Willis 1999. "'Heart' and 'Wing,' Nation and Diaspora: Gendered Discourses in Singapore's Regionalisation Process." *Gender, Place and Culture* 6(4): 355–77.

———, eds. 2004. *State/Nation/Transnation: Perspectives on Transnationalism in the Asia Pacific*. London: RoutledgeCurzon.

———. 2005. "Singaporean and British Transmigrants in China and the Cultural Politics of 'Contact Zones.'" *Journal of Ethnic and Migration Studies* 31(2): 269–85.

Yongyuth Chalamwong. 2004. "Government Policies on International Migration: Illegal Workers in Thailand." In Ananta and Arifin 2004, 352–73.

Yusof, Zaihan Mohamed. 2004. "Sex in the City's Jungle." *The Electric New Paper*, May 7.

Zweig, Ferdynand. 1952. *The British Worker*. Harmondsworth, Middlesex: Penguin Books.

Tape Cassettes, VCDs, and DVDs

Bunchu Buaphang. 2002[?]. "Siang sang chak Taiwan" [A voice from Taiwan]. In *Ruam hits sane Isan* [Collection of Isan-style *lukthung* hits]. Bangkok. [VCD].

Carabao. 1983. "Khon niranam" [Nameless people]. In *Chut tho thahan ot-thon* [Tough soldiers]. Bangkok: AZONA [cassette tape].

———. 1984. "Sawan ban na" [Rice-cultivating villages as heaven on earth]. In *Siang phleng haeng seriphap* [Songs for freedom]. Bangkok: Amigo Studio [cassette tape].

———. 1985. "Sa-udon" [Saudi Arabia/Udon Thani]. In *Ameri-koi* [The greedy American]. Bangkok: Amigo Studio. [cassette tape].

———. 1989. "Singapore." In *Tham mue* [Handmade]. Bangkok: Amigo Studio [cassette tape].

Caravan. 1985. "Pla rai wang" [Homeless fish]. In *1985*. Bangkok: MGM [cassette tape].

Chawiwan Damnoen. 1974[?]. "Chiwit chao na" [The life of Isan rice farmers]. In *Chiwit chao na* [The life of Isan rice farmers]. Bangkok [cassette tape].

Chintara Phunlap. 1987[?]. "Khoi rak chak tang daen" [I wait for my lover working in a foreign country]. In *Ruam hits 8 pi phleng rak chak Chintara* [Collection of eight years of hit love songs from Chintara]. Bangkok: Master Tapes Company [cassette tape].

—————. 1990[?]. "Khoi rak chak Yoeraman" [I wait for my lover working in Germany]. Bangkok: Master Tapes Company [cassette tape].

—————. 1999. "Huang phi thi Kuwait." [I am worried to death for the safety of my lover working in Kuwait]. In *Chut thi 25, phu ni cham* [Vol. 25, An escapee from a lovelorn affair]. Bangkok: Plaeng Thai Group [cassette tape].

—————. 2005. "Ngao chai nai tang daen" [I am lonely in a foreign country]. In *Ruam hits molam, vol. 2* [Collection of *molam* hits, vol. 2]. Bangkok: Master Tapes Company [VCD Karaoke]. First released 1987.

Inthi, David. 2003[?]. "Isan khuen thin"[A call for Isan migrants to return home]. Bangkok [VCD].

It Futbat. 1999[?]. "Chot mai thueng pho" [A letter to my father who works overseas]. In *Prawattisat 20 khon 30 phleng—phleng phuea chiwit* [Songs for life—a historical collection of thirty songs from twenty singers]. Bangkok: C. M. C. Entertainment [VCD].

Khana Nok Yung Thong. 1998[?]. *Sao Taiwan: Lam nitan wannakhadi boran* [The wife of an overseas worker in Taiwan: A storytelling *lam*]. 6 vols. [VCD].

Kittisak Chaichana. 2005. "Fak chai sai song" [I deposit my heart into the remittance envelope I send to my mother]. In *Wan chai raeng ngan: Ruam phleng phro chap chai chak sinlapin Thai wan chai khon su chiwit* [Workers' sweethearts: Collections of beautiful songs from Thai singers dedicated to people who fight to survive]. Bangkok: GMM Grammy [VCD].

Lukphrae and Maithai Uraiphon. 1998[?]. "Khit thueng ban" [Homesickness]." In *Top hits khu ek* [Top hits by the duo stars]. Bangkok: Diamond Studio [VCD].

—————. 2002[?]. "Khwai Thai nai Singkhapo" [Thai buffaloes working in Singapore]." In *Top hits khu ek* [Top hits by the duo stars]. Bangkok: Diamond Studio [VCD].

Lukthung Raeng Chai Raeng Ngan. [*Lukthung* collections intended to delight workers' spirits]. 2003. Bangkok: GMM Grammy [VCD].

Maithai Uraiphon. n.d. "Hen thoe thi Yoeraman" [She was spotted in Germany]. In *Chut bak si doe* [Mr. Upcountry Bumpkin]. Bangkok: Top Line Music [VCD].

—————. n.d. "Khun nai Swiss" [Madam Switzerland]. In *Chut bak si doe* [Mr. Upcountry Bumpkin]. Bangkok: Top Line Music [VCD].

Mike Phiromphon. 2001a. "Thang Biang Ya Siang Doen" [Do not risk your future by taking a side route]. In *Ruam hit khon su chiwit chut thi 1* [Collection of song hits for the fighters in their endeavors to make a living, vol. 1]. Bangkok: GMM Grammy [VCD].

—————. 2001b. "Lakhon chiwit" [A real-life drama]. In *Ruam hit khon su chiwit chut thi 1* [Collection of song hits for the fighters in their endeavors to make a living, vol. 1]. Bangkok: GMM Grammy [VCD].

—————. 2001c. "Ya chai khon chon" [You are the remedy to the heart of an underprivileged man]. In *Ruam hit khon su chiwit chut thi 1* [Collection of song hits for the fighters in their endeavors to make a living, vol. 1]. Bangkok: GMM Grammy [VCD].

—————. 2001d. "Rangwan khon su" [A reward for the fighter in life]. In *Ruam hit khon su chiwit chut thi 1* [Collection of song hits for the fighters in their endeavors to make a living, vol. 1]. Bangkok: GMM Grammy [VCD].

—————. 2001e. "Phuea rak phuea rao" [For our love and for the two of us]. In *Ruam hit khon su chiwit chut thi 1* [Collection of song hits for the fighters in their endeavors to make a living, vol. 1]. Bangkok: GMM Grammy [VCD].

—————. 2001f. "Nueai mai khon di" [Are you tired, my dear?]. In *Khu hit khu rong Mike Phiromphon-Siriphon Amphaiphong* [Collections of super hits from duo stars—Mike Phiromphon and Siriphon Amphaiphong]. Bangkok: GMM Grammy [VCD].

—————. 2002a. "Khoet hot khon klai" [I miss someone who lives far away]. In *Rong rian lang chan* [The school that trains dishwashers]. Bangkok: Grammy Gold [VCD].

—————. 2002b. "Khaen la khon" [A young reed pipe player says goodbye to his home.] In *Rong rian lang chan* [The school that trains dishwashers]. Bangkok: Grammy Gold [VCD].

—————. 2002c. "Khai raeng taeng nang" [Selling my labor to marry my love]. In *Khai raeng taeng nang* [Selling my labor to marry my love]. Bangkok: Grammy Gold [VCD].

—————. 2002d. "Siang khaen, siang khluen" [The sound of *khaen*, the sound of the sea]. In *Khai Raeng Taeng nang* [Selling my labor to marry my love]. Bangkok: Grammy Gold [VCD].

—————. 2003a. "Phu yu bueang lang" [People behind the scenes]. In *Lukthung raeng chai raeng ngan"* [*Lukthung* collections intended to delight workers' spirits]. Bangkok: GMM Grammy [VCD].

—————. 2003b. "Pha khao bon ba sai" [The white towel on my left shoulder]. In *Chut 12 pha khao bon ba sai* [The white towel on my left shoulder]. Bangkok: GMM Grammy [VCD].

Phikun Khwanmuang. 1997a[?]. "Faen tai yu Singkhapo" [My lover was hanged to death in Singapore]. In *Lam phu Thai prayuk* [Modern *lam phu Thai*] [VCD].

—————. 1997b[?]. "Klap Isan thoet ai" [Come home to Isan, my dear brothers]. In *Lam phu Thai prayuk* [Modern *lam phu Thai*] [VCD].

—————. 1997c[?]. "Pai mueang nok hai sue sat" [My dear, you must be honest when you work abroad]. In *Lam phu Thai prayuk* [Modern *lam phu Thai*] [VCD].

Phimpha Phonsiri. 1982[?]. "Nam ta mia Sa-u" [Tears of the wives whose husbands work in Saudi Arabia]. In *Chut nam ta mia Sa-u* [Tears of the wives whose husbands working in Saudi Arabia]. Bangkok: Rota Phaeng Siang Tape [cassette tape].

Phongsit Khamphi. 2000a. "Pho pen kammakon" [My father is an overseas worker]. In *Ruam hits sut chiwit* [Collection of best 'songs for life' hits]. Bangkok: Caravan Company [VCD Karaoke]. First released 1990.

—————. 2000b. "Sao song ok" [Girls to export]. In *Ruam hits sut chiwit* [Collection of best 'songs for life' hits]. Bangkok: Caravan Company [VCD Karaoke]. First released 1990.

—————. 2000c. "Yokohama." In *Ruam hits sut chiwit* [Collection of best 'songs for life' hits]. Bangkok: Caravan Company [VCD Karaoke]. First released 1994.

Phongthep Kradonchamnan. 1990. "Tangke" [Isan fishermen]. In *Khon chon run mai* [The new generation of the poor]. Bangkok: Rot Fai Dontri [cassette tape].

—————. 1992. "Num ko sang" [Construction workers]. In *Khon thi rao rak* [The people we love]. Bangkok: Rot Fai Dontri [cassette tape].

Phonsak Songsaeng. 1979a[?]. "Fak chai pai Singkhapo" [My heart is off to my love who works in Singapore]. In *Ruam lukthung 2* [Collection of *lukthung* hits, vol. 2]. Bangkok: Siang Sayam Phaen Siang [VCD].

—————. 1979b[?]. "Sam wan bin" [Three days to fly]. In *Ruam lukthung 2* [Collection of *lukthung* hits, vol. 2]. Bangkok: Siang Sayam Phaen Siang [VCD].

—————. 1982a[?]. "Ko sang sang sao" [Construction workers' farewells to their lovers]. In *Ruam hit wannakam nam ek* [Collection of gem hits]. Bangkok: JKC [cassette tape].

—————. 1982b[?]. "Sa-u" [Saudi Arabia]. In *Ruam hit wannakam nam ek* [Collection of gem hits]. Bangkok: JKC [cassette tape].

—————. 1986a[?]. "Sao Chan kang kop" [A disgraceful girl named Chan]. In *Chut sao Chan kang kop* [A disgraceful girl named Chan]. Bangkok: Rota [cassette tape].

—————. 1986b[?]. "Sawan ban na" [Rice-cultivating villages as heaven on earth]. In *Chut sao Chan kang kop* [A disgraceful girl named Chan]. Bangkok [cassette tape].

—————. 1986c[?]. "Lam phaen khon klai ban" [A *lam phaen* lament from a person who lives away from home]. In *Lam phaen 14 klon chut 1* [Collection of fourteen *lam phaen* hits, vol. 1]. Bangkok [cassette tape].

Saksayam Phetchomphu. 1975[?]. "Siang bua long krung"[The ex-novice Bua takes a train ride to Bangkok]. In *Lukthung amata chut 1* [Timeless *lukthung*, vol. 1]. Bangkok [cassette tape].

Sam Ton (Thong, Thanom, Bumbim). 1990. "Toei lai tai" [A lament on a mysterious death in Singapore]. In *Chao phap chong charoen* [Long life to the host of the party]. Bangkok: Kita Records [VCD]. Rereleased in 2001.

Sayan Sanya. 1975[?]. "Maem pla ra" [Ma'am fermented fish]. [cassette tape].

Siriphon Amphaiphong. 1987. "Chan rak ban na" [I love my rice-farming village]. In Siriphon Amphaiphong, Vol. 15, *Sao rai po ro faen* [The kenaf plantation girl waiting for her lover]. Bangkok: PGM Records [VCD Karaoke]. Rereleased in 2001.

————. 2001a. "Chot mai chak Chepaen" [A letter from Japan]. In *Ruam hit ruam samai Siriphon, vol. 7* [Siriphon's hits collection, vol. 7]. Bangkok: PGM Records [VCD Karaoke].

————. 2001b. "Parinya chai" [Certificate of the heart]. In *Khu hit khu rong Mike Phiromphon-Siriphon Amphaiphong* [Collections of super hits from duo stars Mike Phiromphon and Siriphon Amphaiphong]. Bangkok: GMM Grammy [VCD].

————. 2002a. "Chotmai phai mue thue" [Letters come second to cell phones]. In *Ruam hit ruam samai Siriphon, vol. 9* [Siriphon's hits collection, vol. 9]. Bangkok: PGM Records [VCD Karaoke].

————. 2002b. "Fak chai pai Taiwan" [My heart is off to my lover working in Taiwan]. In *Ruam hit ruam samai Siriphon, Vol. 12* [Siriphon's hits collection, vol. 12]. Bangkok: PGM Records [VCD Karaoke].

————. 2002c. "Rak num fomaen" [I love the foreman]. In *Ruam hit ruam samai Siriphon, vol. 9* [Siriphon's hits collection, vol. 9]. Bangkok: PGM Records [VCD Karaoke].

————. 2003a. "Phuea mae phae bo dai" [For my mother, I can't give up]. In *Lukthung raeng chai raeng ngan* [*Lukthung* collections intended to delight workers' spirits]. Bangkok: GMM Grammy [VCD].

————. 2003b. "Raeng chai rai wan" [Moral support for my daily-wage worker]. In *Lukthung raeng chai raeng ngan*" [*Lukthung* collections intended to delight workers' spirits]. Bangkok: GMM Grammy [VCD].

————. 2005. "Lam nam lom nao" [A lament of the cold wind]. In *Wan chai raeng ngan: Ruam phleng phro chap chai chak sinlapin Thai wan chai khon su chiwit* [Workers' sweethearts: collections of beautiful songs from Thai singers dedicated to the people who fight to survive]. Bangkok: GMM Grammy [VCD].

Somphot Duangsomphong. 1984[?]. "Mia pa phro Sa-u" [My wife left me because I went to work in Saudi Arabia]. In *Chut mia pa phro Sa-u* [My wife left me because I went to work in Saudi Arabia]. Bangkok: AZONA [cassette tape].

Su Su. 1991. "Lui Kuwet" [Wading into Kuwait]. In *Khon Khem Le Dao* [The siblings of the sea and the sea of the stars]. Bangkok: Center Stage [cassette tape].

————. 1997a. "Khon sing Isan" [Wandering, hard-working Isan people]. In *Khai mot daeng* [Red ants' eggs]. Bangkok: Ra Rai Records [cassette tape].

————. 1997b. "Klap pai Songkran ban na" [Returning to celebrate Songkran in our home villages]. In *Khai mot daeng* [Red ants' eggs]. Bangkok: Ra Rai Records [cassette tape].

Tai Orathai. 2003a. "Kaem daeng raeng chai" [Young girls' moral support to their dear workers]. *Chut thi 1 Dokya nai pa pun* [Vol. 1, A flower in the forest of concrete buildings]. Bangkok: Grammy Gold [VCD Karaoke].

————. 2003b. "Khitthueng pho khitthueng mae khitthueng ban." [I miss my father, my mother, and my home village]. *Chut thi 1 Dokya nai pa pun* [Vol. 1, A flower in the forest of concrete buildings]. Bangkok: Grammy Gold [VCD Karaoke].

————. 2003c. "Sanya na han" [The promise made in front of the *lukthung-molam* concert stage]. *Chut thi 1 Dokya nai pa pun* [Vol. 1, A flower in the forest of concrete buildings]. Bangkok: Grammy Gold [VCD Karaoke].

————. 2003d. "Tho ha nae doe" [Please give me a call, my dear]. *Chut thi 1 Dokya nai pa pun* [Vol. 1, A flower in the forest of concrete buildings]. Bangkok: Grammy Gold [VCD Karaoke].

————. 2003e. "Kin khao rue yang" [Honey, have you eaten yet?]. *Chut thi 1 Dokya nai pa pun* [Vol. 1, A flower in the forest of concrete buildings]. Bangkok: Grammy Gold [VCD Karaoke].

Thepphon Phet-Ubon. 1975[?]. "Isan ban hao" [Isan, our homeland]. In *Phleng amata ngoen lan* [Million baht timeless hits]. Bangkok [cassette tape].

————. 1998a[?]. "Bai si raeng ngan thai pai Singkhapo" [A *bai si* farewell to Thai workers heading for employment in Singapore]. In *Phleng amata ngoen lan* [Million baht timeless hits]. Bangkok [cassette tape].

————. 1998b[?]. "Bai si raeng ngan Thai pai Taiwan" [A *bai si* farewell to Thai workers heading for employment in Taiwan]. In *Phleng amata ngoen lan* [Million baht timeless hits]. Bangkok [cassette tape].

Toi Muak Daeng. 2004. *Mo rock, mo lam* [The king of rock, the king of *lam*]. Bangkok: RS Siam [VCD Karaoke].

Wan chai raeng ngan 2005. [Collections of *lukthung* love songs dedicated to workers]. Bangkok: GMM Grammy [VCD].

Index

3D workers, 3, 50, 53, 116, 123, 146n7

Agamben, Giorgio, 3, 4–5, 6

Bahrain, 37, 141n12
Bangkok
    center of power, 24, 25
    labor migration to, 23–28, 33
    sex workers from, 82, 83
    suburbs, 9, 149n30
    transport to and from, 25
    travel to Singapore, 83
Bangladesh, 12, 14, 21, 15, 110
"bare life," 3–4, 5, 6, 19, 131, 137
Boon Lay, 69, 80
borders, national
    and borderless modern life, 50, 51
    regulations and controls, 84, 155n6
    between Thailand, Malaysia, and
        Singapore, 84, 119
    travel across, 9, 31, 45, 47, 71, 76, 79
Brunei, 58, 125
Buddhism
    merit-making activities, 22, 28,
        57–63
    migrant workers' practice of, 63,
        135
    monkhood, 135
    notion of suffering, 2
    popular beliefs, 42
Bunchu Buaphang, 29, 41

Carabao, 25, 26, 28, 29, 32, 35, 41, 42
Caravan, 25–26
Chawiwan Damnoen, 25, 26, 27
China, 11, 15, 95,110
Chintara Phunlap, 33, 37, 38
Choa Chu Kang, 68–69
Christian churches, 65, 124
City Plaza, 146n7
construction sector (Singapore)
    accidents in, 116–17
    companies, 66–67
    demand for foreign workers, 12
    effect on labor policy, 12
    employment in, 50, 115
    growth of, 12
    sites, 6, 124–25
    types of work, 26, 123–124
    workers, 1, 12, 32, 44, 49, 126
crime, 78, 114, 120, 127

Das, Veena, 4, 6–7
David Inthi, 28
death
    and the bare life, 3, 4, 5, 137
    capital punishment, 5, 36, 42,
        120–21, 127
    causes of, 3, 119
    of domestic workers, 155n9
    as exploitation, 127
    statistics, 118–19, 129
    of Thai workers in Singapore,
        118–23, 125, 128

death (*continued*)
    in transnational labor migration,
        113–23, 127–28
    in work-related accidents, 116–17
    See also sudden unexplained
        death syndrome
domestic workers, migrant
    assistance for, 82
    courtship of, 102–104, 109
    death of, 127
    and emotion, 9
    Indonesian and Filipina, 95–97,
        100, 103–104, 110, 153n7, 155n9
    medical controls on, 79
    numbers of, 21
    Singaporeans' view of, 133
    and village transnationalism, 71
Don Muang International Airport,
    37, 128
dormitories, foreign worker, 16, 70,
    79, 80, 97, 124, 147n16, 156n14

economic development, 21
emotional management, 9
English language course (author's),
    15–16
Europe, 38, 142n19
ethnocultural enclaves, 72, 79, 145n7

factory workers, 9, 10, 70, 83, 142n13
families and home communities
    attachment to, 46, 49, 50, 73
    commitment to, 22, 63
    ideas of, 88
    in *lukthung* lyrics, 26–28, 38, 39–40,
        45
    as recipients of remittances, 19,
        33, 44
    reunions with, 137
    separation from, 9, 10, 35, 44, 56,
        131
    village relationships in
        transnational labor, 43, 58, 63
fieldwork, 14, 16–17
Filipino migrants, 9

flows of labor, 11, 19, 23, 33, 43, 115
football
    in fieldwork, 16
    Football Association of Singapore,
        64
    Football Association of Thailand,
        148n29
    and masculinity, 66, 67
    popularity among Thai migrant
        men, 63
    practice, 66, 67
    team-building, 65–66
    in Thailand, 148n29
    tournaments, 64
    See also Thai Labor Cup
Friends of Thai Workers Association
    (FTWA), 15, 64, 134, 136
Fusionpolis construction site collapse,
    116

gender ideology, 19, 21, 34, 46, 71, 89
gendered agency, 4, 7–9, 18, 108
Geylang
    as ethnocultural enclave, 79
    as fieldwork location, 17
    hotels in, 101, 106, 107
    karaoke bars, 82
    as red-light district, 81, 97, 100, 125
ghosts, 125–126, 127, 144n26
globalization
    cultural, 50
    economic informalization, 90
    global market economy, 3, 5, 23, 69
    power relations in, 76
    and transnationalism, 51
Golden Mile Complex
    alcohol consumption in, 54–55
    comparison to Isan village life, 55
    description, 52
    FTWA office, 15, 64
    history, 53
    karaoke bars in, 82
    as "Little Thailand," 53, 54, 146n7,
        147n15

as location for intimacy, 10, 93, 100, 105, 134
in merit-making projects, 57, 61
negative reputation, 53, 55, 146n8
programs for Thai workers at, 151n7
remittance services, 52, 54, 145n5
as social space, 53, 125
as surrogate community, 56
tradeswomen at, 82, 85
Gulf War, 37

hardship
of internal labor migration, 25
in northeastern Thailand, 23, 26, 27, 139n1 (chap. 2)
of Thai workers in Singapore, 29, 55, 56, 97, 110, 123, 150n43
in transnational labor migration, 3, 19, 36
headnotes, 16–17
healthcare, 80, 151n7
heartnotes, 16, 17
holidays
Chinese New Year, 28, 57, 68
King Bhumibol Adulyadej's birthday, 16
May Day, 16, 136, 141n6
New Year (Western), 28, 57
Songkran, 28, 57
homecomings
as goals, 133, 134
inevitability of, 51, 137
negative, 20, 39, 114, 135–136
for Songkran, 28
successful, 136, 137
Homo Sacer, 4, 5, 6
Hong Huat Hung explosion, 117
Hong Kong, 11, 137
hong pao, 57
host countries, 2, 3, 6, 43, 71, 137
Housing and Development Board (HDB), 12, 54, 61, 69, 124
hunting and gathering, 68–70, 149n39

illegal workers
forest hideouts, 80, 81, 88
and lack of ID papers, 120
numbers of, 13, 155n5
India, 12, 14, 15, 110
Indochinese War, 24, 31
Indonesia, 12, 63, 155n9
Institute of Science and Forensic Medicine (Singapore), 121
International Labor Organization, 117
intimacy
in communication, 44
cultural, 47, 133
emotional, 9, 10
locations for, 10
male migrant, 91, 133
patterns of, 80, 99, 108, 111
in relationships, 99, 102, 107
sexual, 75–81, 88, 89, 91–92, 99, 108, 111
tragic, 39, 135–36
Iraq, 37
Isan
Buddhist roots, 2
ceremonies, 43, 61
internal labor migration from, 9, 23–28
men from, 98
in popular music, 32
provinces included in, 152n1
regional connections, 15, 16
rural-to-urban migration, 11
symbols of, 45, 132
transnational labor migration from, 1, 20, 29
village life, 26–28, 55, 69
women from, 9, 142n19
working in, 29
Israel, 58, 69, 125
It Futbat, 45

Japan, 39, 58, 125
Jit Phumisak, 140n6
job placement agents. *See* recruitment agencies

Jurong, 12, 80

Kaki Bukit, 81
Kallang Riverside Park
    as alternative to Golden Mile, 52
    as fieldwork location, 16–17
    in merit-making activities, 61
    tradeswomen at, 17, 85, 86
Kampoon Boontawee, 23, 149n39
Keppel shipyard fire, 116
khaen, 24, 27, 45, 132
Kleinman, Arthur, 4, 6–7
Kulap Saipradit. *See* Sriburapha
Kuwait, 32, 37, 41

labor migration
    as escape from poverty, 11
    history in Thailand and Southeast
        Asia, 11–13
    internal, 9, 23–28, 30, 46, 142n13
    in popular culture, 47
    rural-to-urban, 11, 23–26, 33
    as self-sacrifice, 1–2
    Thai terminology for, 24, 29,
        141n10
    See also transnational labor
        migration
lai tai, see sudden unexplained
    nocturnal death syndrome
Laos, 24
law enforcement, 1, 42, 88, 111
laws
    bans, 5
    for employers and supervisors, 129
    as expressions of state power, 4–5
    flexibility, 79
    for foreign workers, 6, 51
    violations of, 1, 42
    See also under Singapore
Lim Chu Kang, 80
Linde Gas factory explosion, 116
Little India, 100, 105, 145n7
Lock, Margaret, 4, 6–7
Lucky Plaza, 100, 105, 145n7
Lukphrae Uraiphon, 20, 29

lukthung, 19, 139n1 (chap. 2)
    composers of, 143n20
    heterosexual romanticism in, 34
    importance for Isan workers, 43
    listening to, 131
    lyrics, 25, 29, 31
    singers from Isan, 33
    at Thai Labor Cup, 65
    about transnational romances, 38

Mahidol University (Thailand), 121
Maithai Uraiphon, 20, 29, 38
Malaysia, 15, 63
masculinity
    football and, 66, 67
    hegemonic, 19, 21
    heroic, 19, 20
    male role as provider, 21, 22, 44, 63,
        114, 123
    masculine pride, 8, 10, 20, 34, 40,
        68
    masculine sensitivity, 110
    in popular music, 19–21, 44
    redefining, 2, 4
    and sexual encounters, 91, 92
    in Thai Buddhist culture, 8, 10,
        21–22
    transcendent, 131
media reports
    on death of Thai migrant workers,
        118, 121–23, 125–26
    on foreign workforce in Singapore,
        1, 115, 151n3
    on fraud in *pha pa* projects, 60
    on Golden Mile Complex, 51–52
    on illegal sex work, 80
    on recruitment agents cheating
        migrants, 35, 142n17
    on Thai sex workers, 151n11
    on transnational crime, 120
Mekong River, 24
merit-making activities. See *pha pa*
    projects
Middle East
    job placement agents and, 142n17

labor migration to, 29–30, 31, 35,
40, 69
remittances from, 58, 141n12
SUNDS-like death in, 122
treatment of migrant workers, 92
war in, 37
"migrant foreignness," 92
migrant romanticism, 32, 33, 35, 128
migrant workers. *See* Thai migrant
workers
Mike Phiromphon, 33, 34, 36, 41, 45,
46, 132, 156n1
mobility, 19, 24, 32, 75
modernity
economic, 3
outside one's own locality, 141n11
Thai, 11, 24
Western-style, 9, 25
molam, 19, 139n2 (chap. 2)
composers of, 143n20
importance for Isan workers, 43
lam toei, 41, 144n25
listening to, 27, 131
lyrics, 25, 27, 29
molam rueang, 144n24
narratives, 26
national artists, 24
Phuthai-style, 42
as symbol of Isan, 45
at Thai Labor Cup, 65
MRT (Mass Rapid Transit), 69, 95, 105
muai Thai (Thai boxing), 30, 63
Myanmar, 11, 12, 14, 64

NGOs (non-governmental
organizations), 80, 154n1
Nicoll Highway collapse, 116

Orchard Tower
as ethnocultural enclave, 79
as fieldwork location, 17
as red-light district, 81, 82, 83,
151n11

passes, short-term, 71, 80, 82, 83, 85,
136

pha pa projects
donation amounts, 60
envelope-opening ceremonies
(*poet song*), 61–62
leaders of, 58
organization of, 57
procedure, 58–60
transparency, 60, 62
Phikun Khwanmuang, 27, 42
Philippines, 21, 128, 137, 155n9
Phimpha Phonsri, 39, 40
phleng phuea chiwit, 19, 25, 43, 65, 139–
40nn3–4, 141n6
Phongsit Kamphi, 32
Phongthep Kradonchamnan, 32
Phonsak Songsaeng, 27, 29, 32, 35, 37
police
Singaporean, 53, 80, 83, 87, 88, 95,
147n16
Thai, 59
policy and regulations, foreign labor
(Singapore), 10, 12, 13
double standards in, 88
immigration, 51, 133
as management of economic
assets, 115
medical exams, 79
negotiation of, 89, 91, 92, 103
on sexuality and relationships,
77–79, 95
standardized tests, 14, 152n1
work permits, 1, 6, 42, 51, 78, 100,
115
popular music
as cultural commentary, 47
genres, 19, 140n4
GMM Grammy, 33, 142n16, 156n1
labor migration in, 19–47,
long-distance relationships in, 34,
38
lyrics, 19, 20–21, 23, 26, 37, 45–47,
131
masculinity in, 19–21, 34, 45
narratives, 26–27, 42, 47

popular music (*continued*)
    performative power of, 23
    See also *lukthung; molam; phleng*
    phuea chiwit
Porntipa Atipas, 12, 13, 57
power relations, 6–7, 20, 76, 78

Qatar, 152n1

recruitment agencies
    cheating and overcharging, 35,
       142n17
    fees, 14, 35, 50, 143n19
    role in transnational labor
    migration, 1, 36, 129, 145n4
remittances
    amounts, 60, 126, 145n5, 152n1
    as connection to home, 22, 28, 33,
       39
    economic contributions of, 27, 31,
       60–61, 126
    effect on socioeconomic status, 30,
       45, 143n23
    handling of, 41, 44, 137, 143n22
    merit-making donations, 57, 58,
       60–61, 62
    from the Middle East, 141n12
    to pay off debts, 44, 136
    sending at Golden Mile Complex,
       52, 54
    from sex work, 83
    social, 9, 57, 113
rice farming, 23, 25–28, 30, 45

Saksayam Petchompu, 25
Sala Khunawut, 33
salaries. *See* wages
Saudi Arabia, 29–30, 32, 35, 39, 40,
    141n12
Sayan Sanya, 31
Sentosa Island, 105
sepak takraw, 63
sex workers
    communication of, 10
    dehumanization of, 94
    fees, 81, 95, 100

    independent, 81
    and informal labor market, 90
    in Japan, 39
    location of, 15
    Thai, 31, 97, 135–36, 151n11
    for Thai migrants, 80
    trafficking of, 76
    in transnational labor migration,
       75, 76, 77, 83–84
sexuality
    of female migrants, 38
    homosexuality, 77, 98–99, 153n9
    regulation of, 6, 77–80, 89
    in transnational labor migration,
       75–77, 90
Singapore
    amnesty for illegal workers, 13
    economy, 13, 115
    Employment Act, 124
    Employment of Foreign Workers
       Act, 78, 145n6, 150n2
    fertility rates, 77
    as fieldwork site, 14–17
    forest areas in, 68, 69
    government, 42, 75
    as host country, 6, 49, 133, 134
    immigrants, reliance on, 10–11,
       114–15, 154n3
    Immigration Act, 150n2
    Immigration and Checkpoints
       Authority, 88
    labor migration from Thailand,
       11–14, 41
    migrant workers' death in, 125
    Ministry of Manpower (MOM), 14,
       115, 116, 117, 155n7
    Ministry of Trade and Industry,
       115
    public space in, 53, 54, 78, 93, 109
    regulation of migrants' sexuality,
       77–80, 89
    society and culture, 50, 70, 72, 133,
       154n3
    statistics on foreign workers, 13,
       78, 151n3

as transnational labor market,
10–11, 50, 109, 114, 133
treatment of foreign workers,
72–73, 146n8, 147n16
workforce, 14, 115, 154n5
Siriphon Amphaiphong, 27, 33, 34, 37
social exclusion, 2, 7, 113, 114
Somphot Duangsomphong, 39, 40
Songkran festival, 28, 57
South Korea, 11
Sriburapha, 140n6
state, the
and the bare life, 3, 6
disciplinary measures, 77
ideologies, 77
power of, 4–5
regulation and control, 5–6, 71,
76–77, 154n2
surveillance, 10, 78, 89, 93
workers' experiences of, 51
State of Exception, 4–5
structuration theory, 8
Su Su, 24, 32, 41
sudden unexplained nocturnal death
syndrome (SUNDS), 1, 2–3, 7,
41–42, 114, 119, 121–23
suffering, 2, 3, 5, 6
social, 3, 6–7
in transient life, 25
Sukhothai Thammathirat Open
University, 109, 134
Suriya Smutkupt, 142n14

Tai Orathai, 27, 28, 33, 44
Taiwan, 37, 41, 69, 125, 147n16, 152n1
Tampines Avenue, 80
Thai boxing. See *muai Thai*
Thai embassy in Singapore
Office of Thai Labor Affairs, 13, 14,
15, 64, 134, 151n7
services for undocumented
travelers, 120
sponsorship of FTWA, 15
statistics, 118, 119, 120

Thai Labor Cup (football)
final match (2005), 68
finances, 64
organization, 64
spectators, 64, 67
Thai migrant workers
attitudes on sex, 93, 108
buying sex, 80, 86–89, 108
communication: football as, 66;
with employers, 15, 50; with
home, 28, 109; through mobile
phones, 44, 56, 103, 109,
147n17; with other migrants,
56, 63, 100–101, 103–4, 105
courtship by, 102–8
daily routines, 2
debt incurred by, 50, 136
deportation of, 42
displacement, feelings of, 2, 22, 26,
47, 72, 128
drug use by, 120
as "economic warriors" (*nakrop
settakit*), 1–2, 30
emotional management, 9
entertainment businesses for, 82
female, 9, 10, 33, 46
ideas of home, 45
identity, 3–4, 32, 46, 50, 51, 63, 71
job hazards of, 123–24
as labor commodity, 26
as laborers, 6
language barriers for, 15, 50, 105
living conditions of, 42, 121, 122,
124–25
in long-term relationships, 101–2,
105
merit-making activities, 57–63
numbers in Singapore, 13, 78
in popular media, 47
relationships with domestic
workers, 82, 95–97, 100–101,
102–4
romantic lives, 34, 44, 107–8
in service to the people, 46

Thai migrant workers (*continued*)
  sexual partners, ideal, 94
  sexuality, 92, 93, 100, 107–11
  Singaporeans' view of, 95, 110, 111,
    133, 146n8, 147n16
  social life in Singapore, 16, 17, 52,
    63, 72, 73, 81, 91, 109
  socioeconomic status, 10, 30, 32,
    45, 92, 110
  as sources of economic value, 5
  studies on, 13–14, 46, 57
  time spent in Singapore, 44
  transformation from being rural
    farmers, 25
  vulnerability of, 3, 32, 70, 113, 119,
    129, 154n1
Thailand
  central, 23, 33
  government, 1, 42, 142n17
  Hat Yai, 14, 17, 52, 54, 81, 84, 85
  Khorat plateau, 23, 26
  Ministry of Foreign Affairs, 125
  Ministry of Labor Affairs, 13,
    149n30
  Ministry of Labor and Social Work,
    12
  Ministry of Public Health, 122
  northeastern (*see* Isan)
  northern, 1, 98, 143n19
  Office of the Protection of Thai
    Nationality, 125
  politicians in, 121, 122, 127
    provinces: Buri Ram, 59; Khon
    Kaen, 15; Mahasarakham,
    141n11; Nakhon Phanom, 15,
    59, 68; Nakhon Ratchasima,
    25; Nong Khai, 15, 36, 59;
    Petchabun, 152n1; Sakon
    Nakhon, 15; Ubon Ratchathani,
    25; Udon Thani, 15, 54, 59, 68;
    Yasothon, 59
  Rangsit, 23
  southern, 17, 24, 81–82
  Western cultural influences in, 31

Thaksin Shinawatra, 148–49nn29–30
Thepphon Phet-Ubon, 27
  tradeswomen
  business savvy of, 87
  commuting to Singapore, 84
  cross-border, 10, 14, 17, 71, 85
  identity, 86
  sex work by, 85, 86
  vendors, 52, 53, 61
transnational labor migration
  the bare life in, 3, 5, 6
  consequences of, 20, 127, 136,
    143n22
  as a cultural practice, 11, 41
  death in, 114, 125, 127–28
  decision to engage in, 142n13
  emotional management in, 9
  failure of, 35–36, 114
  human costs of, 114
  loss due to, 40
  masculinity in, 4, 22
  from northeastern Thailand, 20
  in public culture, 22
  sexuality in, 75–77, 90, 108
  as a social force, 21, 30, 43
  social lives in, 91
  in Southeast Asia, 11, 113, 129
  as subject of study, 21, 47, 70,
    75–76, 114, 129
  Thai terminology for, 29, 30–31, 41
  as theater, 131, 137
transnational labor market, 3, 8, 72,
    76
  at turn of 21st century, 51
  as a venture, 1, 36, 43
  See also under popular music
transnationalism, 8, 51, 71, 114, 127,
    131, 134
Tuas, 117, 156n14

undocumented workers, 13, 71, 80,
    113, 120, 155n5
United States, 24, 31

village transnationalism, 49, 50, 68,
    70–73, 144n1

wages
  average (Thai workers in
      Singapore), 50
  for construction work, 148n23
  for domestic workers, 96
  loss of, 40
  management of, 2
  in relation to cost of living, 133,
      150n42
  in Saudi Arabia, 35
  for semiskilled workers in
  Singapore,
      14
  in Thailand, 32
women
  Caucasian, 98
  gender bias against, 88–89, 90
  Indonesian and Filipina, 95–97,
      103–5, 107, 153n8
  male migrants' objectification of,
      94
  migrant workers, 9, 10, 33, 46
  and pregnancy, 79
  selling sex, 75, 76, 82–89, 108
  South Asian, 98
  Thai, 38, 81, 82–89, 97–98, 142n19,
      153n8
  as victims, 90
  See also domestic workers
Wong, Deborah, 12–13, 22, 57
Woodlands Industrial Park, 80
work-related accidents, 115–17, 155n7

The publisher gratefully acknowledges all donations to the Dr. Pattana Kitiarsa Fund to defray the costs of producing and publishing this book: Ian G. Baird, Katherine Bowie, Andrew Brown, Wen-Chin Chang, Susan M. Darlington, C. and T. Fadgyas, Nils Magnus Fiskesjo, John F. Hartman, Charles F. Keyes, Jane Keyes, Leedom Lefferts, Justin McDaniel, John Miksic, Mary Beth Mills, Michael J. Montesano, Oona T. Paredes, Vatthana Pholsena, Andrea M. Pinkney, Visisya Pinthongvijayakul, Craig Reynolds, David E. Strekfuss, Nicola Tanenbaum, Eric C. Thompson, Amy E. Warcup, Erick White, Thongchai Winichakul, and Xiang Biao and Mika Toyota.